OXFORD ENGLISH MONOGRAPHS

General Editors

Anaïs Nin, Fictionality and Femininity

Playing a Thousand Roles

HELEN TOOKEY

CLARENDON PRESS · OXFORD

OXFORD
UNIVERSITY PRESS

Great Clarendon Street, Oxford OX2 6DP

Oxford University Press is a department of the University of Oxford.
It furthers the University's objective of excellence in research, scholarship,
and education by publishing worldwide in

Oxford New York

Auckland Bangkok Buenos Aires Cape Town Chennai
Dar es Salaam Delhi Hong Kong Istanbul Karachi Kolkata
Kuala Lumpur Madrid Melbourne Mexico City Mumbai Nairobi
São Paulo Shanghai Taipei Tokyo Toronto

Oxford is a registered trade mark of Oxford University Press
in the UK and in certain other countries

Published in the United States
by Oxford University Press Inc., New York

First published 2003

British Library Cataloguing in Publication Data
Data available

Library of Congress Cataloging in Publication Data
Tookey, Helen, 1969–
Anaïs Nin, fictionality and femininity: playing a thousand roles / Helen Tookey.
p. cm.—(Oxford English monographs)
Includes bibliographical references and index.
1. Nin, Anaès, 1903–1977—Criticism and interpretation. 2. Feminism and literature—
United States—History—20th century. 3. Women and literature—United States—History—
20th century. 4. Feminist fiction, American—History and criticism. 5. Role playing in literature.
6. Femininity in literature. 7. Women in literature. I. Title. II. Series.
PS3527.I865 Z96 2003 818′.5209—dc21 2002035558

ISBN 0–19–924983–0

1 3 5 7 9 10 8 6 4 2

Typeset by Hope Services (Abingdon) Ltd.
Printed in Great Britain
on acid-free paper by
Biddles Ltd.,
Guildford and King's Lynn

Acknowledgements

This book is based on research undertaken for a D.Phil. thesis, submitted to Oxford University in 2000. I would like to express my gratitude to Rachel Bowlby, who was unfailingly generous with her time, energy, and ideas as a supervisor, and whose ongoing friendship and support I greatly appreciate. More broadly, I am grateful to Rachel and to all those scholars whose work first suggested to me the exciting possibilities at the meeting-points of feminism, literature, and philosophy.

The research for this book was funded by the Arts and Humanities Research Board, and was carried out at Sussex University and Wadham College, Oxford, both of which provided supportive and stimulating environments. I would like to thank Ron Bush, Laura Marcus, Kathleen Wheeler, and an anonymous reader for Oxford University Press for their interest in my work and for helpful comments on earlier drafts. Portions of this book have previously appeared, in slightly different form, in *Anaïs: An International Journal* and in *Women: A Cultural Review*.

Gunther Stuhlmann, Anaïs Nin's Representative, kindly granted me permission to reproduce the illustrations and was generous with his time throughout. His death in April 2002 was particularly sad coming as it did so shortly before the centenary (in 2003) of the author whose work he did so much to promote.

Margaret Tenney, at the Harry Ransom Humanities Research Center, University of Texas at Austin, was most helpful in tracking down articles in *transition* magazine. Noël Riley Fitch was generous with advice on bibliographical matters. I would also like to thank Sophie Goldsworthy, Sarah Hyland, Frances Whistler, and Katie Ryde at OUP.

Support from my friends has been vital in many ways during the research and writing of this book; I would particularly like to thank Suzy Gordon and Matt Bennett, who helped with everything from discussion of the finer points of psychoanalytic theory to babysitting. Lucy Faire and Neil Turnbull have been there for the long haul. I am also very grateful to my parents, Jane and Mick Tookey, both for encouraging my academic aspirations and for generously helping out with the ensuing financial difficulties. Finally, love and thanks to my partner Andrew Kirk and our son Patrick—the former for living with both me and this book, the latter for (to quote Audre Lorde) 'keeping me honest'.

H.T.

Liverpool

Contents

Illustrations

Abbreviations

PFL	The Penguin Freud Library (Harmondsworth: Penguin)
SE	The Standard Edition of the Complete Psychological Works of Sigmund Freud (London: Hogarth Press)

References are given to the Penguin Freud Library where a text exists in that edition, otherwise to the Standard Edition.

References to works by Anaïs Nin in the main text are given for convenience using the following abbreviated titles:

Albatross	*Children of the Albatross*
D. H. Lawrence	*D. H. Lawrence: An Unprofessional Study*
Early Diary	*The Early Diary of Anaïs Nin*
Journals	*The Journals of Anaïs Nin*
Ladders	*Ladders to Fire*
Mystic	*The Mystic of Sex: Uncollected Writings, 1931–1974*
Novel	*The Novel of the Future*
Seduction	*Seduction of the Minotaur*
Sensitive Man	*In Favour of the Sensitive Man*
Spy	*A Spy in the House of Love*
Waste of Timelessness	*Waste of Timelessness and Other Early Stories*
Winter	*Winter of Artifice*

Introduction

Anaïs Nin still seeking Henry Miller.
London Review of Books, personal ads. (18 October 2001)

In *Virginia Woolf Icon* (1999),[1] Brenda Silver explores the proliferating and conflicting versions and cultural images of Virginia Woolf—the ways in which Woolf has come to function as icon, as sign. Silver shows how the various images of Woolf's face, in particular, become a kind of visual shorthand for the multiple meanings of 'Virginia Woolf' circulating in contemporary British and American culture: intellectual, asexual woman/vulnerable beauty/high-cultural snob/feminist pioneer/frightening madwoman/suicide. In the personal ad. reproduced above, the name 'Anaïs Nin' also functions as a kind of shorthand (in this case verbal rather than visual), sufficient on its own, the advertiser trusts, to mobilize a particular fantasy—the perfect name to conjure in the minds of readers the desired combination of the literary, the exotic, and the extravagantly sexual. (And 'Henry Miller'? To the postmodern reader, familiar with Nin from the 1990 Universal film *Henry and June* and the Penguin tie-in edition of the book, Miller can be reimaged, perhaps, as the thinking woman's bit of rough—the gangster-author, always ready for what he famously called 'a literary fuck-fest', but underneath the bravado, a pussycat who always does the washing-up.[2])

One aim of this book is to explore the 'versioning' (to use Silver's favoured term) of Nin—as a modernist, as a woman writer, as a public (and controversial) figure of the women's liberation movement, as a set of conflicting and often extreme representations of femininity. At the same time, I examine Nin's own lifelong fascination with 'versioning',

[1] Brenda R. Silver, *Virginia Woolf Icon* (Women in Culture and Society; Chicago: Univ. of Chicago Press, 1999).

[2] Miller uses the term 'literary fuck-fest' in a letter to Nin dated 30 July 1932 (see Anaïs Nin and Henry Miller, *A Literate Passion: Letters of Anaïs Nin and Henry Miller 1932–1953* (ed. Gunther Stuhlmann; London: Allison & Busby, 1988), 82; the letter is partly cited in *Henry and June*, 213–14. As for the washing-up, Noël Riley Fitch notes that Miller was 'fastidious (in contrast to his literary persona)' (*Anaïs: The Erotic Life of Anaïs Nin* [Boston: Little, Brown, 1993], 104); Mary Dearborn, in her biography of Miller, suggests that '[though] Miller commonly represented it otherwise, his life in Clichy [at the time when he and Nin first became lovers] was thoroughly bourgeois' (*The Happiest Man Alive: A Biography of Henry Miller* [London: HarperCollins, 1991], 151).

with the multiple aspects of identity—the 'thousand roles' an individual might play—and their articulation in and through various forms of representation. In so far as Nin was particularly focused on questions of women's subjectivity and identity, the two main (interweaving) strands of the book can be named as fictionality and femininity.

In her 1998 monograph *Anaïs Nin and the Remaking of Self*, Diane Richard-Allerdyce describes Nin as 'an important Modernist and feminist writer'.[3] However, both attributions—taken separately or together—have proved problematic when applied to Nin. Her current position in relation to what we can call feminist–modernist criticism is perhaps best summed up by her appearance in Lisa Rado's 1994 collection *Rereading Modernism*. Nin is listed, in Rado's introduction, as one of the 'many . . . major writers of the period' whose work can be seen to be informed by 'at least some measure of homosexual identification';[4] but despite her inclusion here as a 'major' writer of the modernist period, Nin does not appear anywhere else in the book. In her introduction, Rado describes the process of 'rescuing' and remembering the 'lost' women of modernism, with the key publication of Shari Benstock's *Women of the Left Bank* in 1986 and Bonnie Kime Scott's 1990 anthology *The Gender of Modernism*.[5] Benstock included a section on Nin, setting her *House of Incest* alongside Djuna Barnes's *Nightwood* and Jean Rhys's *Good Morning, Midnight* in an exploration of the interactions of psychic and political spheres in women's writing of the 1930s. But if Nin was 'rescued', alongside other modernist women, by Benstock, she was more or less 'lost' again afterwards, making fleeting appearances in introductions and conclusions (for instance, alongside Stein, Woolf, and Richardson in the 'Coda' to Sidonie Smith's *Poetics of Women's Autobiography*), but never quite appearing in the main text of feminist–modernist criticism.[6]

[3] Diane Richard-Allerdyce, *Anaïs Nin and the Remaking of Self: Gender, Modernism and Narrative Identity* (DeKalb, Ill.: Northern Illinois Univ. Press, 1998), 4.

[4] Lisa Rado (ed.), *Rereading Modernism: New Directions in Feminist Criticism* (New York and London: Garland, 1994), 13.

[5] Shari Benstock, *Women of the Left Bank: Paris, 1900–1940* (London: Virago, 1987); Bonnie Kime Scott (ed.), *The Gender of Modernism* (Bloomington, Ind.: Indiana Univ. Press, 1990).

[6] See Sidonie Smith, *A Poetics of Women's Autobiography: Marginality and the Fictions of Self-Representation* (Bloomington, Ind.: Indiana Univ. Press, 1987), 175. Nin does edge into the main text of Rado's most recent collection, *Modernism, Gender, and Culture*, though again she gets just one mention, an (inaccurate) reference to *A Spy in the House of Love* and *Seduction of the Minotaur* (Lisa Rado [ed.], *Modernism, Gender, and Culture: A Cultural Studies Approach* [New York and London: Garland, 1997], 292).

In this context, one of my aims is to reassert Nin's place within the feminist–modernist nexus, to show that there are clear links between Nin's work and that of other, now 'canonical', women modernists. In particular, I believe that there are striking parallels between Nin and H.D.: their concern with questions of self-writing and the interrelations between autobiography and fiction; their interest in the narratives and 'legends' of the self created through psychoanalysis, and their moves into analysis (H.D. with Freud, Nin with Freud's former disciple Rank) in the same year; their enthusiasm for film as a new 'synthesis' of art forms and a means of restoring 'magic' and 'value' to language. I examine these parallels at various points in the book.

However, one of the most significant reasons for Nin's marginality in relation to modernist criticism is precisely the fact that she does not fit neatly into the 'modernist period', if this is perceived to have a cut-off point around 1940 (Benstock's book, for instance, is subtitled 'Paris 1900–1940').[7] Nin was certainly not the longest-lived of Benstock's 'women of the Left Bank', nor the last survivor—both Djuna Barnes and Bryher were born in the 1890s and lived into the 1980s. But she was the only one to take on a new lease of public life in the 1960s and 1970s, in a context far removed from that of Paris modernism: US second-wave feminism. So, while Nin is marginalized as a modernist by comparison with H.D., Barnes, or Gertrude Stein, she has a public profile and a degree of fame—or perhaps notoriety—quite unlike theirs. The internet provides a good illustration of this: while searches for 'H.D.' or 'Djuna Barnes' turn up sites produced by and for academics, a search for 'Anaïs Nin' reveals sites with fanzine-style material, such as 'letters' and adulatory tributes to Nin from her fans, mixed in with scholarly information. The name 'Anaïs Nin' also turns up a large number of links to pornography sites and sites advertising erotic publications—in other words, it carries meanings quite unlike those associated with other modernist women writers. Both as a 'real woman' and as a set of representations, Anaïs Nin moved (and moves) across various cultural, historical, and geographical contexts.

I believe that it is precisely this longevity and contextual mobility that makes Nin an interesting and valuable object of study, and particularly so

[7] In a paper given to the English Graduate Colloquium at Sussex University ('Modernizing Modernism', 20 Oct. 1999), Peter Nicholls expressed dissatisfaction with this periodizing tendency, remarking that writers do not always conveniently die (or even stop writing) when the period they are associated with is thought to end. Nin seems a good example of such an 'inconvenient' writer.

in relation to the increasing emphasis on cultural and contextual approaches in feminist literary studies. In *Beyond Feminist Aesthetics* (1989), Rita Felski analysed the interrelations of gender, politics, and aesthetics, specifically in terms of feminist literary theory, and called for a thoroughgoing 'recontextualization' of women's writing, a critical attention to the relations between the 'diverse forms of women's writing' and the 'cultural and ideological processes shaping the effects and potential limits of literary production at historically specific contexts'.[8] In her introduction to the 1994 collection *Rereading Modernism*, Lisa Rado drew on Felski's work in announcing a commitment to 'a more culturally based criticism, a more historical and interdisciplinary approach' for feminist–modernist studies.[9] The title of Rado's most recent collection, *Modernism, Gender, and Culture: A Cultural Studies Approach*, clearly indicates the continuing emphasis on historical and cultural contexts for both modernist studies and feminist literary criticism. Warning against the potentially 'homogenizing' or totalizing effects of critical discourses such as poststructuralism, psychoanalytic criticism, 'and even some forms of Marxism and feminism', Rado argues that historical-cultural criticism is 'the one critical mode that forces us to recognize that individual context matters'.[10] Culturally and contextually informed criticism, then, 'involves not only determining the author's voice, but uncovering the dialogic strands connecting the author to an ongoing conversation with historically specific partners, speakers, and listeners. To "read" a text or a work of art is thus to eavesdrop upon, to hear snatches of a much larger cultural interchange to which we must turn.'[11]

In Nin's case, the history of these 'conversations' is a tangled one, characterized by repeated patterns of displacement, alienation, and adaptation—repeated processes of coming to terms with new countries, new languages, new ideas. Born in Neuilly, near Paris, in 1903, to a Cuban father and French-Cuban-Danish mother, Nin spent the early part of her childhood in various parts of Europe—France, Germany, Belgium, and

[8] Rita Felski, *Beyond Feminist Aesthetics: Feminist Literature and Social Change* (London: Hutchinson Radius, 1989), 48.

[9] Rado (ed.), *Rereading Modernism*, 12.

[10] Rado (ed.), *Modernism, Gender, and Culture*, 4. However, I would suggest that Rado is here being somewhat reductively homogenizing herself, especially since she concedes that 'cultural theory' is 'less a theory than a loosely connected series of critical approaches and methodologies' (3–4). I hope to demonstrate in this book that it is possible to incorporate insights and approaches from psychoanalytic and poststructuralist theory while retaining a basic commitment to the importance of historical and cultural context.

[11] Ibid. 7.

finally Spain. In 1914, following her parents' separation, Nin and her two younger brothers sailed with their mother to New York. Displaced geographically, culturally, and linguistically, Nin at first refused to adapt to America: her earliest diaries were filled with effusive paeans to her 'motherland', France—a patriotism fuelled by the ongoing war. She continued to write in French rather than English until the age of seventeen, but then began to immerse herself in English and American literature and philosophical essays, reading Emerson, Thoreau, Carlyle and Whitman, Mark Twain and Henry James. Emerson, in particular, was an inspirational figure to Nin at this time; in April 1921, having bought for herself Emerson's *Essays*, she wrote in her diary: 'my enthusiasm knows no bounds. I could not part with the little book for all the gold in the world' (*Early Diary*, II, 174). In July of that year, she wrote that the figure of Emerson was 'linked irrevocably with all my theories of life' (*Early Diary*, II, 247).

In March 1923, aged 20, Nin married Hugh Guiler, five years her senior, the American-born son of Scottish parents. Hugo, as he was known, was setting out on a career in banking in order to give himself the financial security to pursue his love of literature and poetry; when he married Nin, a Catholic, he was disowned by his entire family. The following year, Hugo was transferred by his employers, National City Bank, to Paris. Nin prepared for the move by reading Henry James's *The Ambassadors*, feeling caught between different allegiances: '[James's novel] interprets Paris to an American, and I must recognize that I am one of those Americans. I feel it when America is belittled, when American life is libeled. Shall I defend it to the French, I the Frenchwoman by birth and by affection?' (29 July 1924 [*Journal of a Wife*, 55]). On moving to Paris, Nin hated it, feeling herself displaced again, a 'puritan' unable to accept French 'sensuality'. As far as literature went, she found herself 'revolted' by Anatole France ('"I never knew such things had been written"' [45]), 'baffled and bored' by Marcel Proust (51)—who would later become one of her favourite writers and an important literary influence. Instead, she wrote, 'I wave Carlyle and Emerson over my head, like torches or firearms' (117).

Nin remained based in Paris until the outbreak of war in 1939. Having at first rejected Parisian life and French literary culture, she gradually acclimatized, helped by the tuition of Hélène Boussinescq, a teacher of literature who introduced Nin to the 'modern works' she had previously ignored. As Nin began to experiment in her own writing—and in her life—she discovered her own 'modernism' and her affinity with the French 'poetic' writers. Proust, Rimbaud, André Breton, and Henri

Michaux would become important literary figures for her; French 'poetic prose' would become her yardstick for the 'ideal' literary language. The artistic 'revolution' declared by *transition* magazine and by the Surrealist manifestos became Nin's own aesthetic cause. Psychoanalysis too was, for Nin, part of this cultural revolution: her first analyst, René Allendy, also analysed and supported Antonin Artaud, whom he introduced to Nin; her second, Freud's former colleague Otto Rank, was strongly interested in literature and mythology. The influences of the Parisian context—poetic prose, Surrealism, psychoanalysis, and the self-conscious spirit of experiment and innovation, what Nin would later describe as the 'dedicat[ion] to war against the cliché, the obvious, the traditional, and the conventional' (*Novel*, 1)—would remain central to Nin throughout her life.

Forced to return to America, with her husband, at the outbreak of the Second World War, Nin found herself once again culturally alienated, confronted with an emphasis on social and political realism completely at odds with her own preoccupations and aesthetic ideals. She sums up this experience of alienation in the introduction to *The Novel of the Future*:

> I did not realize that with war and emigration to America would come a totally different kind of struggle. In France we felt part of a pioneering group, but in America we found ourselves isolated and in the minority. Literature was for the masses, it was in the hands of the social realists, dominated by the social critics, all more concerned with politics than psychology . . . The climate of the forties was insular, provincial, antipoetic, and anti-European.[12]

Only with the 'jazz writing' of the Beats in the 1950s, and then in the social and cultural upheavals of the 1960s, did Nin begin to feel 'at home' in America. Indeed, she saw the artistic and cultural experiments of the 1960s as in some ways a resurgence of the radical spirit of the Parisian avant-gardes, the flower children of California and Greenwich Village as the spiritual heirs of the Surrealists and *transition* revolutionaries.

More importantly, the rise of the women's liberation movement provided the context for the publication of Nin's diaries and her subsequent fame. This context of second-wave feminism enabled her to situate herself as a woman artist who had struggled for emancipation, for recog-

[12] *Novel*, 1. The 'we' here remains unspecified, but clearly suggests Nin's feeling of belonging to an artistic community in Paris, a 'pioneering group'. There is also a notably elitist tone (characteristic of modernism in general) in the dismissal of American literature as 'for the masses'.

nition, for her own identity. As a radio interviewer remarked in 1971, Nin became, for many women, a figure who 'embodied the notion of personal freedom'.[13] After the long periods of alienation, it seemed that '*this time*, the time was right'.[14]

With the publication of her diaries Nin was transformed, as Diane Richard-Allerdyce writes, 'from a little-known coterie writer of abstract fiction to a spokesperson for the conscience-raising [sic] movements of the 1960s'; she remained 'at the center of a devoted circle of readers', and died 'a cultural heroine'.[15] And yet, in terms of feminism, Nin was a highly controversial figure. Radical feminists, working from a strongly empiricist and social-realist point of view, were hostile to her emphasis on artistic creativity, her ideas about (and enactments of) 'femininity', and particularly to her interest in psychoanalysis—the legacies of her years in France. More than twenty years after her death—and one hundred years after her birth—Nin remains (as I shall show in Chapter 5) a peculiarly charged figure, still capable of inspiring extremes of both adulation and hostility—a demi-goddess to some women, a monster to others.

Suzanne Nalbantian claims that, because of her 'peripatetic' life, Nin remained 'impervious to her epoch and environment'.[16] Rather, I would argue, the result of Nin's many geographical and cultural displacements is a complex layering of contexts and influences, sometimes producing a curious mixture of the anachronistic and the avant-garde. Deirdre Bair suggests that Nin was 'a shining examplar of the modernist dictum "Make it new", for she was prescient enough to poise herself directly in the path of all that was fresh, exciting, and frequently controversial, from D. H. Lawrence to the Beat poets, and to embrace it willingly despite the consequences'.[17] On the other hand, Nin also recognized—an insight she derived from psychoanalysis—that the 'new' always contains the 'not new'. This is the theme of her story 'Ragtime' (1938), in which the protagonist, visiting the ragpickers' camp on the outskirts of Paris, is confronted with fragments of her own past, and with the psychological truth of the ragpicker's endless song, 'in the new not new' ('Ragtime', in

[13] Milton Hoffman, 'An Interview with Anaïs Nin' (1971), in Wendy DuBow (ed.), *Conversations with Anaïs Nin* (Jackson, Miss.: Univ. Press of Mississippi, 1994), 149.

[14] Nin, in ibid. (throughout this book italics are the original author's unless otherwise stated).

[15] *Remaking of Self*, 146.

[16] Suzanne Nalbantian, *Aesthetic Autobiography: From Life to Art in Marcel Proust, James Joyce, Virginia Woolf and Anaïs Nin* (London: Macmillan, 1994), 170.

[17] Deirdre Bair, *Anaïs Nin: A Biography* (London: Bloomsbury, 1995), p. xviii.

Under a Glass Bell, 64). Nin returned frequently to this theme in her writing even as she enacted it in her life, examining psychoanalytic ideas of repeating and re-enacting: in her 1961 novel *Seduction of the Minotaur*, the Mexican Doctor Hernandez describes for Lillian the ways in which people re-enact the same 'dramas', the same plots, throughout their lives.

On the level of cultural influences, while Nin's 'peripatetic' life produced a pattern of displacement and experiences of alienation, she also sought the connections across different temporal, geographical, and cultural contexts, making interesting—sometimes awkward, sometimes bizarre—attempts to graft ideas from one context onto another. Thus, for instance, we can see her early reading of Emerson, which Noël Riley Fitch calls 'the American narrative of self-discovery and [self-] creation',[18] underlying her later interest in Otto Rank's ideas of creative will; in the 1960s, she links the experimental, psychedelic spirit of the American underground back to the French Surrealists' drive to explore the realms of the 'marvellous'; and, in the 1970s, she tries to synthesize her belief in the radical potential of psychoanalysis and avant-garde aesthetics with a predominantly social-realist American feminism. I attempt throughout this book to highlight the ways in which different cultural and historical 'conversations' overlap, intermix or pull against each other throughout Nin's career.

Recognizing these patterns and tensions perhaps also helps with the question, which has dogged the reception of Nin's work, of where to 'place' her in terms of literary traditions, particularly if these are understood in broadly national terms. It is intriguing that Nin has no entry at all in *The Oxford Companion to English Literature* (2000), despite the inclusion of American and European writers considered relevant to 'English' literature.[19] She does get an entry, however, in the more inclusively titled *Cambridge Guide to Literature in English* (1993), where she is described as an 'American diarist, novelist and critic'.[20]

Difficulties and disputes over 'placing' Nin were apparent when the first monographs on her appeared in the 1970s. Richard Centing, in a Foreword to Evelyn Hinz's 1971 study *The Mirror and the Garden*, stressed

[18] Fitch, *Anaïs*, 57.

[19] H.D., e.g., does get an entry, as does Henry Miller. Margaret Drabble (ed.), *The Oxford Companion to English Literature* (Oxford: Oxford Univ. Press, new edn., 2000).

[20] Ian Ousby (ed.), *The Cambridge Guide to Literature in English* (Cambridge: Cambridge Univ. Press, 1993). This is strictly correct, since Nin became a naturalized American citizen in 1952.

the confusions over Nin's 'literary nationality' ('Anaïs Nin had to be excluded from the *Columbia Essays on Modern Writers* because she was no longer a foreigner, while a recent anthology wrongly identified her as a French writer'[21]). Arguing that these confusions had militated against proper literary recognition of Nin in America, Centing stated that 'Anaïs Nin refers to herself as an international writer, but for the sake of literary classification, she must be considered an American.'[22] This is consistent with Hinz's approach in the book as a whole: Philip Jason suggests that Hinz seeks to place Nin inside 'accessible, sanctioned traditions' (that is, accessible and sanctioned for Americans), making connections to James and Emerson rather than to 'scary foreigners'.[23] In contrast, Sharon Spencer's 1977 monograph *Collage of Dreams* approached Nin, as Spencer writes in her Preface, 'from the perspective of one who is deeply involved with twentieth-century fiction, primarily that of Europe and Latin America', paying far more attention to such influences on Nin as Symbolism and Surrealism.[24]

Particularly interesting for my purposes are the shifts and tensions in *feminist* reception of Nin. As I have noted, Nin was interestingly, and awkwardly, positioned between various feminist factions in the late 1960s and 1970s, both held up as an inspiring example of liberated womanhood and feminine creativity, and reviled as an apolitical, individualistic counter-revolutionary complicit with the patriarchy. More recently—that is, at a greater distance from Nin's own participation in the feminist movement—we can discern different strands within academic feminist interest in Nin. As I have indicated, she hovers on the fringes of feminist–modernist studies, and on the fringes of autobiography theory. There is also a recent current of Lacanian psychoanalytic-feminist criticism, which is interested not so much in Nin as any kind of exemplar of womanhood or forgotten literary pioneer, but in the explorations of subjectivity and sexuality in her writings, particularly in her erotica. I discuss this 'Lacanian' connection in Chapter 2.

What is particularly interesting here, I think, is the way in which the disputed object that is 'psychoanalysis' shifts in value. For radical

[21] Richard Centing, 'Foreword: The Recognition of Anaïs Nin', in Evelyn Hinz, *The Mirror and the Garden: Realism and Reality in the Writings of Anaïs Nin* (New York: Harcourt Brace Jovanovich, 2nd edn., 1973 [1971]), p. xi.

[22] Ibid.

[23] Philip K. Jason, *Anaïs Nin and her Critics* (Columbia, SC: Camden House, 1993), 3.

[24] Sharon Spencer, *Collage of Dreams: The Writings of Anaïs Nin* (New York: Harcourt Brace Jovanovich, 2nd edn., 1981 [1977]).

feminists in the 1970s, Nin's association with psychoanalysis was often the crucial sticking point, the one thing they could point to to prove beyond doubt that she *could not* be a feminist. For a recent Lacanian-feminist critic like Richard-Allerdyce, on the other hand, Nin's interest in psychoanalysis is central to her importance as a modernist and a feminist. My suggestion is, then, that looking at the different feminist responses to Nin can also serve to highlight some of the significant tensions within 'feminism' itself—like psychoanalysis, another equally disputed object.

These tensions are also important in Chapter 5, where *femininity* is the central issue. Again, I aim to produce an analysis that moves in two directions: an examination of the different ways in which Nin has been seen to exemplify 'femininity' can also serve as an exploration of some of the difficulties, for women, around notions of femininity and ways of relating to it. In particular, I focus on ideas of costuming and masquerade, which have been important in feminist thinking and are equally significant within Nin's fiction and in relation to her own self-constructions.

If questions around feminism(s) and femininity form one of the main strands in this book, the other is focused on issues of self and writing, identity and 'fictionality'. Here again, I believe that there is a particularly good fit between Nin and the trajectory of feminist literary criticism sketched earlier, because of the critical concern with the relation between the (female) author and her text—one of Nin's preoccupations throughout her writing career.

One of the most important aspects of Rita Felski's call for the recontextualization of women's writing was the attempt to theorize this relation in a more balanced way. Felski saw feminist literary theory as caught between two extreme positions, producing either 'too much' or 'too little' of an author. The first tendency, typical of anglophone feminist criticism, posited a distinctively female self whose texts could be straightforwardly read as expressions or reflections of her gendered experience; thus, Felski claimed, reducing the 'complex meanings of literary texts to the single authenticating source of authorial consciousness', and failing to account sufficiently for the very 'literariness' of texts.[25] The second tendency, more influenced by French feminism, poststructuralist and psychoanalytic theory, was to focus purely on the text and the forces at play within language (what Felski calls 'a kind of erotics of the text'[26]), rejecting the (bourgeois, humanist) conception of 'the author' as historical producer of the text. Felski argued that, by paying more attention to

[25] Felski, *Beyond Feminist Aesthetics*, 28, 30.

[26] Ibid. 23.

the specific cultural and historical contexts of textual production and reception, and to the complex relations between subjectivity and ideological structures (including structures of language), feminist literary critics could avoid these extreme positions. This type of contextual reading would enable critics to reinstate the (female) author as a historically located agent, the producer of her texts, without treating her as the omnipotent Author (as Barthes writes it), both the ground and the limit of all textual meaning.

In paying attention to the contexts of both the production and the reception of Nin's work, I instate Nin both as author and as a historically and culturally located agent. At the same time, however, I try to pay attention to the ways in which texts may escape or ramify beyond authorial control or intention. This may happen at various levels: meanings and interpretations may proliferate both intra- and intertextually. In terms of the latter, the longevity of Nin's career and her geographical and cultural mobility produce some interesting tensions in her own readings of her texts. In Chapter 1, for example, I discuss the tension between Nin's insistence, in the 1970s context, on the 'non-literary' nature of her diary, and her own marked ambivalence on this question in the 1930s. And in Chapter 2, I look at the contrast between Nin's erotica, with their depictions of sexuality as a divisive, conflictual force within the psyche, and her attempts to frame the stories within a cultural-feminist emphasis on women's sexuality as inseparable from love and respect. More obviously, my use of contemporary literary-critical approaches and ideas as tools with which to read Nin's texts (and, particularly in the final chapter, her own self-representations) will produce interpretations which would have been unavailable, even incomprehensible, to her. While Nin remains 'the author', the historically located person whose work and cultural 'conversations' I am examining, she is certainly not 'the Author', the ground and limit of meaning and interpretation.

Precisely these issues of authorship and authority are centrally important *within* Nin's work: the status of the writing subject vis-à-vis her (or his) text was one of Nin's preoccupations from a very early age. Although, as I show in Chapter 1, she sometimes approached questions of self and text in a playful manner, these were also serious and sometimes fraught questions for Nin, with issues of control and power very much to the fore. While her psychoanalytic beliefs, her emphasis on the unconscious, pulled her away from ideas of complete authorial control, biographical evidence suggests that she was fiercely hostile to criticism or 'misinterpretation' of her work, defensively trying to *retain* control of texts and meanings.[27] In Chapter 3, I discuss these issues in relation to Nin's obsessive returns to a Scheherezade-like figure, the tale-spinning but ultimately elusive woman who seems to figure Nin's own ambivalence in her writing, her simultaneous drives towards revelation and concealment. As I will show, a striking passage in the sixth volume of Nin's *Journals* reveals the extent to which, for her, writing and authorship were painfully entangled with feelings of sexual guilt and vulnerability.

The tension in Nin's ideas about authorship and the writing subject's relation to her text is one strand of a wider tension which dominated Nin's thinking and which is central to this book. On the one hand, Nin was pulled towards a fantasy of a coherent, unified identity, a 'whole' self, ontologically prior to and independent of its articulations in writing or in other forms of representation. On the other hand, she was also fascinated by the multiplicity of any 'self'—a multiplicity which could be experienced positively, as a fluidity and freedom from the constraints of identity, or negatively, as conflict and schism. She was also acutely aware of the 'fictionality', in a broad sense, of any self—its formation through stories, enactments, and performances of various kinds.

This awareness can be seen even in Nin's childhood writings, grounded, perhaps, in her early experience of linguistic displacement and her preoccupation, in the face of upheaval, with what would remain her central project: the narrativizing of her life in the diary. In January 1915, aged eleven, Nin records in her diary a remark made by a family acquaintance, M. Emile Villemin: 'he said something that I still remember, that if one knows two languages, one is two people. If one knows three, one is three people. So then, what am I?' (*Early Diary*, I, 41). The immediate relevance of this to Nin's situation—her recent arrival in America, linguistically caught between French, Spanish, and English—is obvious. But two months later, Nin writes that she is 'haunted' by M. Villemin's words (55). His remark had resonated with her not just because of the linguistic and cultural displacement she was experiencing, but also because it clearly suggested the problem that her diary writing was already making

[27] Fitch, for instance, writes that Nin was 'personally hurt by the slightest criticism' in reviews of her books (*Anaïs*, 373). Philip Jason notes that 'Nin could be extremely loyal to her partisans, hostile toward those who could not find only splendor' (*Anaïs Nin*, 12 n. 4). Nin's tendency to feel personally attacked by criticism and to view critics' interpretations as 'misreadings' is clearly apparent throughout her published *Journals*.

her acutely, precociously, aware of: the complex relation between language—writing, story-telling, narrativizing—and identity.

Throughout this book, I trace the ways in which Nin remained fascinated—and sometimes 'haunted'—by the interplay of fictionality and identity, what she would later call 'the plot [or plots] of one's life'. Nin's sense of her life as lived 'within stories' led her to explore the various forms of narrativizing through which identities might be constructed: a text like that of the diary, the stories of psychoanalysis, the roles of the actress, the self-mythologizing of the enigmatic *femme fatale* wrapping herself in veils of words.

The chapters of the book do not form a linear progression, but rather a series of interconnected, though differently focused, analyses of these major issues in Nin's thought—always with an awareness of the importance of different contexts of production and reception. In the first chapter, I consider questions of autobiography and textual personae, comparing Nin's self-narratives with those of H.D. In Chapter 2, I look at Nin's use of psychoanalytic ideas—in particular, Otto Rank's concept of creative will—in relation to questions of identity and psychic division, examining Nin's unique place within the tangled history of those star-crossed twentieth-century lovers, 'psychoanalysis' and 'feminism'. Chapter 3 explores Nin's fascination with figures of actresses and enigmatic women, and analyses the ways in which the seductive but elusive *femme fatale* both recurs in and structures Nin's writing. In Chapter 4, I examine Nin's aesthetics of an ideal prose-poetic language, in terms of both a self-conscious modernism and a concern with gender and creativity. In particular, I trace some of the shifts and tensions in Nin's thinking about femininity, creativity, and a 'radical' artistic practice, and consider the ways in which she has been positioned as an early proponent of *écriture féminine*—between Woolf and Richardson, on the one hand, and Cixous and Irigaray on the other. Finally, in Chapter 5, I look at questions of masquerade, fantasy, and identification in relation to femininity. I suggest that, just as Nin explores in her fiction the ways in which women act as 'mirrors' for each other, reflecting back fantasies of self and of femininity, so Nin comes to play a similar role for other women, becoming 'Anaïs Nin icon'—a kind of place-holder for various fantasies, both positive and negative, of femininity and feminine sexuality.

Susan Stanford Friedman, discussing the textual patterns of repetition and reworking in H.D.'s novels, uses as a model Freud's account of serial dreams, in which the same material is worked over and played out with different focuses, different points of repression: characters, images, and ideas shift from centre to periphery and back again.[28] This is also, I would argue, an illuminating model for Nin's writing and thinking, in which themes and characters recur, narrative lines interweave, loop and return on themselves; and one that she herself, with her emphasis on 'proceeding from the dream', following the unfamiliar and capricious plotlines of the unconscious,[29] would probably have agreed with. I hope that the various narrative threads weaving their way through this book serve not only to cast new light on Nin, but also to suggest some of the ways in which the production and reception of Anaïs Nin and her work can be used to explore questions of modernism, feminism, and psychoanalysis; writing and identity, fictionality and femininity.

[28] Susan Stanford Friedman, 'Return of the Repressed in H.D.'s Madrigal Cycle', in Susan Stanford Friedman and Rachel Blau DuPlessis (eds.), *Signets: Reading H.D.* (Madison, Wis.: Univ. of Wisconsin Press, 1990), 233–52.

[29] See e.g. *Novel*, 27–9.

1

'I Must Live within Stories': Narratives of the Self

Nin's prose poem 'The Labyrinth', first published in 1938, begins with the words 'I was eleven years old when I walked into the labyrinth of my diary' (in *Under a Glass Bell*, 66). Her sense of life and writing as inextricably woven together is apparent even in her earliest diaries, in which she envisages herself and her life as 'a book without an Epilogue, an unfinished book' (13 June 1919 [*Early Diary*, I, 251]), and the future as the unwritten text which will come to fill the blank pages of her diary (1 February 1920 [*Early Diary*, I, 427]). Many years later, Nin described the way in which, through writing the diary, she had always viewed life as 'an adventure and a tale', with herself the protagonist: 'I was telling myself the story of a life' (*Journals*, VII, 266; *A Woman Speaks*, 182).

In this chapter, I shall examine Nin's autobiographical practice in the diary and, more broadly, her insistent drive towards self-narrative. I argue that we find in Nin's writing conflicting views of the diary as text and practice: as 'authentic', spontaneous self-expression, and on the other hand as a literary work with its own generic and formal properties; as site of self-presence and ground of identity, and also as sign of the multiplicity and fictionality of the self. Furthermore, for Nin the diary is not simply a 'record' of lived experience; rather, the 'life' and the writing impact on each other in a process of mutual feedback, creating a life lived, as Nin puts it, 'within stories'. Ultimately, as I shall argue, Nin creates narratives and self-representations which are neither entirely fictional nor entirely historical, but—in Peggy Kamuf's term—'double-jointed', pulling in both directions. In this, Nin is close to her near-contemporary H.D., another writer for whom life and text, fiction and autobiography, were closely entwined; and I shall look particularly at H.D.'s hybrid journal-essay 'H.D. by Delia Alton' in order to draw out the points of connection between the two writers. Finally, I shall examine the ways in which, for both Nin and H.D., psychoanalysis provided another important context for this insistent narrativizing of self, a space for discovering—and for creating—the 'plots' which, for both women, made up their lives.

FEMINIST PARADIGMS OF WOMEN'S SELF-WRITING

Feminist critics, beginning with Estelle Jelinek's edited collection *Women's Autobiography: Essays in Criticism* (1980), have been concerned to examine the specificities of women's self-writing, attempting to theorize the 'difference' of women's autobiography. They have argued that self-writing by women does not conform to the traditional ('male') notion of autobiography, legalistically defined by Philippe Lejeune as 'a retrospective prose narrative produced by a real person concerning his own existence'; a narrative in which the 'identity' of author, narrator, and protagonist guarantees the non-fictional status of the text for the reader, an 'autobiographical pact' which is 'sealed by the proper name'.[1] Sidonie Smith, in her *Poetics of Women's Autobiography* (1987), suggests that the key questions posed by feminist critics are 'how the autobiographer's identity as woman within the symbolic order of patriarchy affects her relationship to generic possibilities—to the autobiographical impulse, to the structuring of content, to the reading and writing of the self, to the authority of the voice and the situating of narrative perspective, to the problematic nature of representation itself'.[2]

Feminist critics, then, seek to examine the interrelations between the problematics of women's place within the symbolic order, and their impulses towards and modes of self-writing. Domna Stanton argues that 'autogynography' (her term for women's self-writing) 'has a global and therapeutic purpose: to constitute the female subject. In a phallocentric system, which defines her as the object, the inessential other to the same male subject . . . the *graphing* of the *auto* was an act of self-assertion that denied and reversed woman's status'.[3] However, Stanton goes on to argue that, despite this aim of self-assertion, this use of writing to constitute and assert subjecthood, autogynography problematizes that subjecthood precisely because of women's symbolic status as marginal 'other':

[1] Philippe Lejeune, 'The Autobiographical Pact', in *On Autobiography* (ed. Paul John Eakin; trans. Katherine Leary; Minneapolis: Univ. of Minnesota Press, 1989), 5.

[2] Smith, *Poetics of Women's Autobiography*, 17.

[3] Domna C. Stanton, 'Autogynography: Is the Subject Different?', in idem (ed.), *The Female Autograph: Theory and Practice of Autobiography from the Tenth to the Twentieth Century* (Chicago: Univ. of Chicago Press, 1987), 14.

'because of woman's different status in the symbolic order, autogynography . . . dramatize[s] the fundamental alterity and non-presence of the subject, even as it asserts itself discursively and strives toward an always impossible self-possession'.[4]

Stanton here suggests a possible connection between women's 'different' placing within the symbolic order and the notions, within women's self-writing, 'of romances, of fictions, of "imagined selves" '.[5] And this connection is in fact central to much feminist theorizing about women's autobiographical practices. Women's historical experience of multiple and *conflicting* roles—classically, the conflict between their allotted roles as wives and mothers within the patriarchal order, and the desire for an independent, creative subjecthood—is seen as informing the writing practice which, in Stanton's words, 'dramatize[s] the fundamental alterity and non-presence of the subject'. Women's marginality and problematic relation to positions of subjecthood are seen as highly relevant to the 'autobiographical impulse' and to the relation to 'generic possibilities', as Smith suggested.

Specifically, women's relation to the problematics of identity is seen to underlie a particular stress on the *fictional* within self-writing—as is suggested in the subtitle of Smith's book, *Marginality and the Fictions of Self-Representation.* For the 'marginal subject', self-writing is not seen as the expression of a pre-given self, but as 'participation in the multiple discourses that establish and reestablish this "self" '. Thus, 'the notion of *fictional* self-writing seems in [some] ways even more congenial to the marginal subject, in that it implies an acknowledgement that the self is always to some extent (and in some senses) a fiction'.[6]

The sense of being caught up in these 'multiple discourses'—of being, in fact, multiply marginal—comes through strongly in a passage from Audre Lorde's autobiographical text *Zami* (1982): '*Being women together was not enough. We were different. Being gay-girls together was not enough. We were different. Being Black together was not enough. We were different. Being Black women together was not enough. We were different. Being Black dykes together was not enough. We were different.*'[7] Lorde continues: 'Self-preservation warned some of us that we could not afford to settle for one easy definition, one narrow individuation of self. At the Bag [the

[4] 'Autogynography', 15.

[5] Ibid. 16.

[6] Molly Hite, Foreword, in Janice Morgan and Colette T. Hall (eds.), *Redefining Autobiography in Twentieth-Century Women's Fiction: An Essay Collection* (New York: Garland, 1991), p. xv.

[7] Audre Lorde, *Zami: A New Spelling of My Name* (London: Sheba, 1984 [1982]), 226.

Bagatelle, a Greenwich Village gay bar], at Hunter College, uptown in Harlem, at the library, there was a piece of the real me bound in each place, and growing.'[8] Several complex issues are raised here. Lorde implies both a struggle for self-definition and acceptance, finding a 'place' within these various discourses, and at the same time a recognition that the (multiply marginal) self cannot be tied to any one discourse or definition. She also invokes the concept of 'the real me', while simultaneously showing the complex and fragmented nature of this 'real' self, which is both material (linked to geographical places) and discursive (being a 'gay-girl' in the 'Bag', for example). As I shall show, the same 'double-jointedness' is evident in Nin's textual explorations of identity.

Laura Marcus, drawing on the work of Rita Felski, also lays emphasis on the role of the fictional in women's autobiographical writing:

> women autobiographers subvert the 'autobiographical pact' by including problematic or ambiguous signals which trouble rather than confirm the distinction between autobiography and fiction, or by making the 'proper name' ambiguous . . . The 'fictional' can become the space for more general identifications, or for the trying out of potentialities and possibilities . . . or it can be a way of suggesting how much fiction is involved in all self-representations.[9]

'Fiction' here should not be taken to imply falsehood as opposed to truth. Rather, it highlights the ways in which any 'self' is bound up with and constructed through particular stories and narratives—there is no 'true', Ur-self lying beyond the realm of constructedness and representation. As bell hooks notes, discussing her experience of writing autobiography, 'I was compelled to face the fiction that is a part of all retelling, remembering. I began to think of the work I was doing as both fiction and autobiography.'[10]

The highlighting of the 'fictional' also suggests the linguistic and grammatical peculiarities involved in representing oneself, saying 'I'—peculiarities highlighted by deconstructionist critics, following Jacques Derrida. In saying 'I', a speaker (or writer) claims both uniqueness and certainty of identity; at the same time, he or she uses a pronoun which is part of a common language, a 'shifter' whose referent can—necessarily—be anyone. In the deconstructionist account, then, representing oneself

[8] Lorde, *Zami*, 226.

[9] Laura Marcus, *Auto/biographical Discourses: Theory, Criticism, Practice* (Manchester: Manchester Univ. Press, 1994), 280.

[10] bell hooks, 'Writing Autobiography', in *Talking Back: Thinking Feminist, Thinking Black* (London: Sheba, 1989), 157.

in language means the 'death' of the (unique, self-identical) self. As Peggy Kamuf puts it, following Derrida, ' "I" spells the death of me; it is already the effacement of a singular nature in a common sig-nature'.[11] The peculiarities involved in saying 'I' are also important within Jacques Lacan's theorizing of the human subject. Arguing that there is a fundamental split, within the psyche, between the *moi*, 'subject of being' or 'subject of identifications', and the *je*, the speaking subject, Lacan highlights both the coexistence of subject and object positions within the individual and the complexity of the 'first person', of saying 'I'. As Ellie Ragland-Sullivan puts it, 'the *moi* of the Lacanian subject normally "speaks" to another about his or her own subject . . . as if *je* were in the third person'.[12]

The centrality of issues of subjectivity and textuality to psychoanalytic, poststructuralist, and deconstructionist theory, together with modernism's self-conscious challenge to 'traditional' conceptions of selfhood and artistic practices, has tended to produce an understanding of autobiographical experimentation as an exclusively twentieth-century phenomenon. Sidonie Smith, in the 'Coda' to her *Poetics of Women's Autobiography*, takes up this contextual point with reference to twentieth-century women writers. Citing the postmodern demystification of the 'metaphysical self', the psychoanalytic shattering of the 'integrity of consciousness', and the poststructuralist disruption of 'the notion of the author and of authority itself', she suggests that, in the twentieth century, 'the teleological conception of selfhood has given way before experimental explorations of experience, memory, language, sexuality, social and political engagements . . . "Autobiography" no longer makes sense culturally. Its structural, rhetorical and imagistic rigidities have been fractured by the heteroglossic possibilities inherent in new ideologies of selfhood.' Women writing in the twentieth century, therefore, 'explore alternative scenarios of textuality and sexuality': Stein's ventriloquism in *The Autobiography of Alice B. Toklas*, Woolf's focus on the heightened moments of self-realization, Richardson's 'long volumes of semiautobiographical narrative', Nin's 'multi-volume outpouring of language and desire'.[13] Similarly, Janice Morgan and Colette Hall argue that, with the throwing into question of the assumptions of the 'fixed reality of the self' and the 'referential power of language' which grounded the firm

[11] Peggy Kamuf, *Signature Pieces: On the Institution of Authorship* (Ithaca, NY: Cornell Univ. Press, 1988), 5.

[12] Ellie Ragland-Sullivan, *Jacques Lacan and the Philosophy of Psychoanalysis* (London: Croom Helm, 1986), 176.

[13] Smith, *Poetics of Women's Autobiography*, 174–5.

distinction between fiction and autobiography, 'contemporary [women] writers have brought the domains of life and literature, experience and textuality, into a much more complex, more mutually creative, in fact complicitous relationship'.[14]

However, we should beware of overstatement here, in terms both of history and of gender. Modernist and postmodernist preoccupations may have enabled (or forced) twentieth-century writers to be more self-consciously aware of, even obsessed by, the fictional aspects of the self and the complexity of self-writing; but this awareness, as well as experimentation with different forms of literary self-representation, was certainly around before the twentieth century. James Olney sees Jean-Jacques Rousseau as prefiguring twentieth-century writers such as Samuel Beckett in his 'fragmentation of the *I*': 'Giving his *I* over to so many voices [in the *Dialogues*], he succeeds . . . in pushing the *I* further and further until it disappears over the horizon, "Nowhere to be found. Nowhere to be sought." His *I* becomes *Not I*. And we thought this was one of the dubious achievements of the twentieth century.'[15]

Nor—as the example of Rousseau already makes clear—is this questioning of the 'I' exclusive to women writers. None of the theoretical factors adduced by Sidonie Smith—the 'demystification' of the 'metaphysical self', the psychoanalytic challenge to identity and self-presence, the poststructuralist questioning of notions of 'author' and 'authority'—is gender-specific; all relate to subjectivity and textuality more generally. Malcolm Lowry is a striking example of a male writer for whom 'fiction' and 'autobiography' were deeply—sometimes tortuously—entangled.[16] Lowry created semi-fictional, semi-autobiographical textual personae, sometimes embedding 'fictions' within 'fictions' (for example, his own autobiographical novel *Under the Volcano* appears, under a different title, in his subsequent, again autobiographical, novel *Dark as the Grave wherein my Friend is Laid*). For Lowry, as for Nin, life and writing were inextricably entwined, forming a labyrinth from which he could not escape.[17] In terms of feminist theories of autobiography, then, we should

[14] *Redefining Autobiography*, 6.

[15] James Olney, *Memory and Narrative: The Weave of Life-Writing* (Chicago: Univ. of Chicago Press, 1988), 236–7. The quotation is from Beckett's play *Company*.

[16] Lowry's biographer Gordon Bowker remarks that 'in very few writers is the work so central to the life, and the life woven so deeply and deliberately into the work' (*Pursued by Furies: A Life of Malcolm Lowry* [London: Flamingo, 1993], p. xix).

[17] In the Preface to his biography of Lowry, Bowker uses the image of a labyrinth which is at the same time a 'hall of distorting mirrors'. He also describes Lowry's compulsive self-mythologizing and endless 'rewritings' of his life, which can be seen as 'his most complex and compelling fictional contrivance of all' (*Pursued by Furies*, p. xv).

resist generalizations suggesting that male conceptions of self and self-writing are 'straightforward' while women's are 'complex'. Blurring generic lines and problematizing 'proper' names may be characteristic of women writers, but are not peculiar to them.

In paradoxical contrast to this deconstruction of identity and exploration of possibilities of (fictional) self-representation, there is a counter-tendency within feminist autobiographical theory which insists on female identity and self-presence and on the 'referential reality' of women's texts. This paradox was suggested in Stanton's formulation: 'autogynography . . . dramatize[s] the fundamental alterity and non-presence of the subject, even as it asserts itself discursively and strives toward an always impossible self-possession'. Stanton goes on to argue that, in contrast to the (male) deconstructionist critics' happy undermining of 'identity', the 'feminist scholar' ('F.S.') is determined to 'affirm' and 'maintain' the notion. She continues:

> the valorized notion of female identity in most readings by F.S. was conjoined with an explicit or implicit belief in the referentiality and truth-value of autogynographies as 'honest records of the moment', or of women's 'inner lives'. It was almost as if . . . the feminist scholar's own identity depended on the referential reality of the woman in the text, as if that woman was the same and different other through whom F.S. needed to construct and relate her self.[18]

As with the emphasis on women's use of fictional strategies of self-representation, so this valorizing of and need for 'identity' is *also* seen as grounded in women's different, historically marginal status in social and symbolic orders: 'Professor Y [the male deconstructionist critic] was feeling paralyzed by the identity that the symbolic order bestowed (or imposed) upon him, whereas F.S. was still struggling, in that recently constructed room of her own, to assert an identity that was denied her'.[19] As we shall see, the kind of reading Stanton is examining here, with its conjoined emphases on identity and referential truth, comes particularly into force both in relation to the specific context of the 1970s women's liberation movement, and in relation to certain forms of women's self-writing, notably 'private' forms such as journals and diaries.

Nin's autobiographical writing may be seen as exemplifying the paradox suggested by Stanton, in that it seems to demonstrate *both* of the paradigms set out above: in Nin's autobiographical impulse, her use of form (specifically, the diary/journal form), her theory and practice of 'the reading and writing of the self', we can see both the drive for identity,

[18] 'Autogynography', 15–16. [19] Ibid. 15.

self-presence, and 'truth', and the recognition of alterity, multiplicity, and ultimately the fictionality of 'the self'—indeed, not merely the recognition of this, but pleasure in the possibilities, even the power, opened up by such a view of selfhood. I shall begin by looking at the significance of the particular reception history of Nin's edited diaries in the early 1970s and the mobilization, both by feminist readers and critics and by Nin herself, of a paradigm of authenticity and representativeness as a means of ascribing feminist value to the texts.

'A WOMAN SPEAKS'

Second-wave feminism of the 1960s and 1970s was a movement grounded in the concepts of testimony, of giving voice; coming to speech and hearing others to speech. At the grassroots level, the women's liberation movement operated through the process of 'consciousness-raising': women would gather in small groups to tell their stories, speak their experiences, and hear the stories and experiences of other women. These experiences would then be brought to bear on the public realm, through the central insight and dictum of the women's movement: that the personal was, after all, the political. Here is Kate Millett, writing in 1976: 'We have been a long time breaking our silence. Contained, muffled for centuries. So long unspoken, our lives, our worlds of experience, the very . . . quality, texture and nuance of our existence undefined, even undescribed. Half the world and mute save for a handful.'[20] Women could break this silence in consciousness-raising groups and on the streets, in rallies and protest marches; but they could also, crucially, break it in writing. Here is Millett again:

> If I look through that special shelf of books that feed me lately—they are all women. And they are all about themselves . . . Women writing their lives, lives as disparate as Sylvia Plath's and Han Suyin's. The energy of women coming full out of their own lives. *Our form is autobiography*, our form in the time of our silence, those burned and discarded diaries, those letters and journals of our obscurity. And now we print them and slip them to each other more and more openly. If men would know us, they are welcome. But we are mad to know each other now, to know ourselves. Now we celebrate, coming into being.[21]

[20] Kate Millett, 'Anaïs: A Mother to Us All: The Birth of the Artist as a Woman', *Anaïs: An International Journal* 9 (1991), 3–8 (3–4). Originally published (in French) 1976.

[21] Millett, 'Anaïs', 4.

Millett puts the phrase 'our form is autobiography' in italics, and this is the crucial point of emphasis: for this context of second-wave feminism, it was women's autobiographical, confessional, 'private' writing which was valued above all other forms of writing as the site of women coming to speech, 'writing their lives'. There are two important aspects to this. The first is the concept of *authenticity* in relation to women's writing. The value of the writing Millett talks about depends on its reference back to the female author—it is a 'true' and 'honest' account of her life and experiences. As Rita Felski argues in *Beyond Feminist Aesthetics*, this authenticity is frequently grounded in a deliberate distancing from the sphere of 'the literary' or of literature—and we can see this in Millett's appeal to the 'non-literary' genres of diaries, letters, and journals.

The second point is that the writing is seen to be *representative*—not just of the individual woman writer but in relation to a wider community of women. The female author writes of experiences shared by other women, with which women can identify; as Felski puts it, the text 'encodes an audience', a 'community of female readers'[22] who can feel themselves to be addressed by the text and to share the writer's personal feelings and experiences. Again, we can see this in Millett's account of reading other women's writing: 'we are mad to know each other—to know ourselves'.[23]

The significance of women's confessional writing for feminism and feminist literary theory, then, lies in its perceived exemplification of 'the intersection between the autobiographical imperative to communicate the truth of unique individuality, and the feminist concern with the representative and intersubjective elements of women's experience'.[24] This accords with Stanton's point, above, that we find in this feminist paradigm the conjunction of a 'valorized notion of female identity' and belief in the 'referentiality and truth-value' of women's texts; and, in this emphasis on the reading community and the 'representativeness' of the texts, corroboration of her suggestion that the feminist reader/critic thinks her own identity 'as a woman' through that of the woman whose texts she reads.

It is this context that was central to the reception of Nin's diary following its publication over the late 1960s and the 1970s, and which encouraged a particular interpretation of the text—not only on the part of the readers but also, interestingly, on the part of Nin herself. Nin had

[22] *Beyond Feminist Aesthetics*, 99.
[23] Millett, 'Anaïs', 4.
[24] *Beyond Feminist Aesthetics*, 93.

returned to the United States from Paris at the outbreak of the Second World War and had struggled throughout the 1940s and 1950s to achieve literary success: her novels had bad reviews and poor sales. But when her diaries were published in the late 1960s and 1970s, in the middle of the burgeoning women's liberation movement, she became a star, taken up as a heroine for women and even as a spokeswoman for the women's movement, touring the US giving lectures and interviews.[25] This is Kate Millett's 1976 account of Nin:

> [If] I were to say what writer matters to us most now, is spread over crammed miles of bookshelves, coast to coast, in the little women's bookstores springing up everywhere . . . is devoured whole in women's study classes, is carried in ragged denim bags from class to coffeehouse . . . is both basic primer and ultimate grace of sophistication, is mother to us all, as well as goddess and elder sister—it would have to be Anaïs Nin.[26]

Nin, she says, is 'the beginner, the shaper[;] giving form to our form, she has laid out her life for us'; in her diary she 'is telling it like it is'.[27] We can see here the importance, in this reception of Nin, of the feminist context I have identified: Nin is valued (even revered) because her diary is perceived to be both an *authentic* account of a woman's experience (she is 'telling it like it is') and *representative* of other women's experience: 'the diary ends by being the voice of woman herself'.[28]

The collection of Nin's interview and lecture transcripts put together by Evelyn Hinz in 1975 under the title *A Woman Speaks* provides equally telling illustrations of this construction of Nin and her text. The title itself is suggestive of the intersection of the personal and the representative from which women's confessional writing is seen to derive its importance: Anaïs Nin speaks *as a woman*. Hinz's introduction illustrates very clearly the emphasis she places on this double aspect of Nin's writing/speaking (that is, both her actual speaking in lectures and seminars and her 'speaking' in the diary): on the one hand, 'each individual comes away with the impression that there has been a personal and intimate conversation with Anaïs Nin'; on the other hand, 'when Anaïs Nin speaks it is a woman who speaks . . . her lectures . . . exemplify the power and range of the authentically feminine voice and vision' (*A Woman Speaks*, pp. xi, xii).

Hinz also emphasizes the reference back to the female author as the grounding meaning or truth of the text, the importance of Nin's public

[25] See Chapter 5 for a more detailed account of this history.
[26] Millett, 'Anaïs', 4.
[27] Ibid. 8, 7.
[28] Ibid. 5.

speaking to 'reassure the audience that there is a continuity between what she has written and who she is':

As she [Nin] came gradually to understand, the need [of her readers to see her 'in person'] reflected an apprehensiveness about the reality of the life portrayed in the *Diary*, a concern that possibly the woman with whose struggles one had identified . . . was not real but a fictional creation, a fear lest this apparently painstaking record of an individual's search for viable truths might be discovered to be partially or totally a masterful fabrication. The need to see her, the writer of the *Diary*, was a need to be reassured that such a life was possible because such a person was real. (*A Woman Speaks*, p. viii)

Having given her audience this guarantee of authenticity, having 'come out of the *Diary* to speak in person', Nin can at the end 'withdraw back again into its pages, leaving her audience with the *Diary* in place of her physical presence, leaving them with the place where she may always be found' (*A Woman Speaks*, p. x). This reassuring construction of the diary as the repository of Nin's authentic self (guaranteed ultimately by the reality of the person 'outside' the text) is strikingly at odds with an entry made by Nin in the diary more than forty years before Hinz's writing: 'Tonight I realize that the diary is a struggle to seize on the most unseizable person on earth. I elude my own detection . . . I cannot write myself out' (19 April 1933 [*Incest*, 141]). Rather than being 'the place where she may always be found', the diary here is the place where, Nin realizes, she can *never* be found. I shall discuss in more detail below the more complex view of the 'self' as constructed in and through the diary that emerges from Nin's writing in the 1930s.

Chapter VI of Hinz's collection, 'The Personal Life Deeply Lived',[29] is particularly useful for considering the ways in which the reception context for the diary impacts upon Nin's own constructions of her text and the aspects of the diary, as both text and practice, that she emphasizes. Here Nin concurs with the view that the importance of the diary lies in its combination of the personal and the representative: 'When I published it I thought it was the story of one woman—one often has the impression

[29] The text of each chapter is, as Hinz explains in her Introduction, a composite construction, excerpts from various lectures and seminars being spliced together (by Hinz) with the stated aim of 'generat[ing] for the reader the *effect* which Nin's addresses have upon her listeners' (p. xii). Hinz's method of choosing 'representative passages' from different texts and arranging these 'in such a way as to reflect the structure of a characteristic lecture' is designed, she states, both to avoid repetition and to create for readers 'the illusion that they are listening to Nin in person' (p. xiv). This seems, ironically, not unlike Nin's own strategy in editing the diary for publication; which, however, she denies emphatically in this text, insisting on the 'spontaneous' and 'authentic' nature of the diary (see below).

of being a solitary human being and unique. But I suddenly found that my diary didn't belong to me, that it was other women's diaries too' (*A Woman Speaks*, 140).

Nin also puts a great deal of emphasis on the nature of the diary as 'spontaneous', 'faithful', 'authentic' writing. Here we see the explicit distancing from 'literature' that Felski draws attention to: 'the writing began to have a living, vital meaning which had nothing to do with literature'; 'not writing as literature but writing as intimately connected with our lives'; 'There was no studying of writing, there was no literary discipline, there was only the reading and receiving of experience' (*A Woman Speaks*, 149, 150). Nin constructs diary writing as artless, unhampered by the constraints of 'literature': 'In writing the diary, I tried to overlook, to forget all procedures of writing. I wanted to make no demands on myself as to whether I'd written it well or not' (*A Woman Speaks*, 166).

THE DIARY AND/AS 'ART'

We find something strikingly different, however, if we shift back from this 1970s context, and the insistence on the non-literary nature of the diary, to the 1930s, and Nin's continuing struggle with the *complexity* of the problem of the diary and, or as, art. Beginning in the late 1920s, her struggles with writing 'fiction' force into prominence the question of the relations between 'fiction' and the diary, and the nature of the diary text. On the one hand, she believes that her best writing is in the diary *because* it is personal, spontaneous, 'natural': it has a 'human authenticity' (10 November 1932 [*Incest*, 28]). 'I am not natural outside of the diary . . . I have no objectivity. I can only write while things are *warm* and happening. When I write later I become artificial' (January 1937 [*Fire*, 374]). At times, carrying this view to an extreme, she makes a distinction between a 'writer' and a 'diarist': 'I am not a writer, or an artist, but a diarist, or *documentaire*'.[30]

However, this view is counterbalanced by her understanding of the diary as a *form*, a notion which at once throws into question the distinction between 'literary' and 'non-literary', and certainly that between 'writer' and 'diarist'. If the diary has a form, it is subject to aesthetic

[30] March 1935 (*Fire*, 49). Nin's conception here of the diary as 'documentary', as an 'objective' record, is interestingly at odds with the more common view of a diary as a highly *subjective* text. In Chapter 4 I discuss Nin's struggle to move beyond the *gendered* polarization of 'diary' and 'fiction' and the problematic opposition of 'woman' and 'artist'.

concerns in the same way as other forms of writing; it may be developed, 'perfected', and this is one way in which Nin, in the 1930s, begins to envisage her writerly enterprise: 'Planning never to come out of the diary again to write novels, but to perfect and expand the diary form' (June 1935 [*Fire*, 99]); 'The diary is my form . . . I must perfect what is natural' (January 1937 [*Fire*, 374]).

This leads, I would argue, to a radical blurring of the lines dividing the diary from 'art', and in particular a blurring of the distinction between 'spontaneous' and crafted writing. Nin describes 'working on' the diaries, presumably a (retrospective) process of rewriting: 'In the morning I work on volume forty-four, expanding the child story, the events following it' (12 February 1937 [*Fire*, 406]). Her descriptions of her writing are often ambiguous: 'I think I have found my style . . . Take the diary and write it more fully, more artistically, but keep the sincerity and directness' (July 1935 [*Fire*, 110]). It is impossible to determine whether this suggests a process of rewriting the diary to produce a more 'literary' work, a different way of writing in the diary, or a way of writing outside the diary which is based on the diary form (which she sometimes notes explicitly: 'I am imitating the diary, approximating the tone of sincerity . . . My father book is written like the diary' [August 1935 (*Fire*, 135, 138)]). The point is precisely that it *is* impossible to determine: 'fiction' and 'diary', 'literary' and 'non-literary' are mutually imbricated.

Nor is this simply a question of a one-directional process, 'literary' reworkings of spontaneous, 'original' diary texts. More radically, the diary text itself may be constituted through the 'literary'. In February 1937, Nin writes: 'I finally wrote the childbirth story which had been preying on me—fifteen pages of naked, savage truth to be inserted in the diary, as part of the diary' (*Fire*, 394). Here the relations between 'diary' and 'art' are at their most complex. The account of the birth, which appears (in slightly differing versions) in *Incest* (377–83) and *Journals*, I (350–6), and which might be considered among the most deeply 'personal' pieces of Nin's writing (and therefore as appropriate to the 'private' diary text rather than the 'public' sphere of 'literary' writing), is written *as a story*, *outside* the diary but *for* the diary. It is crafted as a 'story', but it is also 'naked, savage truth'. Or, to reverse the statement, it is 'truth', which is the province of the diary; but it is also 'art', written as a discrete story three years after the event. So, while Nin's short story 'Birth', published in the magazine *Twice a Year* in 1938 and reprinted in Nin's collection of short stories *Under a Glass Bell* in 1944, may be seen as a literary reworking of the 'original' diary account, it is equally the case that the diary account itself already throws this distinction into question.

This picture contrasts strikingly with the 1970s construction of the diary as fundamentally artless, not subject to aesthetic or literary judgements. The passages considered above suggest, rather, that Nin *is* concerned with the quality of the writing; she wants to 'perfect . . . the diary form'. But, as this phrase makes clear, her aesthetic criteria relate to the *specific form* of the diary, central to which are 'sincerity and directness'. There is a paradoxical element to this. Nin worries about the 'danger' for the diary of 'art': 'Might kill its greatest quality: naturalness' (17 September 1936 [*Fire*, 303]). She goes on: 'No consciousness of perfection must *enter* the diary'. On the other hand, she writes: 'I must perfect what is natural' (10 January 1937 [*Fire*, 374]). In this context, Henry Miller's letter to Nin of 12 October 1933 contains an insightful analysis of the paradox of the diary as art:

> What you are trying to do is a piece of art that is perfect in itself as art and yet retains the imperfections, the *human* fragmented, chaotic characteristics of a diary written on the spot in white heat. I don't know whether it can be done . . . Seems to me, at the moment, that one or other aspect of the work must be sacrificed. And it could be successfully done by the technical trick (a justifiable one!) of maintaining the illusion, for the reader, that he is perusing an intimate journal, but doing your story with infinite care, infinite pains.[31]

We might interpret Nin's statement, above, that 'no consciousness of perfection must *enter* the diary', as suggesting this need to 'maintain the illusion'. In the context of the reception of the diaries in the 1970s—which *depends* on the association of women's confessional writing with intimacy, spontaneity, naturalness—we can see the need to maintain the illusion in Nin's insistence on the spontaneity of the diaries and perhaps in her notably defensive response to questions on this subject.[32]

Miller's letter is also significant in that it explicitly raises the question of the *reader* of the diary. This is important in relation to the association of confessional writing with privacy and secrecy: the diary is seen as an essentially *private* form of writing, and this is seen to guarantee its

[31] Nin and Miller, *A Literate Passion*, 216.

[32] Hinz transcribes these question-and-answer sessions: 'Q. Did you go back over the diaries at all then? A.N. No, I didn't do that. I couldn't go back over the diaries because then their spontaneous quality would have been spoiled' (*A Woman Speaks*, 163). 'Q. In the process of writing your diary and in preparing it for publication have you ever edited or revised it especially to make it more trendy or stylish? A.N. That is a question I shouldn't even be asked! If you've read it, you wouldn't ask that question. It is self-evident. It is quite evident that the diary is not an artificial creation' (169).

honesty and 'authenticity'. In *A Woman Speaks* Nin argues explicitly for the connection between private or secret writing and honesty: 'There was no feeling of censorship, no feeling that someone was looking over my shoulder, so I was truthful. I wasn't really writing for anyone' (*A Woman Speaks*, 140); 'we are never quite sincere if we are writing something which we think someone is going to read. The necessary condition is that it has to be a secret' (*A Woman Speaks*, 146).

However, she also undercuts her own claim not to be writing 'for anyone', that is, without the idea of a reader. The passage cited above continues:

> I wasn't really writing for anyone, even though at first I began the diary as a letter to my father who had left us. The diary was intended to be a description of the new country that I was coming to, a description of America, to entice him to come back, as I didn't believe that he had gone for good. So it began, in a way, for someone else. It was really written for someone else . . . (*A Woman Speaks*, 140)[33]

This account of the original motivation for the diary suggests that for Nin the question of the diary's status as 'literary' was always present. The descriptions of America are written to *entice* her intended reader, her father—thus immediately raising questions, for the writer, of how best to achieve this.[34] This also throws into question right from the beginning the notion of 'truthfulness': the eleven-year-old Nin is writing to create a

[33] In an interview given in 1975 to a magazine called *Helicon Nine: A Journal of Women's Arts and Letters*, Nin put more emphasis on the diary as a text (like any other literary text) with an intended reader. Having stated her original motivation for beginning the diary (to communicate with her absent father), she goes on: 'At the age of sixteen I began writing in English because I wanted to share the diary with a cousin who was also keeping one. Again the diary represented an attempt at communication with someone else: a sense of "the other" pervaded my writing'. (Daniel Stern and Dominique Browning, 'Anaïs Nin: An Interview' [1975], reprinted in DuBow [ed.], *Conversations*, 226). Later in the interview, Nin connects 'self-consciousness as a writer', her literary judgements of her diary (she mentions the rewritten description of arriving in New York; see next note), and awareness of a potential reader: 'At an early age I felt a responsibility to myself as a writer, which means that I was in some way aware of writing for an audience' (230). In looking at *A Woman Speaks*, we should bear in mind the importance of the feminist context not only for Nin but also for Hinz, the editor who has shaped the texts and who clearly wants to stress the 'honesty' and 'spontaneity' of the diaries.

[34] This is further supported by the fact that Nin *rewrote*, several months later, her account of arriving in New York, in a fuller and more detailed version. See *Early Diary*, I: the first account appears on p. 12 under the date 12 Aug. 1914 (the day after the arrival in New York); the revised version is included as an appendix on pp. 501–2, with the date 11 Aug. 1914. According to Nin's text, she wrote the second version on 3 April 1915 (see p. 57). As Nancy Scholar comments, 'the fiction writer was at work editing the diary from the very start' (Nancy Scholar, *Anaïs Nin* [Boston: Twayne, 1984], 19).

particular effect in the mind of her intended reader, rather than producing a disinterested record of events (if such a thing were possible).

Of course, as she goes on to say, over time the diary 'changed roles, it became various things'; she did not persist in the idea of writing specifically for her father. But, as I have been arguing, the issue of the literary status of the diary was always at the forefront for Nin; and bound up with this is the notion of a reader, an audience—as Miller in his letter clearly sees. 'Diary my chief work', Nin writes (March 1935 [Fire, 49]); and the notion of a 'work' surely implies that of a reader. Again, this is paradoxical in the context of the diary, a paradox of which Nin seems to be aware when she says: 'I write for other people, *even* when I say "I am alone" ' (23 January 1929 [*Early Diary*, IV, 156]). Rachel Cottam, discussing the paradoxical 'secrecy' of diaries, argues that any writing in fact presupposes a (possible) reader, even if only the diarist's future self: the very 'writtenness' of the diary's 'secrets', she argues, 'demands at least the possibility of their being read'.[35] Added to this, in Nin's case, is the stronger sense of an audience bound up with her view, in all its complexity, of the diary as a work, a literary creation. The interest of the passage cited above lies in its suggestion that, rather than beginning her diary as a purely 'private' text and then coming to think about it more 'literarily', for Nin issues of form, style, and audience were bound up with the diary-writing practice from its very inception.

THE DIARY AND THE 'SELF'

Nin's diary, Evelyn Hinz suggests, is 'the place where she may always be found'. As we have seen, one feminist paradigm places great emphasis on the self-presence of the writer in her text, the ability of the text to reveal, in Stanton's words, women's 'inner lives', particularly when that text takes the form of diary or journal and can be seen as an 'honest record of the moment'. The text functions as the privileged site of personal expression, of the assertion of (gendered) identity: the voice of (a) woman.

If we turn to the diaries Nin was writing in the 1930s (and earlier), we do find a view of the diary as a crucial site of self-presence and self-identity; it is the one place, Nin sometimes suggests, where all the manifold aspects of her self can be brought together and unified: 'My Journal

[35] Rachel Cottam, 'Secret Scratching: The Diary and its Writing' (D.Phil. dissertation, Sussex University, 1996), 10.

is my true source of balance, my great stabilizer' (18 June 1930 [*Early Diary*, IV, 306]). However, we also find the opposite position: a view of the diary as highlighting, if not actually producing, the alterity, non-presence, and non-identity of the self, and concomitantly, an understanding of the quasi-fictional nature of the self or selves evidenced in the diary.

Nin shows herself highly conscious of the diary's ability to show up the splits within the self; as Rachel Cottam argues, 'while the diary does not in itself split the subject, it certainly intensifies the relation of the self with itself and widens the schism between the self as subject and as object'.[36] Nancy Scholar notes this effect of writing and suggests that Nin is aware of it very early in her diary-writing career.[37] This is supported by Nin's wistful comment from 1920, echoing Thoreau: ' I feel as if all the adventures which succeed one another were unfolding themselves like a play in a theatre—and I, miles and miles away, watching'.[38]

In her early diaries, Nin is already playing with different names and self-characterizations, shifting between first and third person. 'Linotte', from the French expression *tête de linotte*, 'featherhead', is the name she gives to the 'impossible', impractical, literary side of herself; 'Miss Nin' refers to her public faces as housekeeper for her mother and as socialite ('Miss Nin is extremely frivolous and was given a new hat' [10 September 1920 (*Early Diary*, II, 35)]). Nin elaborates on this distinction in a letter to a schoolfriend: 'Miss Nin is the sensible side of me . . . the little housekeeper . . . Linotte is . . . the impossible side which must be hidden' (35). She signs the letter 'Anaïs & Linotte'.

Importantly, 'Linotte' is also 'the verse scribbler' (35)—Nin's identity as a fledgling writer. Thus we can already see here the problematic split between a writerly identity and a practical, dutiful identity ('the little housekeeper'); and we can see the use of different self-characterizations and switches between subject and object positions, which would become frequent textual strategies for Nin.

[36] Ibid. 82.

[37] 'Making her life into an endless story, she perhaps inadvertently condemns herself to the role of spectator of her own existence' (*Anaïs Nin*, 4).

[38] *Early Diary*, II, 77–8; cited by Scholar, *Anaïs Nin*, 4. Cf. Thoreau's reflections in *Walden* (1854): 'However intense my experience, I am conscious of the presence and criticism of a part of me which, as it were, is not a part of me, but spectator, sharing no experience, but taking note of it' (Henry David Thoreau, *The Variorum Walden* [ed. Walter Harding; New York: Twayne, 1962], 122). Nin records buying a copy of *Walden* on 24 May 1921 and finishing reading it on 7 June (*Early Diary*, II, 208, 226). If this chronology is accurate, Nin's comment about 'watching' her own life predates her reading of Thoreau, despite the similarity of expression.

In 1928, grappling with the conflicts between a 'wifely' identity and her desire to write and experiment, Nin talks about creating a diary within a diary, the 'diary of Imagy'. This is the name she now gives to the 'demonic' aspect of herself which is simultaneously problematic for her to acknowledge and at the same time important to her, the side of herself she associates with her writing: 'Imagy lives mostly in images and unrealities. I want to follow her doings because they are the ones which *haunt my writing*' (3 February 1928 [*Early Diary*, IV, 56]). As in her teenage diaries, this self-conscious presentation of her self as different 'characters' reflects the conflicts and divisions she is aware of in her life: 'I live *doubly*. I'll write *doubly*' (56). At the same time, the continuously *written* story (or stories) that is her life enables this 'characterization' of the self, something that will become even more apparent later in the narratives of her complicated simultaneous relationships with her husband Hugh Guiler and lovers Henry Miller and Otto Rank. We can see here a correspondence with Laura Marcus's suggestion that for women autobiographers, use of 'the fictional' can be 'a way of suggesting how much fiction is involved in all self-representations'.[39] After describing 'Imagy', Nin goes on: 'Meanwhile, "me", the real me, has been keeping house' (56). Here there is clearly a tension between, on the one hand, the reassuring idea of a 'real', non-fictional self, and on the other hand the recognition, signalled by the inverted commas and by the deliberately ungrammatical pronoun, that the self who keeps house has no privileged 'reality': she is equally a character in her own story, and can appear as the object ('me') rather than the subject ('I').

In March 1931, Nin experiments again with a 'double' or split diary, this time in the context of her ongoing attempt to find a way to make the diary publishable: 'I get an idea by which I may produce my Journal in disguise—comments, sardonic and mordant, by me, on the "imaginary character" (of Anaïs!) expressed in the Journal. Opposition of two characters, with my signature under the "other" character and "myself" denied!' (7 March 1931 [*Early Diary*, IV, 399]). She goes on: 'The Journal idea: the "Other Woman" is Natasia [a near-anagram of 'Anaïs']. Natasia keeps *this* journal. "I" make the commentaries . . . This is what you might call a dialogue between my two souls—a dramatization of my own duality. I am talking to myself. This procedure is natural enough to me' (18 March; 401). Again, I would argue that Nin is able ('naturally') to envisage the diary as a dialogue between different voices because this is merely

[39] *Auto/biographical Discourses*, 280.

a more explicit elaboration of the way the diary itself functions: the different instances of writing create a heteroglossic text.

The complexity of Nin's multiple relationships is an important factor in this 'characterizing' of herself, her presentation of herself as object, the protagonist of many (simultaneous) stories. On 27 September 1934, she writes: 'Mrs Guiler lives in Louveciennes, has a maid, eats breakfast in bed . . . Mrs Miller peels potatoes, grinds coffee, sweeps, markets . . . Anaïs is caught by Rank's love and wants to go to New York with him' (*Incest*, 389). Here again there is perhaps a tension: we could read 'Anaïs' as the privileged, 'true' self (on the basis of the positioning at the end of the passage, as the 'final' or ultimate statement; and also because 'Anaïs' is the 'personal', most 'proper' name, while 'Mrs Guiler' and 'Mrs Miller' indicate the woman's secondary identity through the man[40]). Yet with the use of the third person, 'Anaïs' is positioned as object, just as the others are. This is demonstrated even more strikingly in the next entry: 'Anaïs went to meet Rank at the Parc Monceau room. She proposed the idea of spending the night en route to Le Havre with Rank' (6 October; 391).

THE 'TEXT' AND THE 'LIFE'

Nin's perception of the multiplicity of her self is intimately bound up with her views on the 'truth' and 'completeness' of what is contained in the diary. Just as she often evinces a desire for personal wholeness and integration ('I am always *between* two desires, always in conflict . . . I would like to feel *whole*' [30 October 1932 (*Incest*, 25)]), so she sometimes sees the diary as containing 'the whole', the 'truth' which cannot be told anywhere else: '[Rank] has understood what a shell the diary is around me, what a weapon of defense. But he has understood, too, that it contains the *truth* . . . which I feel compelled to tell somewhere' (14 January 1934 [*Incest*, 297]). At other times, she recognizes this desire for truth, like the desire for wholeness, as a fantasy: 'It seems to me that I follow only the most accessible thread. Three or four threads may be agitated, like telegraph wires, at the same time, and if I were to tap them all I would reveal such a mixture of innocence and duplicity, generosity and calculation, fear and courage. I cannot tell the whole truth simply because I

[40] Nin's use of these 'patriarchal' names offers confirmation of Nancy K. Miller's point that in women's textual self-representations we find 'traces of the culture of gender, the inscriptions of its political structures' (*Subject to Change: Reading Feminist Writing* [New York: Columbia Univ. Press, 1988], 84).

would have to write four journals at once' (July 1932 [*Henry and June*, 207–8]). She is aware of things left unwritten: 'I have a sense of all that I leave out—the lacunae, especially the dreams, the hallucinations. Also, the lies are left out, a desperate necessity to embellish. So I do not write them down. The journal is therefore a lie' (April 1932 [*Henry and June*, 113]). Here we see the fundamental imbrication of the realm of the 'fictional' with the 'truth' of the self: the journal is a 'lie' because the lies which are left out are part of the 'truth'.

The sense of what is left out is also present in the short story, or prose poem, 'The Labyrinth', Nin's attempt to describe the 'labyrinth' that is the landscape of the diary, the text/world she inhabits: 'I was walking on a carpet of pages without number. Why had I not numbered the pages? Because I was aware of what I had left out; so much was left out that I had intended to insert, and numbering was impossible, for numbering would mean I had said everything' ('The Labyrinth', 67). After being introduced to psychoanalytic ideas of the unconscious by her cousin Eduardo Sánchez in 1931, and reading Freud and Jung, she realizes the *impossibility* of telling the diary 'the whole truth'. There is always something in excess, always another narrative to be lived and written: 'Tonight I realize that the diary is a struggle to seize on the most unseizable person on earth. I elude my own detection . . . I cannot write myself out. I think in a hundred directions' (19 April 1933 [*Incest*, 141]).

In her entry for 2 April 1931, Nin records a 'dialogue' with 'Natasia' as though in the text of a play (recalling the early Thoreauvian lament). This is a technique that she often uses elsewhere in the diaries. In the entry for 7 March 1931, for instance, she sets out a dialogue under the title 'Part I of Play, "Warmth" ', with the characters 'Eduardo and Me' (*Early Diary*, IV, 398); several pages later, in the entry for 24 March, we find another such dialogue, complete with stage-setting: 'Café du Rond-Point. Eduardo, Me, and a few other people—waiters, passers-by; much noise of traffic' (403). Rather than seeing this simply as a convenient, shorthand way of recording a conversation, I think we can see it as indicating the way in which the diary facilitates Nin's 'dramatizing' of her life ('scene-making', as Virginia Woolf called it). It is not simply that she records, after the fact, a conversation with Eduardo in the style of a scene from a play; rather, her habitual diary-writing informs her experiencing the encounter 'as' a scene from a play. The 'life' and the writing impact upon each other in an endless (and beginning-less) spiral. Again, Nancy Scholar notes that something of this understanding may be seen already in Nin's teenage diaries. 'Did you know,' Nin remarks to her diary in September 1920, 'that whatever I do or think I am always forming into words so that I may be able to tell you about it as perfectly as possible?' (28 September 1920 [*Early Diary*, II, 51]). Scholar comments: 'A simple existence is denied her; she must always be reshaping her life to suit the more demanding requirements of art'.[41] I would argue, though, that this is not simply a process of 'reshaping', which suggests a pre-given experiential reality; rather, the 'experience' is *already* 'shaped' by the writing.

Nin's story 'The Labyrinth' is an attempt to describe this textual world. The piece begins: 'I was eleven years old when I walked into the labyrinth of my diary'. Nin goes on: 'I walked with the desire to see all things twice so as to find my way back into them again . . . An anguish about returning, and about seeing these things but once. There was a definite feeling that their meaning could only be revealed the second time. If I were forced to go on, unknowing, blind, everything would be lost' ('The Labyrinth', 66). We can read this as an attempt to describe the complex relation of writing and 'reality'. The writer is seeing and experiencing things 'twice'; the writing is, in one way, a repetition, a recounting or reconstruction of an experience. Paul Ricoeur argues similarly when he describes 'narrating' as a 'secondary' process, following on from a prior experience.[42] But, in another way, the writing is the 'first' experience, the first 'seeing', because it is only in the writing that there is *meaning*, a story, a narrative. Nin acknowledges this in her diary in 1922: 'I do not know what truly happens to me until I see it written' (12 January 1922 [*Early Diary*, II, 375]). Without (or outside) the writing, she is 'unknowing', 'blind'. 'The Labyrinth' literalizes the textual landscape: 'I was walking on a carpet of pages without number . . . I was walking up a stairway of words . . . I was walking on the word obsession with naked feet' ('The Labyrinth', 67).

Nin is self-consciously aware, then, of the endlessly reinforcing spiral between 'life' and 'writing', and her desire or 'demand' for narrative;[43] she writes: 'I must live *within stories*' (18 April 1928 [*Early Diary*, IV, 87]). One episode, from October 1933, suggests particularly well her fascination with and *pleasure* in this spiral. When her husband discovers and reads her diary, detailing her affair with Miller, she claims that this is a *fictional* diary, and that there exists another, 'real' one: ' "You only read the invented journal. It is all invention, to compensate for all I don't do . . . You can read the *real* journal any time" ' (30 September 1933 [*Incest*,

[41] *Anaïs Nin*, 4.

[42] Paul Ricoeur, *Time and Narrative*, I (trans. Kathleen McLaughlin and David Pellauer; Chicago: Univ. of Chicago Press, 1984 [1983]), 77.

[43] Ricoeur speaks of our 'demand for narrative'; *Time and Narrative*, I, 74.

268]). She then begins to compose the 'real' diary, and to delight in the ramifications it suggests. She writes to Miller:

It may turn out a marvellous piece of mystification, the two sides of an attitude, and it becomes so real to me while I write it, for example the determination never to be possessed by you because men remember longest the woman they have not had . . . When you read it you will regret *not* having had me. You won't know after a while whether you did or not. Depends on which journal you read . . . To begin with, try and remember that the *real* journal is the *unreal* one. Wonderful. *This* is the journal of my true feelings. Which one?[44]

And in the diary, she asks herself: 'If I should die and both should be read—*which one is me*?' (2 October; 271).

This understanding of the relations between 'life' and 'text' refuses the notion of an ontologically prior, extratextual 'reality'. Nin's sense of her life as lived in and through her 'stories' produces the addictive aspect of the diary-writing 'habit': 'This is my drug and my vice. This is the moment when I take up the mysterious pipe and indulge in deviations. Instead of writing a book, I lie back and I dream and I talk to myself. A drug . . . I must relive my life in the dream. The dream is my only life' (11 August 1934 [*Incest*, 366]). Here we can see particularly clearly the paradox suggested above in relation to 'The Labyrinth': the dream, the writing, is both a *reliving* of life, and the thing itself, the *only life*. Like a drug, the compulsive writing is intensely pleasurable; it can also be claustrophobic and frightening, the labyrinth the writer is trapped in: 'The landscape did not change, the walk was without corners; the paths so mysteriously enchained I never knew when I had turned to the right or left. I was walking on the word obsession with naked feet: the trees seemed to press closer together, and breathing was difficult' ('The Labyrinth', 67). As Rachel Cottam suggests, 'the diary is inextricably caught up with the life of the diarist, and becomes her very embodiment'. This creates the anxiety bound up in the compulsion to write: 'the diarist sometimes conflates a lack of awareness of the self (in language) with extinction. [Virginia] Woolf imagines death precisely as the end of a narrative.'[45] We can compare this to the feeling Nin sometimes expresses that she does not exist at all outside the pages of the diary—and therefore must continue to write; and also perhaps with the poet H.D.'s urgent self-address in *Hermetic Definition*: 'write, write or die'.[46]

[44] Letter from Nin to Miller, 4 Oct. 1933, in *A Literate Passion*, 212.
[45] 'Secret Scratching', 48.
[46] H.D., *Hermetic Definition* (Oxford: Carcanet, 1972 [1958]), Part 3, 'Star of Day', 49.

'A NEW SPELLING OF MY NAME': SIGNATURE AND NARRATIVE SELVES

In a letter to her friend Viola Jordan in 1927 or 1928, H.D. wrote: 'No-one really much likes my prose but I can't be held up by what the critics think H.D. ought to be like . . . I say WHO is H.D.?'[47] Here we see H.D. questioning the status of her writing signature—a signature which, in its ungendered anonymity and peculiar origins,[48] already seems to be throwing into question the 'proper name' it should represent. The signature, Derrida claims, is 'the point at which both presence and writing are in question'.[49] Objecting to J. L. Austin's argument that the signature functions to 'tether' a written utterance to its 'source' or 'origin' (the writer who signs) in a singular and 'pure' event, Derrida argues that the signature, like every other 'event of discourse', is necessarily 'impure', part of a network of traces and 'citations' referring backwards and forwards beyond itself:

> The effects of signature are the most ordinary thing in the world. The condition of possibility for these effects is simultaneously, once again, the condition of their impossibility, of the impossibility of their rigorous purity. In order to function, that is, in order to be legible, a signature must have a repeatable, iterable, imitable form; it must be able to detach itself from the present and singular intention of its production.[50]

Further, the signature stands in an ambiguous, ambivalent relation to the text, neither clearly 'inside' nor clearly 'outside'. Peggy Kamuf describes the signature as 'double-jointed', operating at the boundary between 'life' and 'text', 'writer' and 'work', and blurring that boundary: 'At the edge of the work, the dividing trait of the signature pulls in both directions at once: appropriating the text under the sign of the name, expropriating the name into the play of the text'.[51] The signature both

[47] Cited in Susan Stanford Friedman, *Psyche Reborn: The Emergence of H.D.* (Bloomington, Ind.: Indiana Univ. Press, 1981), 6.

[48] In her memoir of Ezra Pound, *End to Torment*, H.D. recalls what has become the almost legendary 'naming' scene in the British Museum tea rooms: 'he [Pound] scratched "H.D. Imagiste," in London, in the Museum tea room, at the bottom of a typed sheet, now slashed with his creative pencil, "Cut this out, shorten this line."' (H.D., *End to Torment: A Memoir of Ezra Pound by H.D.* [ed. Norman Holmes Pearson and Michael King; Manchester: Carcanet, 1980 (1979)], 40).

[46] Jacques Derrida, 'Signature Event Context' (1972), in *A Derrida Reader: Between the Blinds* (ed. Peggy Kamuf; Hemel Hempstead: Harvester Wheatsheaf, 1991), 106.

[50] Derrida, 'Signature Event Context', 107.

[51] Kamuf, *Signature Pieces*, 13.

ascribes the text to a writing subject, and pulls that subject into his or her text. Kamuf thus refuses the notion of a prior self that is simply 'expressed' in the text: '[signature is] an always divisible limit within the difference between writer and work, "life" and "letters". Signature articulates the one with the other, the one *in* the other: it both divides and joins. It is this double-jointedness of signature that will be lost to any discourse that continues to posit an essential exteriority of subjects to the texts they sign.'[52]

As Laura Marcus argues, women autobiographers often highlight the ambiguities of signature and identity by 'troubling' or playing with the 'proper name'. Gertrude Stein's appropriation of her lover's name and textual voice in *The Autobiography of Alice B. Toklas* is most easily read as collapsing Toklas's identity into that of Stein (so that Toklas's 'story' is really Stein's); but, I would suggest, it could also be read (more subversively in relation to the widespread perception of Stein's dominance in the relationship) as an acknowledgement, by Stein, of the importance of Toklas in Stein's 'own' story—thus implying the complex way in which the two women's identities are bound up with each other.

Both the title and the subtitle of Audre Lorde's *Zami: A New Spelling of My Name* (1982) indicate the importance of naming in the text. Lorde connects her struggle to escape her mother's definitions with her relation, as a child, to the sign (and signing) of her own name:

> I did not like the tail of the Y hanging down below the line in Audrey, and would always forget to put it on, which used to disturb my mother greatly. I used to love the evenness of AUDRELORDE at four years of age, but I remembered to put on the Y because it pleased my mother, and because, as she always insisted to me, that was the way it had to be because that was the way it was. No deviation was allowed from her interpretations of correct.[53]

Of course, the book tells the story of Lorde's multiple 'deviations' from her mother's script for her, which is simultaneously the story of becoming the writer 'Audre Lorde'. At the same time, Lorde acknowledges the place of her maternal (and Grenadian) heritage within her identity—and finds a way to link this with her identity as a lesbian—through her invocation of the name 'Zami':

> my life had become increasingly a bridge and field of women. *Zami.*
> *Zami. A Carriacou name for women who work together as friends and lovers.*[54]

The title-page of the book, imprinted with the words '*Zami: A New Spelling of My Name* Audre Lorde', thus brilliantly foregrounds both the

[52] Kamuf, *Signature Pieces*, p. viii. [53] Lorde, *Zami*, 24. [54] Ibid. 255.

double-jointed, borderland nature of signature (pulling between textuality and materiality) and the tension (or, ideally, complementarity) Lorde experiences between the individual and the collective aspects of identity and self-naming.

Similarly, bell hooks' accounts, in *Talking Back*, of her reasons for adopting her writing signature (hooks' given name is Gloria Watkins) also reveal an invocation of a collective, maternal heritage to support an identity (as 'writer') that, hooks says, was difficult for her to claim:

One of the many reasons I chose to write using the pseudonym bell hooks, a family name (mother to Sarah Oldham, grandmother to Rosa Bell Oldham, great-grandmother to me) was to construct a writer-identity that would challenge and subdue all impulses leading me away from speech into silence. I was a young girl buying bubble gum at the corner store when I first really heard the full name bell hooks. I had just 'talked back' to a grown person. Even now I can recall the surprised look, the mocking tones that informed me I must be kin to bell hooks—a sharp-tongued woman, a woman who spoke her mind, a woman who was not afraid to talk back.[55]

hooks' reflections, in several of the book's essays, on her own complex relationship with her writing signature highlight the ways in which 'Gloria Watkins' both is and is not 'bell hooks'.[56]

A particularly intriguing example of this 'troubling' of the proper name is the case of the British writer Anna Kavan (1901–68), whom Nin greatly admired. Kavan's given name was Helen Woods; her first novels were published under her married name Helen Ferguson. 'Anna Kavan' was a character in two of these novels; in 1938, following the collapse of her marriage and a period of institutionalization in a psychiatric hospital, Ferguson legally adopted her character's name, under which all of her subsequent work was published. The change of name and signature also marked a striking shift in the writing itself, a move away from 'realist' narrative and characterization, signalled by the disturbing *Asylum Piece*

[55] bell hooks, 'Talking Back', in *Talking Back*, 9. It is interesting to note that for both Lorde and hooks, this (re)claiming of a maternal heritage stands in uneasy tension with their experience of their own mothers as primarily repressive; it is as if both writers can only 'think back through their mothers' once they have achieved enough independence to escape the confines of their mothers' immediate presence and 'interpretations of correct'. It is also, I think, worth noting that whereas both Lorde and hooks link their self-narratives back to wider communities, Stein, H.D., Kavan, and Nin do not. This could be seen to support the accusation of individualism frequently levelled at white feminist thinking by black feminists/womanists.

[56] See particularly the essay 'To Gloria, Who is She? On Using a Pseudonym', in *Talking Back*, 160–6.

(1940). For Kavan, as for H.D., differences of signature are bound up, in complex ways, with differences in writing.[57]

H.D. raises the issues of self-writing and self-identity in an essay that constitutes both a reflection on her own writing practice and a continued questioning of her signature. Written in 1949–50 and published in 1986, the essay is sometimes known as 'Notes on Recent Writing', but its actual title is 'H.D. by Delia Alton'.[58] The title is important because it immediately throws into question the status of the 'proper name' of the author (which in this particular case, as noted above, is already problematic) and therefore her own identity as writing subject. 'Delia Alton' is the protagonist of one of H.D.'s unpublished novels, 'The Sword Went Out to Sea': so there is a displacement here whereby 'Delia Alton' appears as the subject, the narrative voice, and 'H.D.' as the object of discourse, the writer being discussed.

She goes on to link the 'H.D.' signature to a particular aspect of her writing, the 'early poems', the 'tradition of the crystalline legend' ('I grew tired of hearing those poems referred to, as crystalline'[59]). She thus marks a split, a different writing that goes beyond that delimited by the authorial 'H.D.': 'Bryher has suggested that I have a selection of unpublished poems set up. I choose three sequences that differ entirely from the recognized H.D. of the "early poems" . . . these are not fundamentally "H.D. poems" . . . I would like to sign them Delia Alton.'[60]

H.D. goes on to examine the significance of using 'Delia Alton' as a writing signature in an exploration of her interwoven texts and protagonists, a tapestry (as she describes it) in which she herself is woven. Beginning with the protagonists of 'Madrigal' (her original title for *Bid Me To Live*) and 'Hesperia', a different version of the 'Secret Name' story in her novel *Palimpsest*, H.D. writes: 'These are two women, Julia Ashton and Margaret Fairwood. They are of course, they all are, the same woman.'[61] The next sentence begins 'She knows'. This ambiguous, shifting 'she' is the subject of the text. The 'she' also becomes 'I', and even 'we'; she is sometimes named ('Julia Ashton', 'Margaret Fairwood', 'Delia Alton'). She is engaged on a quest, a search for wholeness, for her own identity: 'She can not [sic] yet correlate or relate the various entities that make up her own fragments'.[62] The search 'ends' (but, as I shall indicate, this can only be a provisional 'ending') with Delia Alton. H.D. writes of the novel in which Delia Alton appears, 'The Sword Went Out to Sea':

57 I hope to discuss Kavan's work at greater length in a subsequent study.

58 H.D., 'H.D. by Delia Alton', *Iowa Review* 16 (1986), 180–221.

59 Ibid. 184.

60 Ibid. 199.

61 Ibid. 181.

62 Ibid.

'I feel complete with her. Delia Alton tells the story and Delia Alton signs the book.'[63] And, wanting to emphasize the connection between that novel and the earlier novel 'Madrigal' she says, 'So I sign *Madrigal*, Delia Alton'.[64]

We see here a complex use of a proper (or perhaps improper) name and a sliding of pronouns and subject-positions, just as we saw in Nin's diary. H.D. writes 'Delia Alton signs the book' and then 'So I sign *Madrigal*, Delia Alton'. How are we to understand the relation between these statements? H.D. both is and is not Delia Alton. When she says, 'I feel complete with her', this seems to suggest the importance of the character in H.D.'s search for 'herself', for a sense of completeness and identity. And *writing* is central to this quest—it is through her textual incarnations, such as Delia Alton, that H.D. seeks completeness.[65] But the very form of the sentence ('*I* feel complete with *her*') also signals a split, a difference: the writer and the character cannot be identical. Although H.D.'s protagonists are all engaged in the search for wholeness, and are all in a sense 'the same woman', we can also see H.D. as inscribing herself in an endless series of *different* women, different versions of the narrative. Even the 'completeness' of Delia Alton, then, cannot be final or absolute, as H.D. rather ambivalently recognizes: 'The Sword Went Out to Sea', she says, is 'the final version or rather the new version'.[66]

Just as in Nin's diary, we see in H.D.'s text a play with names, characterizations, and subject/object positions which explores the complex relations between identity and autobiographical writing. Both writers, rather than simply expressing or describing a given, extra-textual identity in writing, show up the ways in which identities are constructed in and through narratives, the various stories they tell of themselves. And we find in both writers' texts the recognition that there is always another story, another narrative to be lived and written: in H.D.'s acknowledgement that 'The Sword Went Out to Sea' is 'the final version *or rather the new version*', and in Nin's words, 'I cannot write myself out'.

The identities constructed through these events of writing are neither entirely fictional nor entirely 'historical' or non-textual; rather, they

[63] Ibid. 191. [64] Ibid.

[65] The importance of writing is, I would argue, implicit in H.D.'s phrase 'she can not yet *correlate or relate* . . . her own fragments' (181, my emphasis): 'relate' here suggests both putting into relation, into connection, and 'relating' in the sense of narrativizing, setting down in writing.

[66] Ibid. 190.

reveal the imbrication of the two spheres, the ways in which a personal history is always a narrativized history. Susan Stanford Friedman argues that H.D.'s 'elaborate play with textual naming . . . negotiates between fictionality and historicity';[67] and Nin's textual strategies do the same. Her use of the 'patriarchal' forms 'Mrs Guiler', 'Mrs Miller', highlights this negotiation particularly well: these names pull towards the fictional (as 'characters', inscriptions in the discursive space of the text) and towards the historical and material situation (both the specific context of Nin's relationships and the wider context of patriarchal marriage). In calling herself 'Mrs Miller', Nin both constructs a particular 'fictional' narrative of herself (she was never, in fact, married to Henry Miller) and embeds that narrative within a wider social and material context.

The narrative selves created by Nin and H.D. are, then, neither entirely products of their texts (as in the Barthesian model of the 'modern scriptor', who 'is born simultaneously with the text, is in no way equipped with a being preceding or exceeding the writing'[68]) nor independent of them; rather they are, in Friedman's words, 'fictive loops that originate in and refer back to a living woman whose identity is inseparable from its many inscriptions'.[69] The 'double' nature of these textual selves, pulling towards both the fictional and the historical/material, parallels Kamuf's account of the signature as 'double-jointed', both connecting and dividing subject and text. As we have seen, H.D. explicitly plays with signature in her essay, exploring the ways in which her textual personae articulate her 'life' with(in) her writing. Nin, too, experiments with displacing her signature, creating a dialogue between textual selves: 'Opposition of two characters, with my signature under the "other" character and "myself" denied!' (*Early Diary*, IV, 399). More broadly, Kamuf's model of the signature as operating at the 'edge' of the text serves to illuminate the 'double-jointedness' of both Nin's and H.D.'s narrative personae, which function for both writers to articulate self and text, life and writing. This notion of double-jointedness, I would argue, provides a way to think through (or beyond) the oppositions in feminist theorizing about women's autobiography—the tension between, on the one hand, the emphasis on fictionality, and on the other hand, the emphasis on 'referential reality' and the valorizing of the woman writer's 'identity'. Nin's

[67] Susan Stanford Friedman, *Penelope's Web: Gender, Modernity, H.D.'s Fiction* (Cambridge: Cambridge Univ. Press, 1990), 68.

[68] Roland Barthes, 'The Death of the Author', in *Image, Music, Text* (trans. Stephen Heath; London: Fontana, 1977), 145.

[69] *Penelope's Web*, 78.

narrativizing of her life, her 'characterizing' of herself in various ways, is part of a spiral in which life and text are mutually interacting; she is, therefore, neither wholly 'outside' nor wholly 'inside' her text.

NARRATIVE AND TEMPORALITY

For both Nin and H.D., then, a 'life' is shaped, and an 'identity' produced, through narrativity, an endless series of writings and rewritings. Nin writes: 'I must live *within stories*'. For H.D., the 'quest' (for identity, for meaning) takes place in writing, across the many narratives she produces of herself; it is through this narrativizing that she can 'correlate or relate' the 'fragments' of herself and her experience. The connections and correlations that H.D. traces in her essay operate among *texts*, or events of writing. This is the key to the sense in which H.D. understands her writing as autobiographical:

> She writes and re-writes various 'novels', that only 'came true' in the late forties. We have written of these novels, the *how* of the writing is almost as important to us now, as the writing itself. When, where and how were these things written? That seems a more adequate autobiographical directive than the when, where, and how did the events described happen, or when, where and how was the dream dreamed.[70]

For H.D., autobiographical 'truth' resides in the event, or rather repeated events, of *writing*; it is the ways in which she writes and rewrites her story that constitute that life-story. Just as we have seen in the context of Nin's diary (and Rachel Cottam argues this point in the context of the diary in general), the distinction between the 'life' and the 'writing' is questioned: there is a relocation or reinscription of the *bios* of 'autobiography' within the *graphē*.

Tracing the connections among her writings, H.D. states that 'we are in the labyrinth'.[71] She writes, not *one* narrative, but multiple narratives; or, if she does see all her writings as part of 'the same' story (as all her protagonists are in a sense 'the same woman'), nonetheless this story is constituted through its many different versions, different narrative inscriptions. Given this multiplicity of stories, it is important to her to be aware of the different *times* of writing (the 'when, where, and how'). However, H.D. does not see the pattern of her texts as straightforwardly linear and one-directional. Rather, the meanings of the texts flow

[70] 'H.D. by Delia Alton', 211. [71] Ibid. 220.

backwards and forwards, creating a spiralling, looping temporality. So, for instance, the early novel 'Madrigal' 'pre-visions' the later novels, 'The Sword Went Out to Sea' and 'The White Rose and the Red'; but, H.D. says, she could only come to understand this relationship at the later date: '*Madrigal* was roughed out in 1939 and left in Switzerland when I returned to the London of [World] War II. But without the answer, the certainty of the War II experience, the War I novel would probably still remain unassembled. It was not until I had recorded the War II mystery in *The Sword* . . . that the War I novel appeared to me authentically part of the sequence.'[72] Here, the meaning of the earlier text is dependent on the later text for its realization. Equally, H.D. writes that the poem 'In Our Town', with its image of 'a sword, a sword, a sword', contains 'a startling prophecy', prefiguring 'The Sword Went Out to Sea'.[73] Meaning is woven backwards and forwards in time; these readings can only be activated or brought into being by later experiences and understandings. Texts come to be part of a sequence, and meaning is affected, or effected, by the place in that sequence.

There are striking similarities between the model of narrativity, and of temporality, that we find in H.D.'s text and those evinced by a diary text such as Nin's. Critical analyses of the diary as a textual form focus on what may be seen as its paradoxical narrative structure, its nature as both fragmentary and continuous. Felicity Nussbaum describes diary and journal as 'serial narrative forms', with 'intermittent form and content'.[74] Rebecca Hogan elaborates on this in more detail: 'A diary is a text composed of "fragments" which nevertheless flow continually through the days . . . A diary is both repetitive and cumulative, each entry discrete (and discreet), and each entry an addition to the flow of days.'[75] The diary text is paratactic, a concept which can itself be seen as paradoxical, containing two 'strands', paralleling the double nature of the diary: 'One [strand] is parataxis as a kind of even, horizontal, metonymic flow of events and entries into the diary; this creates the sense of *continuity* required by diary-keeping. The other is parataxis as a series of related items, events and entries without the use of connecting links; this creates the sense of discrete, separate entries.'[76] The paratactic text, then, is com-

[72] 'H.D. by Delia Alton', 201. [73] Ibid. 213.

[74] 'Toward Conceptualizing Diary', in James Olney (ed.), *Studies in Autobiography* (New York: Oxford Univ. Press, 1988), 128, 132.

[75] 'Engendered Autobiographies: The Diary as a Feminine Form', in Shirley Neuman (ed.), *Autobiography and Questions of Gender* (London: Cass, 1992), 100.

[76] 'Engendered Autobiographies', 104.

posed of *discrete* narratives which are not ordered teleologically or hierarchically; at the same time, it is perceived as having a certain *continuity*.

What model of temporality is suggested by this paradoxical structure—what are, in Peter Brooks's terms, the 'temporal dynamics' of the diary?[77] On the one hand, the diary text emphasizes the *present moment*, the time of each particular event of writing. On the other hand, what Hogan describes as the 'cumulative' character of the diary, the fact that each entry adds to the 'flow of days', months and years, highlights the linear chronology of the text, its continuity over a long stretch of time, a forward-moving process ordered by the dates in the text. In fact, the narrative created in the diary reveals a double chronology: what Jean Laplanche, in his discussion of psychoanalytic temporality, calls 'the time of the human individual', or 'temporality of human being', working within or alongside 'cosmological time', the objective, one-directional chronology represented by the procession of dates.[78]

The most fundamental aspect of the psychoanalytic understanding of human temporality is the insistence on the imbrication of past and present (and even future[79]). Psychoanalysis, Laplanche writes, has 'from its very beginning . . . privileged the movement which begins with the present and turns towards the past'.[80] In his 'Notes on Afterwardsness', Laplanche discusses the different ways in which the past and the present may affect one another, the 'temporal directions' involved in Freud's concept of *Nachträglichkeit*:[81] something in the past may be triggered by something in the present, or an earlier experience may be understood 'retroactively' in the light of a later one—just as we saw in the context of H.D.'s multiple narratives. The methods of psychoanalysis—paying careful attention to associations, memories, and dreams—reflect this fundamental understanding of human temporality as following a labyrinthine path quite unlike the one-directional progression of 'cosmological time' from past to present to future. The 'line' of psychoanalytic temporality is not a straight line but, borrowing J. Hillis Miller's image, a line with

77 Peter Brooks, *Reading for the Plot* (Oxford: Clarendon Press, 1984), p. xiii.

78 Jean Laplanche, 'Psychoanalysis, Time and Translation', in John Fletcher and Martin Stanton (eds.), *Seduction, Translation, Drives* (London: ICA, 1992), 163, 166.

79 In *The Interpretation of Dreams*, Freud makes the point that dreams, as well as making use of material from the past, are also future-oriented, insofar as they represent wishes, which are 'predominantly turned towards the future' (PFL 14, 33).

80 'Psychoanalysis, Time and Translation', 177.

81 Jean Laplanche, 'Notes on Afterwardsness', in *Seduction, Translation, Drives*, 218–19. Freud's term *Nachträglichkeit* is usually translated as 'deferred action'; Laplanche proposes the more literal translation 'afterwardsness'.

'returnings, knottings, recrossings, crinklings to and fro, suspensions, interruptions'.[82]

Returning to the diary, I suggested that we can see within the text a double chronology: the tangled lines of human temporality within the linear ordering of calendar time. Paradoxically, the diary's emphasis on the 'present moment', each particular event of writing, highlights the imbrication of past and future with the present. Although the events of writing in the diary follow linear chronology, what is written about is not determined according to that chronology, but articulates what Felicity Nussbaum calls 'human chronology', what Laplanche calls the 'temporality of human being', and what Nin calls 'an order made by memory, by a chronology of emotion, not of dates' (*Novel*, 48). Nin articulates this particularly well in a passage from one of the question-and-answer sessions in *A Woman Speaks*:

Q. I'm not presently keeping a diary, but sometimes I do feel the need to sit down and write down my feelings. So I decide I will write a diary; I get everything ready, open the book, and then comes the question: where do I start?
A.N. Put yourself right in the present. This was my principle when I wrote the diary—to write the thing I felt most strongly about that day. Start there and that starts the whole unravelling, because that has roots in the past and it has branches into the future . . . The important thing is *today*. Then one day you may have a recollection. Occasionally in the diary something would come out of the past and I would pick it up. Or a dream may throw you back just as it may throw you forward. (*A Woman Speaks*, 155)

Again, she states in *The Novel of the Future* that, for human beings, 'past, present and future are constantly interacting' (123). For Nin, this model of human temporality was explicitly drawn from psychoanalysis. In *The Novel of the Future*, in a section entitled 'The Chronology of Emotion', she recalls: 'When I was being analyzed by Dr Otto Rank in Paris in 1933, I began to perceive a new order which lies in the choice of events, an order made by memory, by a chronology of emotion, not of dates' (48; see also *Incest*, 299). In the diary, with its explicit marking of calendrical time and yet disorderly narrative sequence, the tangled

[82] J. Hillis Miller, *Ariadne's Thread: Story Lines* (New Haven: Yale Univ. Press, 1992), 17. In a passage from *Children of the Albatross*, Nin uses the image of Ariadne's thread to depict Djuna's 'tightly wound memories': 'the thread of Ariadne which led everywhere, right and left, like scattered footsteps in the snow, tugged and pulled within her memory and she began to pull upon this thread . . . as one pulls upon a spool, and she heard the empty wooden spool knock against the floor of different houses' (41–2).

threads linking past, present, and future, this psychoanalytic model of temporality is clearly manifested.

PSYCHOANALYSIS: THE 'PLOTS' OF ONE'S LIFE

If psychoanalysis provided, for Nin, a model of memory and human time that both corresponded to her practice in the diary and offered a radically new structuring principle for fiction,[83] it also confirmed her sense of the discursive, narrative construction of the self. In fact, for both Nin and H.D., this narrative understanding of experience and identity was clearly linked not only to writing but also to psychoanalysis, with its focus on the stories, and their retellings, that make up a self.

Peter Brooks, in *Reading for the Plot*, describes psychoanalysis as 'a primarily narrative art', concerned above all with stories, storytelling and the interpretation of stories.[84] As early as 1895 Freud himself had recognized, not without ambivalence, the literary aspects of his enterprise. In the *Studies on Hysteria*, he writes: 'it still strikes me myself as strange that the case histories I write should read like short stories and that, as one might say, they lack the serious stamp of science. I must console myself with the reflection that the nature of the subject is evidently responsible for this, rather than any preference of my own.'[85]

By the 1920s, psychoanalysis and literary culture were firmly entwined, Freud's writings having been disseminated in English translation through the Bloomsbury context of the Stracheys and Leonard and Virginia Woolf. Elizabeth Abel suggests that Bloomsbury helped to construct 'a singularly literary version of psychoanalysis',[86] and I would argue that for both Nin and H.D., the appeal of psychoanalysis was crucially bound up with this literary aspect, the view of the subject as a primarily narrative construction or creation, a character in its own drama.

To return for a moment to H.D.'s essay, she sums up what she is trying to do in her reflections on her texts and characters: 'I am trying to pin

[83] Proust's use of 'the free associative process of memory' (*Novel*, 119) in *Remembrance of Things Past* was Nin's most important influence in this respect; psychoanalysis and literary modernism went hand-in-hand in offering new structuring principles for representing experience. In Chapter 4, I examine Nin's ideas about the 'revolutionary' new artistic forms which attempt to bring conscious and unconscious into connection.

[84] Brooks, *Reading for the Plot*, p. xiv.

[85] Sigmund Freud and Josef Breuer, *Studies on Hysteria* (1895), SE, II, 160.

[86] Elizabeth Abel, *Virginia Woolf and the Fictions of Psychoanalysis* (Chicago: Univ. of Chicago Press, 1989), 15.

down my map, to plot the course of my journey, to circumscribe my own world or simply to put a frame around my clock-face. I repeat these dates, these names and titles for they are important to me, in this PLOT.'[87] Clearly, the emphasis signals the importance of this notion of 'plot' for H.D.'s conception of her life and writing. It is significant, then, that we find the same word used by Nin, this time with an explicit connection to psychoanalysis. In her diary for 22 April 1935, Nin writes: 'analysis is like a love affair. Produces the same ecstasy, liberation, renewal. *Discovering the plot of one's life*' (*Fire*, 72). We can see here the connection she is making between analysis, with its emphasis on the telling of stories, the emergence of unexpected, 'forgotten' stories from the unconscious, and the view of life as, in Nin's phrase, 'an adventure and a tale' (*Journals*, VII, 266), or rather many tales, and the subject as the protagonist of these tales. More problematically, the subject can also be caught up in endless repetitions of the same 'story', playing out the same plot over and over again. This is an explicit theme in *Seduction of the Minotaur*: Lillian travels to Mexico to escape her past, but comes to realize that psychic patterns must be acknowledged and (in Freud's term) 'worked through' if there is to be a change, a new story. As the Mexican doctor, Hernandez, says to her: 'We may seem to forget a person, a place, a state of being, a past life, but meanwhile what we are doing is selecting a new cast for the reproduction of the same drama . . . And one day we open our eyes, and there we are caught in the same pattern, repeating the same story. How could it be otherwise? The design comes from within us. It is internal' (*Seduction*, 21).

The literary metaphor has clear antecedents in Freud's own writings: in his paper on 'The Dynamics of Transference' (1912), he envisaged this 'internal design' in terms of a printer's 'stereotype plate', producing a text or story which is 'constantly repeated—constantly reprinted afresh—in the course of the person's life'.[88]

Nin expands on the feeling of being both author and protagonist of a literary adventure in the context of her analysis with Otto Rank:

> He would always ask me what I had been doing during the week. It was at this moment his magic would begin to operate, because no matter what I told him . . . Rank would immediately pounce on this fact with the joy of a discoverer, and raise this fragment to a brilliant, complete, dazzling legend . . . all I had done during the week was like a perfect play, or a novel, fostered by Rank's revelation. I felt

[87] 'H.D. by Delia Alton', 220, emphasis in original.

[88] Sigmund Freud, 'The Dynamics of Transference' (1912), SE, XII, 99–100.

like . . . a creator preparing in some dim laboratory a life like a legend, and now reading the legend itself from an enormous book. (*Journals*, II, 44)

The key word here is 'legend'; and this is also the key word used by H.D. in relation to her analysis with Freud in 1933 and 1934. In his Foreword to her book *Tribute to Freud*, Norman Holmes Pearson cites H.D.: '"For me, it was so important," she wrote, repeating, "it was so important, my own LEGEND. Yes, my own LEGEND."' Pearson goes on to gloss this: 'She used "legend" multiply—as story, a history, an account, a thing for reading, her own myth.'[89] As a written key to a map, 'legend' also links back to H.D.'s image of the map on which she plots the 'course of her journey'—to 'plot' in its related senses of a spatial location and the charting of that space. Like Nin, H.D. is, through analysis, discovering the plot of her life.

However, we might question the idea of psychoanalysis as a 'narrative art' given the fact that it seems to be *suspicious* of narrative, of coherent stories. In his discussion of 'secondary revision'—the attempt by the psyche's 'censoring agency' to make a dream 'approximate to the model of an intelligible experience'—Freud insists that we must disregard this apparent coherence: 'it remains an essential rule invariably to leave out of account the ostensible continuity of a dream as being of suspect origin.'[90] As Adam Phillips puts it, in his discussion of the connections between autobiographical writing and psychoanalysis, 'it is the continuity of our life-stories that we use to *conceal* the past'.[91] In analysis, the story is broken down, fragmented, into the non-narrative forms of free association. But then, of course, another story begins to appear from these fragments—the analysand 'exchanges one story for another that is, at least provisionally, better'.[92] And this story is not so much 'discovered' as, in a sense, *created* through the dialogue of the analyst and the patient, and through the transference which operates between them. (Again, Freud employs a literary metaphor in his account of transference: the emotion the analysand feels for the analyst, he writes, 'consists of new editions of old traits'.[93]) In psychoanalytic treatment, as Phillips says, 'it takes two to make a life-story'.[94] Indeed, it perhaps takes more than two, if we think about the interactions between the conscious and the unconscious that

[89] H.D., *Tribute to Freud* (Manchester: Carcanet, rev. edn., 1985), p. v.
[90] Freud, *Interpretation of Dreams*, 630, 642.
[91] Adam Phillips, *On Flirtation* (London: Faber & Faber, 1994), 67, my emphasis.
[92] Ibid. 68.
[93] Sigmund Freud, 'Observations on Transference-Love' (1915), SE, XII, 168.
[94] *On Flirtation*, 68.

are involved here; and Nin, at least, often wrote of the unconscious as playing out its own dramas, following its own 'plots': 'In this world of the unconscious there is . . . a different plot from the one we are familiar with' (*Novel*, 28). We get a sense of the dialogue, the joint creation, between analyst and analysand in Nin's description of her analysis with Rank: 'all I had done during the week was like a perfect play, or a novel, fostered by Rank's revelation'. This is not to suggest that the analyst is in some sense forcing an interpretation, a particular story, on the analysand—though, of course, this may happen. Rather, it is that the interaction between the two produces particular stories: 'With a different analyst one would speak different life-stories', Phillips writes,[95] and we could equally say that a different analyst would *hear* different life-stories.

This idea that we could tell different stories about ourselves is at the heart of the way we should understand psychoanalysis as a 'narrative art', and is also, I would argue, the key link between analysis and the kind of self-writing I have ascribed to Nin and H.D. Psychoanalysis is suspicious of the idea of a coherent and complete narrative because there is always something in excess, another story that could be told. Phillips writes: 'from a psychoanalytic point of view our lives are always other lives (and always in the making). The psychoanalyst, like the patient and the autobiographer, is always having to manage the fact that too many autobiographies make a life; that one's life might be different at every moment . . . There is no cure for multiple plots.'[96]

The awareness of this multiplicity of plots, the fact that one can never have a final or complete story, is exactly what we saw in Nin's and H.D.'s self-writing. While both autobiographical writing and analysis involve, in Phillips's term, a 'self-telling',[97] both also highlight the impossibility of any *one* story or any final story. Further, just as the personae created through writing 'negotiate' between fiction and history, the textual and the extra-textual, so too the self-narratives of psychoanalysis are not simply there to be 'discovered', but are formed and re-formed in the interactions of analyst and analysand, conscious and unconscious. When Nin writes, therefore, that in analysis one is 'discovering the plot of one's life', we should add two caveats: first, that the 'plot' is not simply given, but is realized through a process of negotiation; and second, that there is in fact no single plot, but rather 'multiple plots'.

95 *On Flirtation*, 72. 96 Ibid. 75. 97 Ibid. 69.

2

'As Fluid as Mercury': Psychoanalysis, Feminism, and Questions of Identity

In April 1932, Nin began her first analysis with René Allendy after being introduced by her cousin to the writings of Freud and Jung. In September that year, she wrote to Henry Miller: 'I have not decided yet whether analysis simplifies and undramatizes our existence, or whether it is the most subtle, the most insidious, the most magnificent way of making dramas more terrible, more maddening . . . psychoanalysis, when grasped by the artist, becomes another device by which to create chaos.'[1] One on level, we can see here another manifestation of the tension I located, in the previous chapter, within Nin's autobiographical practice: the pull towards 'wholeness' or unity of identity, and simultaneously the recognition—even the celebration—of its impossibility. On another level, Nin's remark may be seen as containing, in microcosm, the history of psychoanalysis in the twentieth century—a history of conflicting interpretations, battles over definitions, rival claims on the disputed object that is 'psychoanalysis'. At various points in space and time, this tangled history intersects with the equally tangled history of another equally disputed 'object': feminism. In particular, feminism and psychoanalysis connect, entwine, or battle it out (depending on one's point of view) over questions of *identity*, in terms of both gender identity and 'personal' identity: the cohesion, or lack of cohesion, of a 'self', and the understanding and experience of that self as female or male. In the words of Jacqueline Rose, 'the question of identity—how it is constituted and maintained—is . . . the central issue through which psychoanalysis enters the political field'.[2]

[1] Letter dated 29 Sept. 1932; *A Literate Passion*, 111–12.

[2] Jacqueline Rose, 'Introduction: Feminism and the Psychic', in *Sexuality in the Field of Vision* (London: Verso, 1986), 5.

The aim of this chapter is twofold. I shall examine Nin's use of psychoanalytic ideas in relation to the question of identity, particularly in relation to the issue of psychic conflict and division. As we shall see, there is no one resolution of this issue in Nin's writings. Rather, different contexts produce different images of the self: in the context of the women's liberation movement of the 1970s Nin tends to stress positive notions of a self that is fluid and changeable but not conflictual or fragmented; in other writings, and particularly in her erotica, we find a picture of the self as divided by the difficulties of sexuality (a picture that has a considerable affinity with Lacanian feminist thought).

At the same time, I shall set the specific case of Nin, and that of her most important psychoanalytic mentor, Otto Rank, within the wider context of the tangled history of psychoanalysis and its complex relation to feminism. In particular, I shall trace some of the historical, cultural, and geographical outlines of the schism between 'Lacanian' versions of psychoanalysis and US-based 'ego psychology', and shall explore the intriguing position that both Nin and Rank occupied in this fraught history of cross-cultural clash, claim and counter-claim.

'RICHNESS' OR 'DISEASE': PSYCHIC CONFLICT AND THEORIES OF EGO

In 1954, Nin wrote confidently: 'Analysis is one of the powerful elements I have complete faith in to attain harmony and wholeness' (*Journals*, V, 219). On the other hand, she could also write: 'Through the microscope of analysis I see the dispersed and sundered being, every little piece leading a separate life. Occasionally, like mercury, they fuse, but remain elusive, unstable, and not welded' (*Journals*, III, 251). Nin's fascination, throughout her writing, with the elusive and multiple aspects of the self contains both positive and negative aspects, both fear and desire; if the self is perceived as elusive and unstable, this is not always seen as something to be overcome, 'healed', welded into a solid whole. In 1946, when a section of *Ladders to Fire* was printed in *Harper's Bazaar* and Leo Lerman asked her for a 'short autobiography' to go with the article, she wrote back: 'My life is not possible to tell. I change every day, change my patterns, my concepts, my interpretations. I am a series of moods and sensations. I play a thousand roles . . . My real self is unknown' (*Journals*, IV, 198). Here we can clearly see at work an *erotics* of multiplicity and elusiveness, a fantasy of an unlimited proliferation of selves and possibilities.[3] But Nin evinces a quite different viewpoint in the following passage from 1937: 'It seems to me that I traverse a hundred quarters a day, breathe a hundred different airs, am so sensitive to changes, *suffer* from my dualities and triplicities' (*Journals*, II, 261, my emphasis). Here the emphasis is rather on conflict and division, the 'dislocation' Nin describes more graphically in *House of Incest*:

> I am a marionette pulled by unskilled fingers, pulled apart, inharmoniously dislocated; one arm dead, the other rhapsodizing in mid-air . . . I see two women in me freakishly bound together, like circus twins. I see them tearing away from each other. I can hear the tearing, the anger and love, passion and pity. When the act of dislocation suddenly ceases—or when I cease to be aware of the sound—then the silence is more terrible because there is nothing but insanity around me, the insanity of things pulling, pulling within oneself, the roots tearing at each other to grow separately, the strain made to achieve unity. (*House of Incest*, 187)

Nin summarizes this difference of attitude towards the 'dualities and triplicities' of the psyche: 'I have always been tormented by the image of the multiplicity of selves. Some days I call it richness, and other days I see it as a disease' (*Journals*, I, 54).

This opposition—understanding the psyche in terms of an erotics of multiplicity or a painful dislocation, an irreducible conflictedness or an aberration to be cured, 'richness' or 'disease'—could be said to lie at the heart of the history of psychoanalysis through the twentieth century. The roots of this conceptual schism can be traced back to Freud's changing 'topographies' of the psyche, and in particular to what came to be known as the 'turning point' of 1920, when Freud apparently abandoned his earlier topography of unconscious, pre-conscious, and conscious in favour of his new classification, id, ego, and super-ego.[4] Elisabeth Roudinesco sums up the importance of this moment for the future development of psychoanalysis:

> Two options were available after Freud's 1920 revision of his theories. One was to see the ego as the product of a gradual differentiation of the id, acting as a representative of reality and responsible for controlling the drives (ego psychology); the other rejected any idea of making the ego autonomous and instead looked to find its genesis in identification. The first alternative meant trying to extract the

[3] See Chapter 3 for a discussion of June Mansfield, Henry Miller's wife, as representing for Nin a fantasy of an elusive and unbounded self.

[4] Jean Laplanche and J.-B. Pontalis, in *The Language of Pyscho-Analysis* (trans. Donald Nicholson-Smith; London: Hogarth Press/Institute of Psycho-Analysis, 1973), emphasize that this should not be seen as a clear-cut 'turning point', stressing the continued complexity of Freud's views of the ego.

ego from the id and making it the instrument of the individual's adaptation to external reality, while the second option moved the ego closer to the id and sought to show it structuring itself in stages by means of imagoes borrowed from 'the other'.[5]

As Roudinesco notes, the first position, broadly speaking, came to be known as 'ego psychology', associated with Anna Freud and, in particular, with a group of analysts exiled from Europe to the US during the Second World War: Heinz Hartmann, Ernst Kris, and Rudolph Loewenstein. The second position was that taken up, although in different ways, by Melanie Klein and by Jacques Lacan. Lacan, in particular, saw it as his avowed mission to root out what he considered to be a 'repudiation of psychoanalysis', a pragmatic and reactionary system of thought aimed at 'the adaptation of the individual to the social environment'[6] and, worst of all, based on an erroneous understanding of Freud's work. 'Thirty-five years of cohabitation with the ego under the roof of the second Freudian topography', Lacan remarked sardonically in 1955, had produced 'a drawer . . . filled to overflowing with old novelties and new junk the sheer mass of which is certainly entertaining'. '[The ego] is autonomous!' he went on derisively: 'That's a good one!'[7] Lacan rejected both the conception of the ego as an agent of psychic mastery and unification, and the understanding of psychoanalysis as a means of 'curing' the individual, 'unifying' his or her psyche and reconciling him or her to societal norms. In his 1955 lecture on 'the return to Freud', he insisted that 'the practice [of psychoanalysis] in the American sphere has been so summarily reduced to a means of obtaining "success" and to a mode of demanding "happiness" that it should be pointed out that this constitutes *a repudiation of psychoanalysis*'.[8] For Lacan, Roudinesco suggests, psychoanalysis was 'above all an intellectual epic, a discovery of the mind, a theoretical journey'[9]—perhaps even, as Nin put it, 'a device by which to create chaos'.

[5] Elisabeth Roudinesco, *Jacques Lacan: An Outline of a Life and a History of a System of Thought* (trans. Barbara Bray; Cambridge: Polity Press, 1997), 111.

[6] Jacques Lacan, 'The Function and Field of Speech and Language in Psychoanalysis' (1953), in *The Four Fundamental Concepts of Psycho-Analysis* (ed. Jacques-Alain Miller; trans. Alan Sheridan; London: Hogarth Press and the Institute of Psycho-Analysis, 1977), 38.

[7] Jacques Lacan, 'The Freudian Thing, or the Meaning of the Return to Freud in Psychoanalysis' (1955), in *Four Fundamental Concepts*, 131, 132.

[8] Ibid. 127, my emphasis.

[9] Elisabeth Roudinesco, *Jacques Lacan & Co.: A History of Psychoanalysis in France, 1925–1985* (trans. Jeffrey Mehlman; London: Free Association Books, 1990), 119.

PSYCHOANALYSIS, FEMINISM, AND THE 'RESISTANCE TO IDENTITY'

In Lacan's claim that American ego psychology constituted a 'repudiation of pyschoanalysis', we can see the structure of argument that had characterized psychoanalysis, as an 'institution', almost from its inception, and would continue to do so after Lacan's own intervention. The history of psychoanalysis is a history of claims and counter-claims, attempts to define both the nature and the function of the disputed object, 'psychoanalysis', and to stake a claim to it—or to stake out one's territory in opposition to it. Freud himself laid the foundations for this with his conception of his followers as 'sons', and the rebels among them (notably Adler, Jung, and then, as we shall see, Rank) as traitors, turning on and betraying their 'father'—and, in so doing, putting themselves beyond the pale of what could legitimately be called 'psychoanalysis'.[10] In his 'History of the Psychoanalytic Movement' (1914), Freud describes the painful 'secessions'[11] of Jung and Adler and the hopes he had placed in Jung as his heir, the 'younger man, who would then as a matter of course take my place after my death'.[12] For his part, Jung, as the relationship between him and Freud was breaking down, angrily rejected his positioning as 'son' to Freud's 'father': 'You go around sniffing out all the symptomatic actions in your vicinity, thus reducing everyone to the level of sons and daughters who blushingly admit the existence of their faults. Meanwhile you remain on top as the father, sitting pretty.'[13] By contrast, in the 1920s, Ernest Jones and Karl Abraham would manoeuvre against Rank as part of a jockeying for position within Freud's inner circle. The structure would be played out again after Freud's death with Anna Freud and Melanie Klein, in bitter dispute over their rival claims to the status of 'daughter', the faithful inheritor of the father's ideas; and again, as we

[10] See Sigmund Freud, 'On the History of the Pyschoanalytic Movement' (1914), PFL 15, 108–28. It is noteworthy that Freud insists that Adler's and Jung's theories cannot be seen as *developments* of psychoanalysis but represent 'an abandonment of analysis and a secession from it' (127). It is also important to note that Freud makes this a personal matter by explicitly tying 'psychoanalysis' to himself: 'I [do] not recognize the innovations of the Swiss as legitimate continuations and further developments of the psychoanalysis that originated with me' (121). Adler and Jung were both eventually forced to adopt new names for their theories ('individual psychology' and 'analytical psychology' respectively).

[11] Freud, 'History of the Psychoanalytic Movement', 108.

[12] Ibid. 102.

[13] Letter from C. G. Jung to Sigmund Freud, 18 Dec. 1912, in *The Freud/Jung Letters* (ed. William McGuire; Harmondsworth: Penguin, 1991 [1974]), 292.

have seen, in Lacan's campaign against ego psychology and claims for himself as the true disciple, inaugurating the 'return to Freud'. And in 1974, feminist critic Juliet Mitchell would make a decisive intervention on behalf of (a strongly Lacanian) Freud, claiming psychoanalysis for feminism and opening a new, often intensely bitter, chapter in this fraught history.

Within this history, certain issues recur: the conflict of 'theory' against 'therapy'; the political status of different kinds of psychoanalytic practice and discourse (conservative and normative, or radical and subversive); the ultimate aim of psychoanalysis; and above all, as I have outlined, the nature of the psyche, of the 'ego', and of 'identity'.[14] The schism between Anna Freud and Melanie Klein brought to the fore the opposed understandings of the ego and of the psyche as a whole developed out of Freud's 'second topography'; Anna Freud's book *The Ego and the Mechanisms of Defence* (published in 1936 but partially delivered as lectures from 1929 onwards) was a seminal text for what was to become American ego psychology. Defending her position (that is, defending it as the 'truest' form of psychoanalysis), Anna Freud wrote: 'From the beginning analysis, as a therapeutic method, was concerned with the ego and its aberrations: the investigation of the id and of its mode of operation was always only a means to an end. And the end was invariably the same: the correction of these abnormalities and the restoration of the ego to its integrity.'[15] Anna Freud's version of psychoanalysis was primarily therapeutic (rather than theoretical), pragmatic, and *normative*; the analysand (or perhaps better 'patient') is to be *cured* by means of the 'correction of [his or her] abnormalities'. Psychic division and conflict were, for Anna Freud, aberrations to be cured. For Melanie Klein on the other hand, who understood the ego as developed through identifications with the 'other' (particularly, the mother), they were inherent parts of the human psyche.

For Jacques Lacan, Anna Freud's (and the later ego psychologists') pragmative and curative version of psychoanalysis constituted a *repression*

[14] See, among others, Mari Jo Buhle, *Feminism and its Discontents: A Century of Struggle with Psychoanalysis* (Cambridge, Mass: Harvard Univ. Press, 1998); Rachel Bowlby, 'Still Crazy After All These Years: Travels in Feminism and Psychoanalysis', in *Still Crazy After All These Years: Women, Writing and Psychoanalysis* (London and New York: Routledge, 1992); and Lynne Segal, *Why Feminism? Gender, Psychology, Politics* (Cambridge: Polity Press, 1999), esp. ch. 6, 'Cautionary Tales: Between Freud and Feminism', for accounts of the relationship between feminism and psychoanalysis.

[15] Cited in Lisa Appignanesi and John Forrester, *Freud's Women* (London: Weidenfeld & Nicolson, 1992), 294.

of what was truly radical, and therefore discomfiting, in Freud's work. As Elizabeth Grosz puts it,

> Lacan affirms the more notorious, unpalatable components of Freud's work—those very components purged, removed, silenced, or left unarticulated by the Neo- and revisionist Freudians . . . Lacan claims that Freud's work is in danger of itself being repressed . . . He stresses the neglected, unrepresented, or undiscussed elements of Freud's work—those which generated psychical or intellectual resistances on the part of psychoanalysts themselves.[16]

This was an argument over the status of the unconscious—the 'notorious, unpalatable' element in psychoanalysis—and, concomitantly, over the notion of *identity*, the 'integrity' (to return to Anna Freud's term) of the psyche. As Jacqueline Rose puts it, 'In terms of Lacan himself, the history begins with his critique of American ego-psychology, the assimilation, as he saw it, of the concept of the unconscious into a normative or adaptive psychology which took identity at its word and tried to strengthen it.'[17] Lacan saw his 'intervention' within psychoanalysis, Rose goes on to argue, as 'a return to the concepts of psychic division, splitting of the ego, and an endless (he called it "insistent") pressure of the unconscious against any individual's pretension to a smooth and coherent psychic and sexual identity'. For Lacan, 'psychoanalysis does not offer an account of a developing ego which is "not *necessarily* coherent", but of an ego which is "necessarily *not* coherent", that is, which is always and persistently divided against itself.'[18]

The first point I want to make about Rose's account here is that, although she attributes the understanding of ego psychology as conservative and normative specifically to Lacan ('as he saw it'), it is important to note that this understanding is equally present in the work of the Lacanian-influenced feminist theorists, such as Elizabeth Grosz, Juliet Mitchell, and Rose herself, writing from the mid-1970s onwards. A clearly politicized opposition is thus set up whereby Lacanian psychoanalysis is constructed as the radical, subversive other to the conservative, normalizing 'mainstream' that is ego psychology (what Grosz calls neo-Freudian 'orthodoxy'[19]). To note the way in which this opposition has been entrenched, post-Lacan, is not to suggest that it is historically invalid; we

[16] Elizabeth Grosz, *Jacques Lacan: A Feminist Introduction* (London: Routledge, 1990), 9–10.

[17] Rose, 'Feminism and the Psychic', 4–5.

[18] Jacqueline Rose, 'Femininity and its Discontents', in *Sexuality in the Field of Vision*, 94–5.

[19] *Jacques Lacan*, 8.

should be aware, however, that it may not always have been so clear-cut as later commentary may suggest. The case of Otto Rank, Nin's analyst and psychoanalytic mentor, illustrates this particularly well: as I shall go on to show, although Rank has been claimed by at least one commentator as a 'forerunner' of ego psychology, his ideas do not fall neatly onto either side of this politicized divide.

The second important point is that Rose's account of the history of Lacan's 'intervention' is embedded within a discussion of the importance of psychoanalysis for feminism (and vice versa).[20] The question of identity is the crucial point of connection between psychoanalysis and feminism (and political thought more broadly); Rose writes that 'the question of identity—how it is constituted and maintained—is . . . the central issue through which psychoanalysis enters the political field'.[21] Her general argument is that the political relevance of psychoanalysis lies in its emphasis on the 'divided and disordered subjectivity'[22] which must be seen as common to all; on the *inevitable* 'failure' of any identity and, *a fortiori*, of any normative gender identity:

> The unconscious constantly reveals the 'failure' of identity. Because there is no continuity of psychic life, so there is no stability of sexual identity, no position for women (or for men) which is ever simply achieved. Nor does psychoanalysis see such 'failure' as a special-case inability or an individual deviancy from the norm . . . 'failure' is something endlessly repeated and relived moment by moment throughout our individual histories . . . Feminism's affinity with psychoanalysis rests above all, I would argue, with this recognition that there is a resistance to identity at the very heart of psychic life.[23]

For Rose (following Lacan), psyche and culture are isomorphic, with the unconscious as the dissident within: 'The critique of autocracy and the critique of the ego should be taken together, since an ego in place which has held off the challenge from the unconscious, or transformed it into something which can simply be known and controlled, will be autocratic above all else.'[24]

On this view, what psychoanalysis offers feminism is an account of this 'resistance to [or failure of] identity', a theoretical support for feminism's project of undermining the linked structures of bourgeois individualism, phallic autocracy, and common-sense empiricism which seek to define

[20] In fact, there are two analyses of these issues within *Sexuality in the Field of Vision*: in the introduction, 'Feminism and the Psychic', and in ch. 3, 'Femininity and its Discontents'. I am considering the two together as complementary essays.

[21] 'Feminism and the Psychic', 5.

[22] 'Femininity and its Discontents', 101.

[23] Ibid. 91.

[24] 'Feminism and the Psychic', 5.

the norms of gendered identity, set women in their place, and keep them there. However, Rose also concedes that feminists have not always welcomed this offer. Indeed, she suggests that feminists, rather than putting the concepts of the unconscious and psychic conflict to subversive political use, have subscribed instead to a 'utopianism of the psyche', rendering psychic conflict 'either an accident or an obstacle on the path to psychic and sexual continuity', and persistently returning to 'this concept of psychic cohesion as the ultimate object of our [i.e. feminists'] political desires'.[25]

Rose is conceding, then, that the issue of 'identity', the territory on which psychoanalysis meets feminism in the political arena, may be far from clear-cut for feminists. I shall set Nin's attempts to negotiate the tensions around this issue alongside those of the psychoanalytic feminism exemplified by Rose's work, arguing that there are certain significant parallels between their 'interventions' in these issues of psychoanalysis, subjectivity, and feminism. In the final section of the chapter, I shall look at Nin's erotica and her depictions of the psychic difficulties surrounding sexuality, depictions which show considerable affinity with the Lacanian feminist understanding of subjectivity. First, however, I shall focus on Nin's association with Otto Rank and the key ideas about subjectivity and creativity (and about analysis itself) which she took from Rank and which informed her own work.

OTTO RANK: ONE OF 'THE GREAT "MADMEN" OF FREUDIANISM'

In a lecture given to the Otto Rank Association in October 1972, Nin described her debt to Rank, as analyst and as thinker:

There are books which we read early in life, which sink into our consciousness and seem to disappear without leaving a trace. And then one day we find, in some summing-up of our life and our attitudes towards experience, that their influence has been enormous. Such a book is *Truth and Reality*, by Otto Rank, which I read in my early thirties . . . the meaning of this book, its guiding principles, sank into my unconscious and I did not read it again until, thanks to Virginia Robinson and Anita Faatz,[26] I rediscovered it and found that my whole life as a woman

[25] 'Femininity and its Discontents', 101.

[26] Virginia Robinson and Anita Faatz were former colleagues of Rank at the Pennsylvania School of Social Work and founded the Otto Rank Association, dedicated to preserving and publishing Rank's work.

artist had been influenced by it, and proved its wisdom. ('On Truth and Reality', in *Sensitive Man*, 47)

Nin goes on to discuss the concept of 'creative will', which was, she argues, 'Rank's great contribution to the psychology of woman' ('On Truth and Reality', 52). The lecture suggests both her lasting respect and affection for Rank and the central importance of his work and ideas for what she saw as her ongoing creative project: 'my whole life as a woman artist'.[27] Although she read both Freud and Jung avidly, and was analysed by several people after Rank, notably Martha Jaeger and Inge Bogner, it was Rank's ideas, his emphases on literature and myth, the conflicts of the artist, and above all creativity and *self*-creation, that fitted perfectly with Nin's own concerns. Rank's thought, she wrote in the context of her analysis with him in 1933, formed 'a metaphysics of the artist' (*Journals*, I, 303); her lifelong concern was with the 'metaphysics' of the woman artist.[28]

When Otto Rank presented himself to Freud in the spring of 1905 with the manuscript of *Der Kunstler*, Freud was so impressed that he arranged for Rank to be funded through a university degree, and in 1906 made him the secretary of the Vienna Psychoanalytic Society. By 1923, Rank had become 'virtually indispensable' to Freud,[29] both administratively (he was vice-president of the Society and director of Freud's *Verlag*) and personally. As Freud himself wrote in a letter to Sandor Ferenczi in March 1924, '[Rank is] the person nearest to me in so many respects. His work

[27] Sharon Spencer makes the same point in her article 'Delivering the Woman Artist from the Silence of the Womb: Otto Rank's Influence on Anaïs Nin', *Psychoanalytic Review* 69/1 (1982), 111–29. She writes that 'all of her mature life [Nin] was grateful to Rank whose influence as a man, a therapist, and a thinker was profound and enduring' (112).

[28] It is also possible to see in this concern with self-creation the underlying influence of Nin's earlier American 'mentors', particularly Emerson. Noël Riley Fitch writes: 'Despite her later acknowledgement of her three European "gods of the deep" (Dostoyevsky, Proust, Lawrence), Anaïs also belongs to the American tradition of Emerson, Thoreau, and Whitman . . . The search for happiness, the primacy of the self, the American narrative of self-discovery and [self-] invention—are these not her hallmarks?' (Fitch, *Anaïs*, 57). Nin never referred to Emerson in her lectures and seminars, always crediting Rank as the crucial influence on her thinking about self and creation. Nonetheless, I think we can see a connection here; as I suggested in the introduction, Nin frequently 'grafted' ideas from one cultural and historical context onto another. In Chapter 4, I discuss one critic's placing of Emerson as a link between the German Romantic preoccupation with the 'vital creative force' and a psychoanalytic (or, strictly speaking, Jungian) account of unconscious energies.

[29] Robert Kramer, 'Introduction: Insight and Blindness: Visions of Rank', in Otto Rank, *A Psychology of Difference: The American Lectures* (ed. Robert Kramer; Princeton: Princeton Univ. Press, 1996), 12.

has been invaluable, his person would be irreplaceable'.[30] Freud praised Rank and Ferenczi's joint work *The Development of Psychoanalysis: On the Inter-Relationship between Theory and Practice*, written in 1923 and published in 1924; and he was initially full of praise for Rank's book *Das Trauma der Geburt* (*The Trauma of Birth*), which was dedicated to Freud and presented to him by Rank in November 1923. But it was this book, with its then-radical emphasis on the pre-Oedipal mother–child relationship[31] and on the separation from the mother at birth as the prototype for all later anxiety (an idea Rank developed from Freud's own suggestion in a footnote to *The Interpretation of Dreams*[32]), that was to result in Rank's being ostracized from the psychoanalytic world.

Interestingly, it was not Freud himself but his disciples Ernest Jones and Karl Abraham who objected to Rank's new ideas and, indeed, viewed them as posing 'a mortal threat to the scientific foundation of psychoanalysis'.[33] The conflict over Rank appears, again, as a conflict over status, a jockeying for position as the 'purest Freudian', the most faithful disciple—and therefore, perhaps, the designated heir.

Although Rank at the time saw *The Trauma of Birth* as a contribution to Freudian theory, Jones and Abraham thought otherwise, and began a campaign to persuade Freud that Rank's theory amounted to 'a blatant denial of the Oedipus complex',[34] and thus a denial of the whole psychoanalytic edifice of which the Oedipus complex was the cornerstone. As Freud, urged by Abraham and Jones, began to reconsider his positive attitude towards Rank, Ferenczi, concerned for his own position, began to distance himself from Rank. In April 1924 Rank sailed to the USA to give a series of lectures, in which he saw himself as spokesman for Freud while at the same time emphasizing his own 'contribution' to Freudian

[30] Letter dated 20 March 1924, cited in E. J. Lieberman, *Acts of Will: The Life and Work of Otto Rank* (New York: Free Press, 1985), 218.

[31] Robert Kramer sees Rank as foreshadowing the work of Melanie Klein in his emphasis on the mother–child relationship, particularly as elaborated in his 1926 article 'The Genesis of the Object Relation'. Kramer notes, however, that it would have been 'politically' impossible for Klein to have acknowledged Rank's ideas even if she had read this text, since by the time it was published Rank was persona non grata in the psychoanalytic world. His name was, however, linked to Klein's by Edward Glover in 1944 during the 'Controversial Discussions' in the British Psychoanalytic Society: Glover accused Rank and Klein of a similar 'deviation' from psychoanalysis (Kramer's note, in Rank, *A Psychology of Difference*, 150).

[32] Freud, *Interpretation of Dreams*, 526–7 n. 2.

[33] Kramer, 'Visions of Rank', 16. See *Journals*, I, 288–9 for Nin's account of this conflict, as told to her by Rank. She stresses Freud's vision of Rank as his 'son' and 'heir' and the jealousy of the other 'disciples' (Jones and Abraham).

[34] Kramer, 'Visions of Rank', 25.

thought. In an exchange of letters between Freud and Rank in July–August 1924, Freud pleaded with Rank to 'leave open a way back'. Rank responded with what Kramer calls 'a declaration of independence'.[35] By April 1926 Rank had resigned his posts in Vienna and effectively severed his connections with Freud and the Freudians.

In May 1930 Rank spoke at the First International Congress on Mental Hygiene, a huge psychoanalytic conference in Washington, DC. In a ten-minute summary speech, he set out his 'undefinable position' in relation to psychoanalysis: 'I am no psychiatrist, no social worker, no psychoanalyst, not even an ordinary psychologist'. He went on to castigate Freudian psychoanalysis for its overvaluation of intellectual understanding, its aim of a 'scientific comprehension of the individual', and its attempts to impose order on the essentially disorderly human psyche:

> The error [of 'scientific psychology', i.e. psychoanalysis] lies in the scientific glorification of *consciousness*, of intellectual knowledge, which even psychoanalysis worships as its highest god—although it calls itself a psychology of the *unconscious*. But this means only an attempt to rationalize the unconscious and to intellectualize it scientifically . . . in order to pretend that control and prediction are possible, one has to deny the individual's own will, his emotional instability, and the large part chance plays in the sphere of our psychical life.[36]

Roudinesco suggests that this attack on the scientistic aspirations of Freudian psychoanalysis can be understood as one of the 'occultist crises', through which not only Rank but other notable 'dissidents' such as Ferenczi and Wilhelm Reich—'the great "madmen" of Freudianism', who 'could not manage to submit to the etiquette of the movement's "notables"'—broke with Freudianism, attempting to rectify 'the rationality of an institution intent on adapting to the ideals of science' by means of an emphasis on 'irrationalism'.[37]

After Rank had spoken, A. A. Brill, the president of the American Psychoanalytic Association, addressed the conference, saying: 'I was particularly impressed by one remark of Dr Rank's—namely that he is no longer a psychoanalyst . . . all the stuff to which Dr Rank treated us this morning is but an indication of his own present maladjustment'.[38] At the

[35] Kramer, 'Visions of Rank', 31.

[36] Otto Rank, Speech at First International Congress on Mental Hygiene, in *A Psychology of Difference*, 222–3.

[37] Roudinesco, *Jacques Lacan & Co.*, 11. In his last book, *Beyond Psychology* (New York: Dover, 1958 [1941]), Rank wrote: 'This book is pleading for the recognition and the acceptance of the irrational element as the most vital part of human life' (15).

[38] Cited in *A Psychology of Difference*, 227 n. 8.

meeting of the APA the same evening, in response to a motion proposed by Brill, Rank's name was struck from the list of honorary members (the only others being Freud and Ferenczi). In an ironic foreshadowing of what was to happen to Jacques Lacan in 1968 at the hands of the International Psychoanalytic Association,[39] the APA ruled that any of their members who had been analysed by Rank must be re-analysed by a recognized Freudian in order to retain their status. As far as the psychoanalytic establishment was concerned, 'Rank was dead'.[40]

NIN AND RANK: NEUROSIS AND CREATIVITY

It is clear that Nin's account of her 1933–4 analysis with Rank as it appears in the first volume of the *Journals* cannot be considered a verbatim report, or even an accurate reconstruction, of her analytic sessions. Rather, it must be viewed as a composite account, perhaps pieced together and revised at many different times—an account of Rank and his ideas as Nin saw them. Parts of the account, indeed, read like an essay on Rank's thought designed to introduce his ideas to a wider public and, perhaps, to defend him against a culture hostile to psychoanalysis by emphasizing his difference:

> Otto Rank should not be confused with the other psychoanalysts. He . . . transcends the psychoanalytical theories and writes more as a philosopher, as a metaphysician . . . the preoccupation becomes a metaphysical or creative one. It is this emphasis I want to make clear, for a great popular confusion tends to classify all psychoanalysts more or less in the same pragmatic category: as doctors and not as seers, as healers and not as philosophers. (*Journals*, I, 307)

Nin appears here to be addressing herself (possibly writing in the early or mid-1960s, as the first volume of the *Journals* was being edited for publication) to an American audience with a specific concept of 'psychoanalysis' as a pragmatic treatment for mental illness and, perhaps, a suspicion of 'psychoanalytic theories'. It is important to be aware, then, that her accounts of Rank's ideas and her analysis with him are being presented at a time and in a culture very different from those in which she first encountered Rank. It is also the case, of course, that her presentations of Rank reveal those aspects of his thought that she focused on and applied to her own case; so that, although her accounts cannot be taken

[39] The IPA did not expel Lacan but refused to recognize the qualifications of analysts trained by him; see Grosz, *Jacques Lacan*, 16.

[40] Kramer, in *A Psychology of Difference*, 227 n. 8.

as historically accurate reports of what Rank actually said in the analytic sessions, they *can* be taken as guides to the ways in which Nin was influenced by and made use of Rank's ideas in her life and writing. This is equally true of the account of the analysis that appears in the 'unexpurgated' diary volume *Incest*. Nin admits the impossibility of an accurate transcript of what was said in the sessions: 'I find it difficult to retain exact phrases . . . I feel as I write that I am missing the overtones' (20 January 1934 [*Incest*, 301, 302]). And she describes Rank's 'bold stroke' of taking the diary away from her (temporarily), so that her descriptions of sessions with Rank are in any case reconstructions from some temporal distance (*Incest*, 294), focusing always on what appeared to her the crucial points, the key ideas.

The overriding idea that Nin took from Rank, which had fired her interest in his work before she met him, was that of the central importance of *creativity*, of what Rank was to call the 'creative will'. Describing their first meeting, she writes exultantly: 'Immediately I knew that we talk the same language . . . There is—beyond sexuality, beyond lesbianism, beyond narcissism—creation, *creation*' (7 November 1933 [*Incest*, 292]). In the earliest days of her interest in psychoanalysis, Nin had been attracted to Jung, whose article 'Psychology and Poetry' had appeared in *transition* in 1930, because of his emphasis on creativity and the artist:

> [Freud] has not studied enough of the transposition, sublimation, transfiguration of our physical and mental elements. Forcibly, being a doctor, he would seek to point out where and how such elements destroy us, and how, through knowledge, we can master them; but *how the artist uses them* is another matter, which Jung magnifies as it should be magnified. (1 January 1931 [*Early Diary*, IV, 372])

Although Nin admired Freud greatly (she called him 'the greatest thinker among psychologists' [1 August 1931 (*Early Diary*, IV, 449)]), and continued to defend the importance of his ideas for the rest of her life, she did not find in his work the interest in creativity that was so central to Rank. Indeed, while Freud did write about creative artists, he himself suggested that the creative drive, which he saw as resulting from the sublimation of the libido, lay outside the scope of psychoanalysis, bordering on biology: 'Instincts and their transformations are at the limit of what is discernible by psychoanalysis. From that point it gives place to biological research . . . Since artistic talent and capacity are intimately connected with sublimation we must admit that the nature of the artistic function is also inaccessible to us along psychoanalytic lines.'[41]

[41] Sigmund Freud, 'Leonardo da Vinci and a Memory of his Childhood' (1910), PFL 14, 229.

Ironically, although Freud did not profess any great interest in 'the artistic function', he was more successful in analysing creative artists (such as Gustav Mahler) than some analysts who thought of themselves as 'specialists' in artists—including Nin's first analyst, René Allendy. Allendy was one of the founder members of the Société psychanalytique de Paris, and analysed not only Nin but also the Surrealist writer René Crevel, as well as being a friend and mentor of Antonin Artaud, whom he introduced to Nin. The first generation of Paris analysts, as Roudinesco notes, 'entertained a variety of relations' with that group of artists and writers who were seizing eagerly on Freud's ideas as offering new possibilities in the exploration of the mind and the realms of the 'marvellous'—the Surrealists. The opportunity seemed to be there for a great meeting of minds; and yet, Roudinesco suggests, the 'first generation' of Paris analysts were too close to what was happening, unable to understand the connection between themselves and the Surrealists, retreating into conservative, 'psychobiographical' forms of analysis.[42] Certainly Nin was scathing about Allendy: in calling her, patronizingly, '*petite fille littéraire*', he had demonstrated his 'great limitation': 'Allendy is not interested in literature, art, or artists' (*Incest*, 293).

Otto Rank, in his *Art and Artist* (published in English in 1932), had focused in great detail on the psychology of the artist and of creativity, and had elaborated his radical view of neurosis as a failure in creativity, the 'neurotic' as an *artiste manqué*.[43] Nin had been immediately attracted to this idea: 'He considered neurosis a failed work of art, the neurotic a failed artist . . . It was this concept which appealed to me' (*Journals*, I, 280). In the published account, she depicts herself arriving at Rank's door with the following self-declaration: 'I am one of the artists you are writing about, Dr Rank' (280). She thereby depicts herself as also confirming Rank's own statement that the first act of the creative personality is an act of self-nomination: 'he, so to say, appoints himself as an artist'.[44]

Rank's appreciation of her self-conception as an artist was crucial to Nin's enthusiasm for him as an analyst. Having dismissed Allendy as 'not interested' in artists, she writes of Rank that, on the contrary, 'he does not separate me from my work . . . He seizes me through my work' (*Incest*, 297). Allendy was seeking normality, an adaptation to ordinary life: 'With Allendy, I was an ordinary woman, a full human being, a simple and

[42] Roudinesco, *Jacques Lacan & Co.*, 5–8.

[43] See Otto Rank, *Art and Artist: Creative Urge and Personality Development* (New York: Norton, 1989 [1932]), 25–7.

[44] Ibid. 27.

naïve one; and he would exorcise my disquietudes, vague aspirations, my creations which sent me out into dangerous realms' (*Journals*, I, 291). The aim of that analysis was 'the formation of my human self': 'normalcy' (292). Nin had rejected this ideal: 'If psychoanalysis is going to divest me of all decoration, costume, adornment, flavor, characteristic, then what will be left?' (127). She chose instead, she writes, 'to retrogress into . . . neurosis and obsessions', seeing these as 'more inspiring' than Allendy's normality (292). Rank, in contrast, focuses on the 'vast, amorphous, restless realm' of fantasy and imagination as providing 'the key': 'Allendy would say, "You must separate these games of your fantasy. They are just games." But in the fantasy lay the secret desires and the seed of positive creation' (292–3).

Nin suggests that she does not want a 'cure' from Rank. Typically, as she sits in the train on her way to her first meeting with Rank, she plans the lies and fantasies she will spin for him, noting the paradox: 'I meditate lies as others meditate confessions. Yet I am going to him to *confess*, to get help in the solution of my conflicts.' She then immediately contradicts herself, suggesting a different motivation for going to analysis: 'I am going to Rank . . . not to solve, but to aggrandize, dramatize my conflicts, to see all that they contain, to seize them in full' (7 November 1933 [*Incest*, 293]). And she finds a parallel to this in Rank's own technique:

> It is exciting to see . . . how he enlarges the problems like a creator who is there to add, to invent, to multiply, to expand rather than analyze into nothingness. He does not raze the ground by analysis; he explores and quickens into life, he illumines—and partly because he is not seeking a definite, static conclusion. He does not work for a determined finality of judgment, but to arouse, awaken, stimulate, enrich. (20 January 1934 [*Incest*, 301–2])

These descriptions clearly recall her suggestion to Miller, in 1932, that perhaps psychoanalysis, rather than simplifying things, might prove to be 'the most subtle, the most insidious, the most magnificent way of making dramas more terrible, more maddening'. In the same passage, she had made the link that was to be so important in her analysis with Rank: 'psychoanalysis, *when grasped by the artist*, becomes another device by which to create chaos'.

For Rank, the artist and the neurotic are two sides of the same coin, each the shadow of the other; if the neurotic is an *artiste manqué*, the artist is the 'productive neurotic'.[45] (The same link is made by Freud in

[45] Rank, *Art and Artist*, 27.

his discussion of the character Norbert Hanold in Jensen's *Gradiva*: he was 'destined . . . to become an artist or a neurotic; he was one of those whose kingdom was not of this world'.[46]) They are closer to each other than either is to the 'average type', who 'accepts himself as he is' and accepts 'reality', the external world, as it is, seeking merely to adapt to that reality in the best possible way. The artist and the neurotic, however, do not accept themselves, but 'exercise their volition in reshaping themselves'.[47] This project of self-construction or reconstruction is, in Rank's account, central to the development of the creative personality, beginning with the act of self-naming as an artist and continuing in an endless process, what Rank calls 'the artist's lifelong work on his own productive personality'.[48] The 'life' and the 'art' are therefore bound together in the creative process:

creativeness lies equally at the root of artistic production and of life experience. That is to say, lived experience can only be understood as the expression of volitional creative impulse, and in this the two spheres of artistic production and actual experience meet and overlap. Then, too, the creative impulse is manifested first and chiefly in the personality, which, being thus perpetually made over, produces art-work and experience in the same way.[49]

The neurotic is blocked in relation to this creative and self-creative process, either through fear, or through an excess of constraining will. The role of the analyst, then, is not to encourage a process of adaptation to 'normality', the 'average', but to enable the neurotic to accept his or her own individuality as the first stage of the creative process. As Nin puts it, 'the act of self-creation which the neurotic must make with the analyst is only possible *if he is convinced that the invention of his illness is a symptom of the power to create*, and not a symptom of impotence' (*Journals*, I, 309).

Rank elaborated on this idea in his 1935 lecture 'Neurosis as a Failure in Creativity'. Beginning with Freud's idea of the possible 'gain from illness', Rank describes neurosis as '*self-willed*, a sort of creation that can find expression only in this negative, destructive way'.[50] This view has vital implications for the understanding of neurosis and the neurotic

[46] Sigmund Freud, 'Delusions and Dreams in Jensen's *Gradiva*' (1907), PFL 14, 40.

[47] *Art and Artist*, 41.

[48] Ibid. 37. Cf. Nin's statement in her diary in 1931: 'The time for self-creation is never over' (March 7 1931 [*Early Diary*, IV, 399]).

[49] *Art and Artist*, 38.

[50] Otto Rank, 'Neurosis as a Failure in Creativity' (lecture given at the California Academy of Medicine, 9 Feb. 1935), in *A Psychology of Difference*, 252.

person, the thwarted creator: 'This evaluation of illness as an expression of the individual's *creative will* leads to a totally different conception of the neurotic, to a rehabilitation, I might say, of the neurotic'.[51] The therapeutic aim, then, is not normative, but is individually oriented and creative: 'My aim is rather to enable the individual first to find himself and then to develop himself . . . to create himself and then to go on and create externally'.[52]

Rank's emphasis on the continuous process of creation, the personality which is 'perpetually made over', leads to an emphasis, seized on by Nin, on movement and change. This is one of the strongest threads running through her accounts of Rank. Her first impression of him is one of fluidity: 'Immediately I felt air, space, movement . . . The swift-changing colors of his moods. The swiftness of his rhythm of thought, because it is intuitive and subtle' (14 January 1934 [*Incest*, 297]). This fluidity in Rank himself and his technique of analysis ('Impossible to analyze his way of analyzing, because of its spontaneity, its unexpectedness, its daring' [20 January 1934 (*Incest*, 299)]) is linked to his belief in the fundamentally fluid, changeable nature of the psyche and his encouragement, as Nin feels, of this fluidity: 'There is a pre-Rank vision, and there is an after-Rank swimming. Perhaps, at last, he has made me swim in life' (20 January 1934 [*Incest*, 299]; or, in the previously published version, 'Perhaps he has the secret of mobility and change' [*Journals*, I, 300]). This view is confirmed in a striking passage from Rank's 1929 Yale lecture:

> There is nothing fixed in the field of psychology, everything changes, everything is different at different moments. It is constantly moving . . . a patient may tell you something in one minute, which he says he is sincere in telling, while an hour later he may say to another person something quite different, the opposite of what he said before, and this is again true in this particular situation with regard to this person. It is true, he is not lying, he is not lying in a psychological sense, he is true here to himself and true there to himself.[53]

This passage has strong resonances with Nin's writing, recalling the multiple and contradictory stories ascribed to the elusive, changeable Sabina in the novels.[54] More generally, it hints at some of the difficulties,

[51] Rank, 'Neurosis as a Failure in Creativity', 252.

[52] Lecture given at Yale University, 28 Feb. 1929, in *A Psychology of Difference*, 244. Ironically, while Rank has (as I shall show) been linked with ego psychology, a version of psychoanalysis frequently accused of being 'normative', he accused Freudian psychoanalysis of being itself normative: 'Freud tries to reform the individual to the normal standard' (Yale lecture, 241).

[53] Ibid. 246.

discussed in Chapter 1, around linguistic self-representation and what James Olney calls 'the fragmentation of the *I*'.[55] In the diary, Nin raises the problem of speaking 'truthfully' or 'sincerely': 'How difficult it is to be "sincere" when each moment I must choose between five or six souls. Sincere according to which one, reconciled to which one?' (*Journals*, I, 126).[56]

We have seen that the task facing the neurotic, according to Rank, is one of self-creation or re-creation. But when the neurotic frees his or her power to create, it is not just the self that is re-made, but the world. Rather than simply adjusting to circumstances—adapting to 'reality'—the creative person '*adjusts the circumstances to himself*';[57] in other words, uses 'creative imagination . . . in order to change the world according to his own ideals'.[58] The creative will involves what Nin calls 'the capacity to alchemize and transform ordinary daily living, the human condition, into something else' (*A Woman Speaks*, 185). For Nin, this desire—even need—to 'create a world' is the fundamental motivation for artistic creation, for writing:

> I believe one writes because one has to create a world in which one can live. I could not live in any of the worlds offered to me . . . I had to create a world of my own, like a climate, a country, an atmosphere in which I could breathe, reign, and re-create myself when destroyed by living. That, I believe, is the reason for every work of art. The artist is the only one who knows the world is a subjective creation, that there is a choice to be made, a selection of elements. It is a materialization, an incarnation of his inner world. (*Journals*, V, 149[59])

Nin's claim here recalls Oscar Wilde's plea, in his 1889 essay 'The Decay

[54] See Chapter 3 for more detailed discussion of Sabina's contradictory and evasive speech, and her status as the *femme fatale* who represents an 'epistemic trauma', a block to knowledge.

[55] Olney, *Memory and Narrative*, 236.

[56] This questioning of the notion of 'sincerity' also throws into question the notion of 'authenticity' appealed to by some feminist critics in the context of women's writing (see Chapter 1), since 'authentic' seems in part to mean 'true to oneself (as a woman)'. Here Nin and Rank are saying that there can be no one 'truth' of the self, or rather there can be as many 'truths' as there are aspects of the self; and, since there exist within the subject *unconscious* desires and fantasies, the question of sincerity is not amenable to rational, conscious determination. (Although Nin's formulation here perhaps gives the impression of a conscious 'choice' between 'souls' or selves, she is always aware of the importance of unconscious determinants in the human psyche.)

[57] Yale lecture, 244.

[58] 'Neurosis as a Failure in Creativity', 258.

[59] This text also appears as part of 'The New Woman', a lecture given at the Celebration of Women in the Arts, San Francisco, April 1974; published in *Ramparts*, 1974; reprinted in *Sensitive Man*, 11.

of Lying', for a return to 'imaginative reality', in which 'the visible things of life are transmuted into artistic conventions'.[60] Rather than 'art' imitating 'life', it should be the other way around, with our creative fantasy determining our experience of reality: 'Art takes life as part of her rough material, recreates it, and refashions it in fresh forms, is absolutely indifferent to fact, invents, imagines, dreams'.[61] Life, in fact, *becomes* 'art', Nin's 'subjective creation'; in Wilde's memorable phrase, '[art] makes and unmakes many worlds'.[62]

Nin stresses 'the importance of the *wish*', the 'creative dream', in instigating this process of transforming reality (*A Woman Speaks*, 115). (Similarly, in 'Jensen's *Gradiva*', Freud notes the future orientation of dreams: 'the dream . . . revealed itself to [me] as a wish of the dreamer's represented as fulfilled; and who could deny that wishes are predominantly turned towards the future?'[63]) The wish, the 'image',[64] serves as the guide for the 'subjective creation' which is one's life. Thus Nin gives the example of her fascination with the idea of living on a boat: 'dreaming about the houseboat, then seeing it, then getting it, then living in it, and then writing about it' (*A Woman Speaks*, 119; see also *Novel*, 20–1). This is, indeed, a particularly good example, showing the spiralling pattern which, as I argued in Chapter 1, links 'life' and 'writing' for Nin. A visit to Brittany, where she saw a fishing boat washed up in a garden and dreamed of sleeping in it, inspired the early story 'Waste of Timelessness', in which the protagonist's mystical journey by boat represents her attempt to sail away from the banal, everyday world 'down some strange wise river into strange wise places' ('Waste of Timelessness' [1930], in *Waste of Timelessness*, 4). Nin's renting a houseboat moored on the Seine in 1936, for assignations with her lover Gonzalo More, can thus be seen as already informed by her associations of a boat with psychic as well as physical journeys, and in turn inspired the story 'Houseboat', in which Nin interiorizes the flows and different moods of the river, uniting them with the protagonist's dreams and desires: 'Once inside the houseboat, all

[60] Oscar Wilde, 'The Decay of Lying', in *Complete Works of Oscar Wilde* (Glasgow: HarperCollins, 1994), 1076, 1080. Wilde's use of the word 'transmute' connects to Nin's list of 'magic words' beginning with the prefix 'trans' and suggesting change or movement; see below.

[61] Ibid. 1078.

[62] Ibid. 1082.

[63] Freud, 'Jensen's *Gradiva*', 33.

[64] Her use of this term here (119) is important in its associations with dreams as presentations of images, and the possibility of 'a language of images' (120) derived from the unconscious. In Chapter 4, I discuss Nin's ideas (closely parallel to H.D.'s) about film as the best medium for presenting the imagistic sequences of dreams and the unconscious. In an analysis of the film of Venice made by Ian Hugo (the pseudonym of her husband Hugh Guiler), Nin states: 'We are living in the age of the image' (*Journals*, V, 136).

the voyages began' ('Houseboat', in *Under a Glass Bell*, 11). Finally, the journey by boat is one of the key structuring symbols of *Seduction of the Minotaur*, as Lillian, in the 'flowing' experience of Mexico, manages to exorcise her recurring dream of attempting to push a boat on dry land, a dream that plagued Nin herself: 'she was fully aware that the dream of pushing the boat through waterless streets was ended. In Golconda she had attained a flowing life, a flowing journey' (*Seduction*, 26).[65] Nin's example of the image of the boat thus illustrates well the interaction she is claiming between art and life through the 'creative dream', the fantasy that propels the subject towards 'making a world'.

The need to re-make the world according to one's own 'creative imagination', which, as we have seen, Rank stresses in his Yale lecture and in his paper on neurosis, is also an important theme in his book *Truth and Reality*—the book that Nin claimed had influenced her 'whole life as a woman artist'. Rank argues that the neurotic and the creative person cannot live with what is generally called 'truth' or 'reality', but must transform the world, creating their own 'truth': 'While the average well adjusted man can make the reality that is generally accepted as truth into his own truth, the creative searcher after truth seeks and finds his own truth which he then wants to make general—that is, real. He creates his reality, as it were, from his truth.'[66]

Esther Menaker, on the first page of her 1982 study of Rank, writes that 'his emphasis on individuation made him the forerunner of ego psychology'.[67] She understands Rank's emphasis on the mother–child relationship and on the 'development of individuation' as crucial to this history: 'he opened the way to an ego psychology, since many of the current problems of identity, with which we make frequent clinical contact with our patients . . . hark back to struggles and conflicts surrounding separation from the mother and the formation of an autonomous, delimited, and relatively independent ego'.[68] Yet we can see how far Rank is from the ego-psychological idea of adaptation to the norm: for Rank, the process of 'adaptation' moves in the opposite direction, as the subject 'adjusts the circumstances to himself'.

We can also clearly understand the enormous appeal of his writings for

[65] The original title for the main part of the book was 'Solar Barque', referring to the Egyptian myth of the barques that carried the dead on to the afterlife. Nin uses this myth in the book as an image of psychic journeys.

[66] Otto Rank, *Truth and Reality* (trans. Jessie Taft; New York: Norton, 1978 [1929]), 43.

[67] Esther Menaker, *Otto Rank: A Rediscovered Legacy* (New York: Columbia Univ. Press, 1982), p. ix.

[68] Ibid. 67.

Nin, who saw her whole life as an attempt to create a world she could live in, and stubbornly refused to 'adapt' to the 'normality' that she saw Allendy, for instance, attempting to impose on her. In the first volume of the *Journals*, she portrays Rank expatiating on this theme of adaptation: '"In Allendy's analysis he tried to adapt you to the social ideal. Not enough emphasis has been put on the differentiations, because the object of the 'cure' has been adaptation. The error here is that there is an individual solution for each case . . . it is the adaptation to the self that is important, not the adaptation to the average"' (*Journals*, I, 293).[69]

Nin emphasizes Rank's interest in the realm of fantasy and imagination as the key to each individual drama: 'Rank prizes the variations as precious indications of the character, color, nature of the neurotic's imagination, a key to be used later in helping him to construct his own world' (*Journals*, I, 307). While Allendy dismissed Nin's elaborate lies, fantasies, and roles as 'just games', Rank, she suggests, focused precisely on these 'games' as containing the key to her fantasy and therefore her reality: 'in the fantasy lay the secret desires and the seed of positive creation' (293). It is the 'revelation of the artist and the creative process', Nin claims, that runs through all of Rank's thought and enables him to 'travel so much further' than Allendy (292); a 'metaphysics of creativity' that both inspired her personal project of self-creation and, she later came to believe, could inspire other women to fulfil the potential that the feminist movement was beginning to awaken.

CREATIVE WILL: A 'WAY OUT' FOR WOMEN

In her 1972 lecture on *Truth and Reality*, Nin refers to the concept of creative will as Rank's 'great contribution to the psychology of woman'. She comes back to the idea of creative will in many of the lectures, seminars, and interviews that she gave in the early 1970s in the context of feminism and the women's liberation movement: it is a central theme of the texts collected by Hinz in *A Woman Speaks*, particularly in the chapters entitled 'A New Center of Gravity', 'Proceed from the Dream', and 'The

[69] As I have already noted, it is important to bear in mind that Nin's account of her analysis with Rank cannot be treated as a verbatim report; here she is obviously using the convention of direct speech to convey what she sees as the significant difference of Rank's thought, not only from that of Allendy at the time of the analysis, but probably also from what had become (by the 1960s when she was editing this text for publication) the dominant ideology of psychotherapy in the US.

Artist as Magician'. In this section, I want to examine how this emphasis on creative will impacts on the questions, with which I began the chapter, of psychic division and feminist investment in, or resistance to, 'identity'. I shall begin by looking at Rank's own model of the psyche, and shall then turn to consider Nin's appropriations of and departures from Rank's thought.

Esther Menaker describes Rank's concept of 'will' as 'an original, uniquely human "given" . . . which is representative of the life force';[70] it is a concept that is both absolutely central to Rank's work, developed out of his early interest in Schopenhauer and Nietzsche, and, in its existential force, difficult to define precisely. For Rank, Freudian psychoanalytic theory, in ignoring the human will (concentrating rather on the interplay of 'drive' and inhibition), misses the most crucial aspect of the human individual: 'In psychoanalytic theory the person . . . is missing in action: "The real I, or self with its own power, the will, is left out" '.[71] As this quotation suggests, Rank's notion of the will cannot easily be mapped onto Freudian conceptions of the structure of the psyche, whether the model of the conscious, preconscious and unconscious systems developed in *The Interpretation of Dreams* (1900), or the later model of ego, super-ego, and id as elaborated in *The Ego and the Id* (1923).

Rank does sometimes present the will as the *controlling* force of the psyche: 'an autonomous organization to control primarily the impulsive self'; 'the supreme autonomic organizing force in the individual'; the 'supreme creative and controlling power of the personality'.[72] This might seem to make will equivalent to the 'strong, masterful, autonomous ego' (as Elizabeth Grosz describes it) that is the ideal of ego psychology. However, Rank's notion of will is both richer and more complex than this formulation would suggest. It is not straightforwardly a unifying force; as the creative drive, it also *produces conflict* within the individual. Esther Menaker notes this point: 'It is the creative urge, expressed through the individual will, that at one and the same time produces the conflict and attempts its resolution through all the manifestations of creativity'.[73]

The principle of creative will is, in fact, fundamentally bound up with

[70] *Otto Rank: A Rediscovered Legacy*, 39.

[71] Kramer, citing Rank's *Will Therapy*; 'Psychoanalysis as General Psychology', in *A Psychology of Difference*, 62 n. 2.

[72] 'Neurosis as a Failure in Creativity', 253; 'Modern Psychology and Social Change' (1938), in *A Psychology of Difference*, 268.

[73] *Otto Rank: A Rediscovered Legacy*, 34.

Rank's view of the human subject as essentially in conflict with itself, conflict that can be ameliorated but never completely resolved, since it is inherent in the human condition. I have noted that Rank traces all anxiety back to anxiety at the primal separation from the mother. This separation represents both an end of life—the end of the prenatal unity with the mother—and a beginning of life as an independent individual. As such it is the prototype for all subsequent life events that involve change, a movement away from something and simultaneously a movement towards something, and that therefore inspire in the subject both fear (the fear of the unknown, of loss, of separation) and desire (the desire for new experience, for difference and individuality). Although, as we have seen, Menaker sees the concerns of ego psychology foreshadowed in Rank's account of separation and, as she puts it, 'the formation of an autonomous, delimited, and relatively independent ego', Rank's own account in 'The Genesis of the Object Relation' paints a rather different (and far more Kleinian) picture: 'Every object relation . . . holds destructive elements within it, since the deposit of overcome and renounced ego phases always involves a breaking up and reorganizing of the ego structure, which we know and fear as the destructive side of love'.[74] For Rank—as for Klein, as for Lacan—the ego never can be 'autonomous', but is constantly subject to the forces of projection and identification, remoulding itself in others' image. As Kramer notes, the fundamental conflict that Rank perceives in psychic life—the opposed desires for individuality and belonging, sameness and difference—is also constantly played out 'in the relationship between "ego" and "object", I and Thou'.[75]

For Rank, this fundamental duality is what characterizes human existence. In *Will Therapy*, he expresses this in terms of 'primary fear', with its double aspect:

> primary fear corresponds to a fear of separation from the whole, therefore a fear of individuation, on account of which I should like to call it fear of life, although it may appear later as fear of the loss of this dearly bought individuality, as fear of death, of being dissolved again into the whole. Between these two fear possibilities, these poles of fear, the individual is thrown back and forth all his life.[76]

The existential conflict can also be expressed positively: in Menaker's

[74] Rank, 'Genesis of the Object Relation', in *A Psychology of Difference*, 148–9.

[75] Kramer's note to 'Genesis of the Object Relation', in ibid. 149.

[76] Otto Rank, *Will Therapy & Truth and Reality* (New York: Knopf, 1947), 124. Cited by Menaker, *Otto Rank: A Rediscovered Legacy*, 80.

words, the 'primary dilemma' is a conflict between 'the impulse toward emergence, i.e. individuation, and the pull towards embeddedness'.[77] The fear of death, of being 'dissolved into the whole', is also the desire for immortality, which, Rank argues in *Art and Artist*, is the driving force behind artistic creation: 'the creative impulse . . . attempts to turn ephemeral life into personal immortality. In creation the artist tries to immortalize his mortal life.'[78] And yet this striving for immortality is, inevitably, accompanied by guilt; creation and guilt, Rank argues in chapter 6 of *Truth and Reality*, 'belong together . . . indissolubly'.[79]

We can now begin to understand the paradoxical nature of the creative will. As the dynamic existential principle within the individual, the will is essentially an *assertion of difference*. As such, it inevitably throws the subject into conflict—not only with others, with the surrounding society, but also with itself, since the human subject also seeks embeddedness, belonging, unity. And yet the creative will is also the means by which the subject seeks to resolve these conflicts, to ameliorate guilt, to achieve a productive self-realization. The creative person, Rank argues, is his or her own therapist: 'The only therapeutic possibility with our modern individual neurotic type is to permit him to develop and accept his own individuality, in other words, to allow the individual to mold himself into that which he is, that is, to affirm his own will and therewith his own individuality.'[80] In the affirmation of his or her 'own will', the individual uses guilt creatively (Rank in fact uses the paradoxical expression 'creative guilt'[81]), rather than experiencing it as neurotically inhibiting: the guilt is 'atoned for through new creation',[82] though of course this can never be a final resolution, but only part of a continuous process.

Taking his cue from Rank's own description of his work in *Beyond Psychology*,[83] Robert Kramer entitles his edited collection of Rank's lectures *A Psychology of Difference*. For Kramer, Rank's psychology, centred as it is on what Rank calls 'the will-guilt problem',[84] is concerned with the pain and the possibilities of human individuality or difference: 'For Rank, will means nothing other than "difference", and "difference" always brings guilt in its wake'.[85] This 'difference', I would argue, is not only difference from others, but also difference from 'oneself'. Since the

[77] Ibid. 5. [78] *Art and Artist*, 39. [79] *Truth and Reality*, 67. [80] Ibid. 82.
[81] Ibid. 67, 83. [82] Ibid. 83. [83] See *Beyond Psychology*, 29.
[84] See for instance *Truth and Reality*, 74.
[85] Kramer, in the notes to 'Emotional Suffering and Therapy' (1927), *A Psychology of Difference*, 176 n. 3. In this lecture Rank argues that 'we cannot entirely remove the cause of emotional suffering . . . because suffering is in the nature of human emotional life' (168).

human subject, for Rank, is always caught up in conflicting fears and desires, both striving towards 'difference' and afraid of it, the creative will is also a principle of conflict within the individual. Further, it cannot simply be identified with *conscious* desires or motivations. Just as Freud saw the unconscious motive for illness lying behind the patient's conscious desire to get well, so Rank sees the neurotic's symptoms as thwarted expressions of his or her 'difference', which, however, the patient does not consciously wish to recognize and affirm. Kramer, in his interpretation of Rank, puts considerable emphasis on Rank's respect for unconscious factors in human psychical life, perhaps reacting against interpretations such as Menaker's which, in claiming Rank as a 'forerunner' of ego psychology, stress rather his concern with *conscious* factors.[86] In discussing Rank's criticism of the psychoanalytic 'glorification of consciousness', Kramer suggests that Rank is philosophically closer to Lacan on this issue: 'This repression of the "existential" unconscious, forgetting the mystery of *Dasein*, which remains forever unknown and unknowable, is precisely the criticism later leveled by Lacan against the American form of ego psychology'.[87] These competing interpretations of and claims for Rank can be seen as metonymic of the whole structure of claim and counter-claim that is the history of 'psychoanalysis'; they also suggest the difficulty, or impossibility, of placing his thought in a neatly defined box. Rank's last work was entitled *Beyond Psychology*, and Menaker, despite her claiming of Rank as forerunner of ego psychology, acknowledges that, in his broad focus on human being, Rank must finally be understood as a philosopher (she refers to him as an existentialist[88]) rather than narrowly defined in the terms of psychoanalytic factions.

Returning to Nin, the key associations with the creative will in her 1970s texts are the ideas of change and movement (just as she writes, in the edited diary account, 'Perhaps [Rank] has the secret of mobility and change' [*Journals*, I, 300]). So in 'The Artist as Magician' she identifies what she calls 'a whole set of magic words . . . in the dictionary under the prefix *trans* which means change or movement—transforming, transposing, transcending, translucent, transfiguring, transmitting'. This

[86] Menaker, for instance, tends to oppose Rank to Freud's 'determinism': 'It is not hard to realize that while the discovery of unconscious motivation and its effect on conscious functioning was of the utmost importance and had definite validity . . . it altogether obscured the fact that human beings can also be motivated by self-determined conscious impulses of the will' (*Otto Rank: A Rediscovered Legacy*, 42). She does, however, go on to say that Rank 'never denied the existence of unconscious factors'.

[87] In the notes to 'Psychoanalysis as General Psychology', 65 n. 6.

[88] Menaker, *Otto Rank: A Rediscovered Legacy*, 120, 122.

'magic' of change and movement is then linked to creativity: 'creativity is so necessary to our human life because it shows us the capacity for change'.[89]

The creative will, then, is 'a possibility, a potential to change ourselves' (*A Woman Speaks*, 2). But, as I have already shown, this change extends beyond the self to the world: the creative will engenders 'the transformation of life, the transcending, the metamorphosis of everything' (*A Woman Speaks*, 128). Despite the emphasis on the self, Nin is at some pains to argue that this world of 'imaginative reality' can become an *intersubjective* world, rather than remaining a solipsistic one: 'I was creating the world I wanted, and into this world, once it is created, you invite others and then you attract those who have affinities and this becomes a universe, this becomes not a private world at all but something which transcends the personal and creates the link'.[90] The implicit context here is the accusation, frequently made against Nin by more directly political second-wave feminists, of an over-emphasis on the personal and the individual at the cost of the collective and the political. For example, feminist literary critic and activist Estelle Jelinek, in a strongly negative assessment of Nin written in 1974 and published in 1978, writes that Nin 'lives for individual solutions [and therefore] is not going to believe in any form of collective action'.[91]

Nin is also at pains to make the point that her understanding of 'creativity' is a very broad one, encompassing more than strictly 'artistic' creation: 'By creating I don't mean only or specifically painting or com-

[89] *A Woman Speaks*, 172–3. The text here is taken from a lecture or seminar called 'Magic Women', given at Sonoma College, California, in April 1973. Cf. also the use of the word 'tropic' in *Seduction of the Minotaur*: 'According to the definition, tropic meant a turning and changing, and with the tropics Lillian turned and changed, and she swung between the drug of forgetfulness and the drug of awareness, as the natives swung in their hammocks, as the jazz players swung into their rhythms, as the sea swung in its bed turned changed' (110).

[90] *A Woman Speaks*, 182. Here again we find, perhaps, an echo of Nin's early interest in Emerson. Jeffrey Steele argues that for Emerson, restoring 'wholeness' to the individual self will result in 'wholeness' on a wider scale: 'the salvation of self is seen also as the salvation of society' ('Interpreting the Self: Emerson and the Unconscious', in Joel Porte [ed.], *Emerson: Prospect and Retrospect* [Harvard English Studies, 10; Cambridge, Mass.: Harvard Univ. Press, 1982], 99).

[91] Estelle C. Jelinek, 'Anaïs Nin: A Critical Evaluation', in Cheryl L. Brown and Karen Olson (eds.), *Feminist Criticism* (Metuchen, NJ: Scarecrow Press, 1978), 316. The issue of whether Nin's emphasis on personal creativity and psychological 'liberation' amounted to a rejection of collective political action recurs frequently in interviews she gave around this time. See, e.g., Nancy Williamson, Evelyn Clark, and Barbara Reyes, 'A Conversation with Anaïs Nin' (1971 interview), reprinted in DuBow (ed.), *Conversations*, 75. Here Nin insists: 'I am not speaking against political action: I am speaking of a better preparation for it'.

posing music or writing books. I mean creating everything . . . For me creativity is an all-encompassing word' (*A Woman Speaks*, 35). Here, again, Nin is countering the objection that a concern with 'creativity' is both apolitical and exclusivist; as Jelinek puts it, 'Nin is appealing to middle-class women who have the leisure to lavish attention upon their creative talents'.[92] In answer to a question 'what of the woman who can't create?', Nin states, 'There is always creation to be done' (*A Woman Speaks*, 54–5). Rather than speaking specifically of artistic creation, Nin's polemical aim is to bring to her female readers and audiences what she saw as Rank's inspiring emphasis on the inherent human drive towards and capacity for effecting change, what Kramer calls 'the "drive" for newness and difference'.[93] If we understand the concept of creative will in this way, its relevance to the specific context of the women's liberation movement becomes much clearer, particularly if we keep in mind Nin's emphasis on women's *psychological* 'liberation' as a vital part of the feminist programme for change in women's lives. Women have been constrained, both by external circumstances (the misogynist system of patriarchy) and by their own lack of confidence and positive self-images—or, rather, the oppressive ideology of patriarchy works, like any ideology, both 'externally' and 'internally' in a feedback loop that is difficult to break. But, Nin wants to say, the creative will can play a key role here. If women have been hedged around by restrictions and hampered by their own internalization of a limiting ideology of gender, held within a pattern 'very rigid and very limited' (*A Woman Speaks*, 33), nonetheless there is the possibility of liberation, of movement and change, and that possibility lies in the Rankian concept of creativity: 'there is always a way out, there is always a way out through the creative will' (*A Woman Speaks*, 212).

We can see, in the accusations of apoliticism and exclusivism levelled at Nin and her repeated attempts to defend herself against these charges, a specific instance of what has been, since the upsurge of the women's liberation movement, a central and intractable issue: the attempt to decide, as Rachel Bowlby puts it, 'what is to be considered truly political for feminism'.[94] Bowlby goes on to say that one of the 'baselines' of this ongoing argument is 'the implied legitimation in terms of the gesture of "more political than thou"',[95] and we can clearly see this gesture at work in Estelle Jelinek's criticisms of Nin, cited above. Jelinek's overall claim in her article (one that was levelled against Nin many times) is that, despite

[92] Jelinek, 'Anaïs Nin', 318.
[93] Kramer, *A Psychology of Difference*, 63 n. 2.
[94] Bowlby, 'Still Crazy', 134.
[95] Ibid.

Nin's status and popularity in the women's liberation movement, she is *not* a feminist because her concerns are not collective and not political.[96]

Nin's 'apoliticism' is seen to be bound up with her focus on creativity, subjectivity, and psychoanalysis: for Jelinek, '[t]he fact that Nin . . . can still extol psychoanalysis shows how dated and unfeminist she really is'.[97] Bowlby sums up the argument between 'pro-psychoanalytic' and 'anti-psychoanalytic' feminist factions as follows:

> Psychoanalytic feminism takes non-psychoanalytic feminism to be too simple in its notion of subjectivity for it to be capable of achieving the very political goals it sets itself; while anti-psychoanalytic feminism sees in the psychoanalytic stress on subjectivity a needless detour from feminism's real concerns, if not a pernicious undermining of the tough, coherent agents needed to carry through political action with a subjectivity united at both the individual and the collective level.[98]

Nin, in the 1970s, was awkwardly—perhaps, among feminist writers, uniquely—situated in relation to this debate. American feminists' hostility to psychoanalysis was at least partly a consequence of the particular history of the psychoanalytic movement in the US, where it had become (against Freud's original wishes) strongly medicalized, linked to the psychiatric establishment, and thus both masculinist and socially conservative. In France, on the other hand, psychoanalysis had been understood—by the Surrealists, and through them by Lacan and his followers, including feminists—as a *radical* discourse occupying 'a position of contestation in relation to bourgeois culture and norms'.[99] If, as we have seen, the first generation of analysts in France found it difficult to perceive the common ground between themselves and the Surrealists, the Surrealists themselves had no difficulty in making the link; Surrealism, as Roudinesco puts it, 'accompanied the adventure of the Freudian unconscious', and laid the groundwork for Lacan's interpretation of Freud: 'the Surrealist experiment brought to light, for the first time in France, an

[96] Jelinek writes: 'From reading [Nin's] diaries and novels and now having heard her in person, I can see, despite what I have been told, that she holds views that are anathema to me and the women's liberation movement' ('Anaïs Nin', 314). The 'cult' surrounding Nin, Jelinek argues, is 'a regressive aspect of the women's liberation movement'; and Nin's own involvement in the movement is 'insincere because she is not a feminist. She holds views that are contrary to those held by true feminists' (322). The terminology here, with its almost religious overtones, positions Nin as the leader of a 'cult', a kind of false prophet preaching a debased form of the 'true faith'. For a contemporary discussion of feminist hostility to Nin because of her perceived antipathy to collective action, see Williamson, Clark, and Reyes, 'A Conversation with Anaïs Nin'.

[97] 'Anaïs Nin', 319.

[98] 'Still Crazy', 134.

[99] Rose, 'Feminism and the Psychic', 17.

encounter between the Freudian unconscious, language, and the decentering of the subject'.[100]

The Surrealists' aim was to detach psychoanalysis from medicine, linking it rather with the avant-garde project of exploring the unconscious in order to subvert both the bourgeois social order and the supposedly rational subject at the heart of that order. For Nin, whose formative years as a writer had been spent in 1930s Paris, who had read Jung's article on 'psychology and poetry' in *transition* in 1930, 'psychoanalysis' was indissolubly linked with Surrealism and the avant-garde project—a project, as Roudinesco puts it, whose aim was 'to open the individual to a Rimbaldian "elsewhere"'.[101] In *The Novel of the Future*, Nin constantly links the project of psychoanalysis with the project of 'the poets', explicitly connecting Freud and Breton in 'the quest for other dimensions' (*Novel*, 15, 51). Surrealism and psychoanalysis are invoked together as crucial historical influences, the twin inspirations for her artistic project. For Nin, psychoanalysis was an oppositional discourse, what Rose calls '[a] form of radical enquiry'.[102] For second-wave American feminists, on the other hand, psychoanalysis was located firmly within an oppressively normative, reactionary medical establishment. Nin thus found herself struggling with a cultural clash, attempting to invoke psychoanalysis positively in a feminist context which, as Bowlby states, tended to view psychoanalytic ideas either as self-indulgent and irrelevant or, worse, as 'pernicious' and anti-political.

The crucial issue, then, is that of subjectivity: the dilemma for feminism is how to acknowledge and work with the problems of subjectivity and identity raised by psychoanalysis, while also demanding for women both an escape from the limiting psychic structures imposed by patriarchy and, more positively, a coherent and satisfying personal and political agency. In her texts of the 1970s, Nin attempts to deal with these issues through invoking the creative will.

As we have seen, the refusal of any adaptive or normative model of the subject is crucial to Nin's affinity with Rank's thought: the creative self makes its own patterns rather than conforming to accepted norms. The emphasis is always on fluidity and change rather than any fixedness, which was anathema to Nin, associated (as I show in Chapter 3) with confinement and constraint: the fear of 'definition' and thus constraint is the force driving what I earlier called Nin's erotics of multiplicity, her fantasy

[100] Roudinesco, *Jacques Lacan & Co.*, 26.

[101] Ibid. 25.

[102] Rose, 'Femininity and its Discontents', 87.

of the ever-elusive, boundless self. However, for Rank the creative will is also a principle of *conflict.* The human subject remains caught between incompatible—sometimes unconscious—desires, pulled in opposite directions, never able to resolve its conflicts finally or completely. Nin explicitly acknowledges the conflict Rank identifies between the desire for individuation and the desire for belonging, the opposed wishes 'to stay close to others' and 'to create something which may alienate us from our culture'. And, in a particularly interesting passage, she talks about 'the will to create, or creative will, which *pursues the artist and haunts the artist*' (*A Woman Speaks*, 2, my emphasis). Here the terminology of pursuing and haunting clearly suggests a conflict, a psychic division; and recalls, perhaps, Nin's early characterizing of her 'demon', Imagy: 'Imagy lives mostly in images and unrealities. I want to follow her doings because they are the ones which *haunt my writing*' (*Early Diary*, IV, 56). It is the very drive to create that 'haunts' the artist, pursuing him or her like a shadow—at once both disruptive and threatening, and a vital part of the person, what Nin elsewhere calls 'the necessity to be the artist' ('The New Woman', in *Sensitive Man*, 14). More broadly, it is the drive for difference that haunts everyone, producing an insoluble conflict with the equally universal desire for 'sameness' and belonging.

On the whole, however, Nin plays down this conflictual aspect, emphasizing instead the importance of the creative will in the positive movement towards psychic harmony and 'synthesis'. Even when she invokes the unconscious (in the form of the dream-image or 'wish') as instigator of the creative process in art and life, she does not focus on this as raising the possibility of internal psychic conflict, but rather emphasizes the unconscious as a source or locus of 'richness',[103] and stresses the creative will as a means towards psychic stability and wholeness: 'a center of gravity in your own soul, an axis in an unstable world, a core' (*A Woman Speaks*, 2). This emphasis on the positive, harmonizing role of creativity is clearly related to the feminist context and aim of these 1970s texts (lectures, seminars, articles, and interviews). The original titles of some of the seminars (listed by Hinz) give a good idea of their focus: 'Womanspace'; 'The Emerging Woman'; 'Adventurous Women'; 'Magic Women' (all 1973). Implicit here is the importance for feminism of a positive identity for women; that is, a positive identity that is both a *personal* identity and a *gender* identity—a sense of oneself as a woman. What Nin

[103] *A Woman Speaks*, 130. See also Chapter 4 for a discussion of the selective nature of modernist appropriations of the psychoanalytic idea of 'the unconscious'.

is envisaging as the ideal is an identity that is fluid enough to encompass change and difference, but does not disperse completely or fragment into conflict. We find an image of this ideal self in a diary passage from 1953 describing Nin's friend, the Viennese artist Renate Druks: 'Renate can penetrate any experience or role without dissolution of her self. They are extensions, dilations, expansions, not dissolutions. She can play various roles with none disconnected from each other. She is as fluid as mercury, which can move in all directions and yet not be divided' (*Journals*, V, 131).[104]

The image of mercury is an attempt to contain the principle of internal difference, the 'hauntedness' I identified above, within a self that, while avoiding fixity and constraining boundaries, does not split or fragment. Both of these aspects are, in Nin's view, vital for the feminist project, because women have suffered both from a sense of self (and of 'woman') that is too narrow and too rigid, *and* from a painful psychic fragmentation (the former, we might think, the result of a relatively 'successful' internalization of a patriarchal norm; the latter perhaps a symptom of difficulty with or refusal of such an internalization).

We might see Nin here as invoking what Jacqueline Rose calls a 'utopianism of the psyche': the dimension of psychic *difficulty* is underplayed as a result of the perceived feminist need for a strong, positive sense of personal and gender identity. But Rose herself acknowledges the force of this demand; she even acknowledges it as a *necessity*: 'the concept of the unconscious [does not] sit comfortably with the necessary attempt by feminism to claim a new sureness of identity for women'.[105] Again, discussing the harnessing of Lacanian accounts of the divided subject to the Marxist attack on 'bourgeois individualism', Rose writes: 'Feminists could legitimately object that the notion of psychic fragmentation was of little immediate political advantage to women struggling for the first time to find a voice, and trying to bring together the dissociated components of their life into a political programme.'[106] There is, of course, a particular historical moment under discussion here. Rose is referring specifically to the 'struggles' of second-wave feminists in the late 1960s and 1970s—the same women Nin is addressing. She is acknowledging the necessity,

[104] This description also raises the question, so central to Nin's work, of 'playing roles'; here, the different aspects of Renate's self are both 'authentically' part of her, and at the same time 'roles', with all that term's connotations of acting and dissimulation. I shall look at questions of acting and identity in Chapter 3, and at concepts of 'masquerade' and identity as performative in Chapter 5.

[105] Rose, 'Femininity and its Discontents', 103.

[106] Ibid. 94.

at this stage of the feminist movement, for an emphasis on coherence and 'sureness of identity', a place from which to speak. But it is not clear what happens, or what 'should' happen (on Rose's view), to this emphasis as the historical narrative of feminism moves on. Rose writes, using the present tense this time: 'it remains the case that—without reifying the idea of a pure fragmentation which would be as futile as it would be psychically unmanageable for the subject—only the concept of a subjectivity at odds with itself gives back to women the right to an impasse at the point of sexual identity, with no nostalgia whatsoever for its possible or future integration into a norm.'[107]

The notion invoked here of a 'right to an impasse' is a difficult one. An impasse—literally, a place with no way out—seems a strange thing to claim a 'right' to, and a problematic alternative to the autocratic system of normative gender identity that feminism seeks to dismantle; it also forms a striking contrast to Nin's emphasis on a 'way out' for women. But the phrase itself also seems to bring together incompatible registers or discourses: while the notion of 'rights' belongs to the discourse of political or juridical theory, and implies a strong concept of the subject or agent, the 'impasse at the point of sexual identity' pulls against this discourse, invoking the *problems* of subjectivity. Rose's phrase, with its internal tensions, thus seems to re-stage the whole dilemma, the problem for feminism of how to articulate psychoanalysis and politics.

We can certainly see both Nin and Rose as attempting to address this issue, and, more particularly, as attempting to introduce a concern with subjectivity into a more conventionally political setting. I have already described Nin's awkward positioning in relation to the feminist context she was addressing in the early 1970s. Somewhat similarly, Rose's position a decade later was also one of straddling different contexts. A British academic working out of a predominantly French tradition of psychoanalytic thought, she makes clear in both 'Feminism and the Psychic' and 'Femininity and its Discontents' that she is putting an argument to the American feminist tradition *and* to the British Marxist and socialist-feminist traditions—different contexts, but equally opposed to psychoanalysis.[108] In a sense, then, we can see both Nin and Rose as occupying positions of some tension in relation to these debates; and this provides an interesting meta-level reflection on both the tensions within their

[107] Rose, 'Feminism and the Psychic', 15.

[108] See 'Femininity and its Discontents', 83 n. 1, where Rose explains the genesis of the article and sets out the context of the British Left's 'repudiation' of Freud and the rejection of psychoanalytic thought by socialist feminists.

work and the tensions of subjectivity that they are concerned with. For Rose, writing in the early and mid-1980s, the value of psychoanalysis for feminism is precisely that 'it allows into the political arena problems of subjectivity (subjectivity *as* a problem) which tend to be suppressed from other forms of political debate'.[109] There remains, however, the uneasy fit between this claim and Rose's acknowledgment of the strategic necessity, for feminism, of women's claim to a 'new sureness of identity'. For Nin, writing and speaking in the early 1970s, notions of psychic fixity and normative gender identities must be replaced by a model of the self as fluid enough to encompass difference and change, but cohesive enough to represent a 'center of gravity', a basis for liberation. In these texts Nin generally played down the conflictual aspects of subjectivity, finding it difficult to incorporate such ideas into the context of women's liberation. However, an emphasis on the conflicts of the psyche, and in particular of sexuality, emerges strikingly in Nin's erotica, producing a picture of the 'divided, disordered' subject with a close affinity to that found in Lacanian feminist thought.

SEXUALITY: 'FANTASIES, IMPASSES, CONFLICT AND DESIRE'

'The reality of the unconscious', states Lacan, 'is sexual reality—an untenable truth.'[110] For Lacanian critics, sexuality is the most crucial arena of conflict and division within the subject; sexuality, as above all what must be repressed in the process of 'civilization', is the strongest element in that 'insistent pressure' which, as Elizabeth Grosz puts it, 'subverts, renders ambiguous, and resists the ego's conscious ideals'.[111] Rather than reading Freud's accounts of human sexuality (as anti-psychoanalytic feminists such as Kate Millett and Shulamith Firestone had done) as prescriptive, teleological accounts of the development of normal (normative) sexuality, Lacanian feminist critics, following Lacan's own interpretation, focus on Freud's emphasis on the *difficulties* of this path to 'normality' (especially in the case of feminine sexuality), on his descriptions of sexuality as the 'most unruly of all the instincts', the 'weak spot' of 'human cultural development'.[112] On this account, sexuality is above all an anti-social force; there is, Freud claims, an 'inverse rela-

[109] 'Femininity and its Discontents', 103.

[110] Lacan, *Four Fundamental Concepts*, 150.

[111] Grosz, *Jacques Lacan*, 59, 27.

[112] Sigmund Freud, *Three Essays on the Theory of Sexuality* (1905), PFL 7, 75, 61.

tion holding between civilization and the free development of sexuality'.[113] And, insofar as the individual comes to identify consciously with the mores of 'civilization', sexuality, constrained within the limits of the 'so-called normal'[114] by repression, is also a force pushing against the coherence of the conscious ego or super-ego: the site, as Rose puts it, of 'fantasies, impasses, conflict and desire'.[115]

It is precisely in her concern with sexuality that Nin both diverges the furthest from her mentor Rank and comes closest to the preoccupations of psychoanalytic feminist thought. Whereas Rank consistently played down the role of sexuality in the human psyche, simplistically seeing Freud's emphasis on sexuality as a form of biological determinism that denied agency, Nin was interested in the ramifications for the human subject of sexuality and sexual desire; in particular, given her overall preoccupation with questions of female identity, she was interested in the tensions of *feminine* sexuality. Her affinity with Lacanian feminist thought lies in the fact that she depicts sexuality as a crucial but highly problematic site of subjectivity, one that undercuts rationality and operates in a realm of fantasy, role-play, and illusion. If women (and men) face an 'impasse' in the sphere of identity, it is sexuality that, more than any other force in the psyche, produces that impasse.

Nin's novel *A Spy in the House of Love* (1954) is probably her best-known and most sustained exploration of the tensions of feminine sexuality, the story of Sabina, actress in life who fakes a career as a professional stage actress in order to pursue her multiple desires. Sabina is depicted as torn by her desire for wholeness and her desire for the endless multiplications of desire itself: 'Sabina . . . felt germinating in her the power to extend time in the ramifications of a myriad lives and loves, to expand the journey to infinity, taking immense and luxurious detours as the courtesan depositor of multiple desires' (39). The wholeness she wishes for can only be another role, staged for the benefit of her husband: '*play the role of a whole woman, at least you have always wished to be that, it is not altogether a lie*' (21). Eventually, Sabina experiences a dissolution and loss of identity which is frightening rather than pleasurably liberating (recalling Nin's image of the marionette torn apart):

The entire sky a warm blanket of eyes and mouths shining down on her, the air full of voices now raucous from the sensual spasm, now gentle with gratitude, now doubtful, and she was afraid because there was no Sabina, not ONE, but a

[113] Freud, *Three Essays*, 168. [114] Ibid. 80.
[115] 'Feminism and the Psychic', 15.

multitude of Sabinas lying down and yielding and being dismembered, constellating in all directions and breaking . . . she was weeping, 'Someone hold me—hold me, so I will not continue to race from one love to another, dispersing me, disrupting me . . . *Hold me to one . . .*' (96)

There is no resolution, within the novel, to this conflict; indeed, Nin returns to the figure of Sabina in later works (notably *Seduction of the Minotaur* [1961] and a short story, 'Sabina', in the *Chicago Review* [1962]), demonstrating her own fascination with, and perhaps inability to resolve, the conflicts represented by Sabina.

It is, however, Nin's two volumes of erotica, *Delta of Venus* and *Little Birds* (written during the 1940s and published posthumously in 1977 and 1979), that have received the most attention from psychoanalytic feminist theorists, with articles by Judith Roof in 1991 and Karen Brennan in 1992, and a projected study by Diane Richard-Allerdyce.[116] As this critical interest suggests, there is indeed an affinity between the Lacanian feminist framework and Nin's depictions, in these stories, of the vicissitudes of sexuality. In fact, we can see a particularly interesting tension at work between the understanding of sexuality and subjectivity within these texts and Nin's own framing of them in the context of second-wave feminism. In the 'Postscript' to *Delta of Venus*, written in 1976, Nin explains her ideological problems with the erotica and her eventual decision to release them for publication:

I believed that my style [in the erotica] was derived from a reading of men's works. For this reason I long felt that I had compromised my feminine self. I put the erotica aside. Rereading it these many years later, I see that my own voice was not completely suppressed. In numerous passages I was intuitively using a woman's language, seeing sexual experience from a woman's point of view. I finally decided to release the erotica for publication because it shows the beginning efforts of a woman in a world that had been the domain of men. (14)

Nin's claims here can clearly be situated in the context of the feminist interest, burgeoning in the 1970s when Nin is writing, in questions of women's authorship and feminine language (issues that I shall focus on in Chapter 4). But there is another aspect to her ideological confusions over the erotica. In the 'Postscript', Nin writes:

[116] Judith Roof, 'The Erotic Travelogue: The Scopophilic Pleasure of Race vs. Gender', *Arizona Quarterly* 47/4 (Winter 1991), 119–35; Karen Brennan, 'Anaïs Nin: Author(iz)ing the Erotic Body', *Genders* 14 (Autumn 1992), 66–86. Richard-Allerdyce notes in the introduction to her 1998 monograph on Nin that she does not discuss the erotica because she plans 'a separate study' devoted to them (*Remaking of Self*, 170 n. 20).

Women, I thought, were more apt to fuse sex with emotion, with love, and to single out one man rather than be promiscuous . . . But although women's attitude towards sex was quite distinct from that of men, we had not yet learned how to write about it . . . If the unexpurgated version of the *Diary* is ever published, this feminine point of view will be established more clearly. It will show that women (and I, in the *Diary*) have never separated sex from feeling, from love of the whole man. (14)

This claim is picked up in the back-cover blurb of the 1990 Penguin edition of *Delta of Venus*, which states that '[Nin's] vibrant and impassioned prose magically evokes the essence of female sexuality in a world where only love has meaning'.

Nin thus frames her erotica with a claim for the wholeness, and wholesomeness, of feminine as opposed to masculine sexuality: rather than being promiscuous and objectifying, women's desire is bound up with 'love' and a regard for the 'whole man'. This claim can clearly be seen as motivated or informed by what we can call the cultural feminist agenda (a strong current of US second-wave feminism through the late 1970s and early 1980s), with its valorizing of femininity and feminine sexuality as positive, even redemptive forces.[117] But the framing is strikingly at odds with the depictions of sexual desire within the stories themselves. It is precisely Nin's depictions of (feminine) sexuality as an 'equivocal, vacillating' force that 'wreak[s] havoc on consciousness',[118] operating in the realms of fantasy and cinematic or theatrical stagings, that make her erotica interesting to psychoanalytic feminist critics. Contrary to the romantic claim of the cover blurb, the stories themselves suggest that, in the face of sexual desire, the conscious realm of 'love' has very little meaning or power. There is no 'whole man', and there certainly is no 'whole woman'; Nin's stories depict, rather, the constant slippage of identity and identifications, even across gender boundaries, and the psychic divisions caused by fantasy and desire. The interesting tension here between the stories and their framing suggests again, I would argue, the tensions of Nin's positioning in relation to the feminist context of the 1970s.

'Elena', the longest story in *Delta of Venus*, and one that is discussed by Brennan, raises the same conflict that Sabina struggles with in *A Spy in*

[117] Mari Jo Buhle describes cultural feminism as developing 'a theory of [female] empowerment configured around mothering', emphasizing 'women's special relational capacities and sensibilities'. Cultural feminists sought to affirm women's difference from men and to celebrate a 'sublime' femininity. See *Feminism and its Discontents*, 254, 260, 261–2.

[118] Brennan, 'Anaïs Nin', 77, 75, partly quoting Mary Jacobus.

the House of Love. Elena wants 'eroticism mixed with love' (122); she wants 'to be whole' (130). But her lover Pierre is 'fully aware of her . . . attraction to the demonic and the sordid, to the pleasure of falling, of desecrating and destroying the ideal self' (122). Elena, embarked on a series of sexual encounters with men and women, cannot maintain the 'wholeness' of love she consciously wants: 'She thought of Pierre's flesh, his flavor, the love they had, and at the same time she heard Jean's adolescent laughter, trusting, sensitive, and she saw the potent charm of Leila. She was afraid. She was afraid because she was no longer securely tied to Pierre but to an unknown woman lying down, yielding, open, spreading' (132). The 'ideal self' is destroyed: 'she had little interest in the rooting of love, in its fixity. She wanted only the moment of passion from everyone' (143). Elena fantasizes herself in the place of Bijou, the 'whore of whores', wanting sex without romanticism, 'bestial and direct'; while Bijou fantasizes herself as Elena, the woman who 'poetized and dramatized love' (138–9). Elena also fantasizes herself as occupying the male position: 'She was thinking that when Pierre turned his back to her, he became like a woman for her, and she would have liked to rape him' (151). 'Enchanted' by the homosexual Miguel, she identifies herself with Miguel's lover Donald, and 'she began to enjoy subtly and mysteriously Miguel's making love to him—for her . . . Was Miguel aware that he was making love to a twin brother of Elena, to Elena in a boy's body?' (106). Eventually she becomes the voyeur of Miguel's and Donald's lovemaking, positioned, as Brennan puts it, 'off-scene' in the bathroom which adjoins the bedroom: 'The scene in the dark affected her strangely. She felt part of herself sharing in it, as a woman, she as a woman within Donald's boy's body, being made love to by Miguel' (109).

There is a clear cinematic dimension to this 'scene in the dark', with Elena as the spectator fantasizing herself part of the scene, 'identify[ing] simultaneously with both the spectacle and the gaze', as Brennan puts it, drawing on Teresa de Lauretis's analysis of the female spectator.[119] Judith Roof, in her article 'The Erotic Travelogue', focuses particularly on the importance of looking relations (scopophilia, voyeurism, exhibitionism) in Nin's erotica (and pornography generally—Roof sees Nin's writing, in fact, as 'in many ways a meta-discourse of pornography'[120]), and on Nin's emphasis on sexuality as 'staged spectacle'; she notes that the first story in *Delta of Venus* 'begins, perceptively, in a bordello-like Peruvian theatre'.[121] Sexuality operates in the sphere of stage-sets and mirrors,

[119] Brennan, 'Anaïs Nin', 68–9.
[120] Roof, 'The Erotic Travelogue', 120.
[121] Ibid. 120.

specular identifications and 'the infinite possibility of multiple layers of watchers'.[122] Here we can see a clear link with Nin's fascination throughout her writing with the figure of the actress, with staging, illusion, and role-play.

As a final illustration, I want to turn to a story from Nin's second collection of erotica, 'Two Sisters' (which neither Brennan nor Roof discusses). Early in this story, the antagonistic tension between Dorothy and her sister's lover, Robert, explodes in a sexual encounter once again in a bathroom. This time Robert (and the reader) is the voyeur, watching Dorothy (who, we are told, 'think[s] herself alone' in the house; though everything suggests that, unconsciously, she knows differently) via the mirror on the bathroom door:

> She went into the bathroom to take a bath. Edna had left her door open, and Dorothy, thinking herself alone, did not trouble to close it. On this door there was a mirror. Dorothy came into the bathroom and dropped her kimono . . . Every move she made before the mirror brought out the provocative full, taut curves of her breasts and buttocks. Her hair was full of lights . . . her breasts danced as she moved . . . And Robert, on awakening, found himself looking at this spectacle from the bed, everything mirrored before him. (*Little Birds*, 36)

When Robert comes into the bathroom, Dorothy '[makes] no outcry' (again suggesting that this was her unconscious, if not conscious, desire), and they indulge in violent and passionate sex.

Later in the story, when Dorothy is married to Robert, in love with him but unable to desire him (out of guilt, she believes, for taking him away from her sister), she re-stages this scene with another man. Noticing that this man, Donald, also has a mirror on his bathroom door, she requests that he go into the bathroom and watch her in the mirror while she, naked except for a fur coat, exposes herself to another man in the living room:

> Seeing Dorothy in the mirror, seeing the hair of her sex like the hair of the fur, Donald felt that if John touched her between the legs he would strike him. He came out of the bathroom, his penis exposed and erect, and walked towards Dorothy. This was so much like the first scene of her passion for Robert that she moaned with joy, tore herself from John and turned fully upon Donald, saying: 'Take me, take me!'
>
> Closing her eyes, she imagined Robert crouching over her, tigerlike, tearing open the fur, and caressing her with many hands and mouths and tongues, touching every part of her, parting her legs, kissing her, biting her, licking her. (42)

[122] Ibid. 133. Here she is referring to Nin's story 'The Veiled Woman', which is also analysed in some detail by Brennan.

After this deliberate re-staging, in which Dorothy re-creates herself in fantasy as mirrored spectacle for Robert's gaze, she returns home to her husband, who, overjoyed to see her so desirous, immediately makes love to her: 'She was convulsed. The moment seemed to have come. He forgot his watching in his own wave of pleasure. And Dorothy carried off her deception, unable to reach the orgasm she had had only an hour before while closing her eyes and pretending it was Robert who was taking her.' (43) Here Nin clearly depicts sexuality as, in Rose's words, the 'site of fantasies, impasses, conflict and desire', the force that 'wreaks havoc' with the unity of consciousness and leaves the subject split by her own incompatible desires, an actress whether she wants to be or not.

3

Sphinxes and Scheherezades: The Actress and the *Femme Fatale*

Reflecting, in his preface to the 1921 edition of *The Tragic Muse* (first published in serial form in 1889–90), on the novel's origins and in particular on his creation of the actress protagonist, Miriam Rooth, Henry James wrote: 'I had desired for her, I remember, all manageable vividness—so ineluctable had it long appeared to "do the actress" '.[1] Twenty years later, in June 1941, Nin wrote in her diary, in the context of her friendship with Hollywood actress Luise Rainer, 'Nothing fascinates me more than the actress' (*Journals*, III, 122). Through the nineteenth and into the twentieth century—encompassing James, in the 1880s, planning the novel in which he would, as he put it, ' "do something about art" . . . some dramatic picture of the "artist-life" ',[2] and Nin, at what is usually seen as the close of the 'high modernist' period, reflecting on her own fascination with the figure of femininity which occurs again and again in her writings—the figure of the actress takes centre stage as the quintessentially modernist (patriarchal) fantasy of the feminine. As Nietzsche enjoined his readers in *The Gay Science*, seven years before the appearance of the first instalments of James's novel, 'Reflect on the whole history of women: do they not *have* to be first of all and above all else actresses?'[3]

The paradoxical notion of women as essentially inessential, as mere surface, illusion, acting, the appearance of mystery which conceals no real substance—Oscar Wilde's 'sphinxes without secrets'[4]—has a long

[1] Henry James, 'Preface', in *The Tragic Muse* (London: Macmillan, 1921 [1889–90]), p. xviii.

[2] James, 'Preface', p. v.

[3] Friedrich Nietzsche, *The Gay Science* (New York: Vintage, 1974 [1882]), 317.

[4] See Wilde's story 'The Sphinx without a Secret' (1891), in *Complete Works*, 205–8. In *The Picture of Dorian Gray*, when the Duchess of Monmouth teases Lord Henry Wotton with the challenge 'Describe us as a sex', he replies, 'Sphynxes [sic] without secrets' (*Complete Works*, 143).

history in male thought. It is particularly visible, though, in the late nineteenth and early twentieth centuries, as male anxieties about the place of women within the new urban contexts of modern culture crystallized in the fin-de-siècle obsession with figures of actresses and prostitutes, 'problematically public'[5] women who seemed to pose a threat—simultaneously social, sexual, and epistemic—to the hegemonic order. Taking this perceived threat to the limit, male artists and writers of the period produced endless representations of the 'fatal woman', the beautiful but deadly *femme fatale* (personified above all in the 'exotic', alluring, and amoral figure of Salome); this was a period characterized, as Bram Dijkstra writes, by a 'fascination with woman as the embodiment of evil'.[6]

'Nothing fascinates me more than the actress', writes Nin; and indeed her own life and self-constructions are frequently read in terms of the actress or the related figure of the veiled woman, the mysterious, mythmaking (and mythic) *femme fatale.* In this chapter, I shall explore the ways in which the figures of the actress, the duplicitous, role-playing woman, and the *femme fatale*—seductive and problematic fantasies of the feminine—not only recur in Nin's writing but can also be seen to structure it. I shall try to show that Nin's own investment in the figure of the *femme fatale* is a complex one, raising issues of seduction, self-mythologizing, power, and control.

'CREATURES OF SHOW': MODERNITY AND FEMININITY

In a section of *The Painter of Modern Life* (1863) entertainingly titled 'Women: Honest Ones, and Others', Baudelaire describes the courtesan, a 'shady type of beauty . . . dwelling on the fringes of regular society', concealing 'trickery and struggle' beneath her 'surface finery'. He goes on: 'These reflections about the courtesan may, to a certain extent, be applied to the actress; for she too is a creature of show, an object of public pleasure'.[7] The figure of the female performer, Rita Felski argues,

[5] This term is used by Rachel Brownstein; see her *Tragic Muse: Rachel of the Comédie-Française* (Durham, NC and London: Duke Univ. Press, 1995), p. ix.

[6] Bram Dijkstra, *Idols of Perversity: Fantasies of Feminine Evil in Fin-de-Siècle Culture* (New York: Oxford Univ. Press, 1986), 235.

[7] Charles Baudelaire, *The Painter of Modern Life* (1863), in *Selected Writings on Art and Literature* (Harmondsworth: Penguin, 1992), 430, 431. Baudelaire does, however, go on to note that the actress must also be considered an artist: 'If, on the one hand, the actress comes close to the courtesan, on the other she reaches up to the poet' (431). See below on Henry James's portrait of the actress Miriam Rooth, which emphasizes above all her status as artist.

easily lent itself to appropriation as a symptom of the pervasiveness of illusion and spectacle in the generation of modern forms of desire. Positioned on the margins of respectable society, yet graphically embodying its structuring logic of commodity aesthetics, the prostitute and the actress fascinated nineteenth-century cultural critics preoccupied with the decadent and artificial nature of modern life.[8]

This 'pervasiveness of illusion and spectacle' was nowhere more visible than in the great exhibitions and 'expositions'—at the Crystal Palace in 1851, in Paris in 1889 and 1900. With the Crystal Palace Exhibition, Thomas Richards argues, '[t]he era of the spectacle had begun'.[9] The Exhibition showed that 'the capitalist system had not only created a dominant form of exchange but was also in the process of creating a dominant form of representation to go along with it';[10] that, in other words, the commodity and the spectacle would now go hand in hand. In the Paris expositions, the 'sensual pleasures of consumption' were paramount; the 'consumer revolution', as Rosalind Williams argues, 'displayed a novel and crucial juxtaposition of imagination and merchandise, of dreams and commerce, of collective consciousness and economic fact'.[11] The Trocadéro section of the 1900 display, featuring a 'gaudy and incoherent jumble' of colonial locations and exhibits, provided an enticing and spectacular 'vision of the exotic'.[12] Similar strategies were employed in the department stores, depicted most famously by Zola in *Au Bonheur des Dames* (1883). To this end, as Williams notes, there was great reliance on fakery and artifice ('fake mahogany, fake bronze, fake marble'); the aim was purely to attract consumers' attention, to create a surface effect, a 'sense of the lavish and foreign'.[13] At least one contemporary observer, a journalist named Maurice Talmeyr, objected precisely to this 'inherent and pervasive trickery', noting that the expositions, rather than creating any real art or architecture, used only 'stage sets'.[14]

As the name of the store in Zola's novel clearly suggests, however, there was a strongly feminine inflection to this new consumerism and to the commodified, specularized culture of modernity. Williams describes the way in which the 1900 Paris exposition overtly displayed and reinforced this perceived link between femininity and consumption in the symbolic

[8] Rita Felski, *The Gender of Modernity* (Cambridge, MA: Harvard Univ. Press, 1995), 20.

[9] Thomas Richards, *The Commodity Culture of Victorian England: Advertising and Spectacle, 1851–1914* (London: Verso, 1991), 3.

[10] Richards, *Commodity Culture*, 3.

[11] Rosalind Williams, *Dream Worlds: Mass Consumption in Late Nineteenth-Century France* (Berkeley: Univ. of California Press, 1982), 12.

[12] Ibid. 62. [13] Ibid. 71. [14] Ibid. 72.

figure of 'La Parisienne': 'This penultimate [sic] female, the symbol of the 1900 exposition, was perched atop the Monumental Gateway [the massive and elaborately arched entrance on Place de la Concorde], an icon both sexy and remote, goddess and slut . . . a hybrid streetwalker-princess.'[15] Women became stereotyped as the creatures of consumption par excellence, seduced in their hordes into the boudoir-like space of the department store depicted by Zola; conversely, consumption itself, and the modern society of which it is characteristic, become feminized; in Felski's words, 'the idea of the modern becomes aligned with a pessimistic view of an unpredictable yet curiously passive femininity seduced by the glittering phantasmagoria of an emerging consumer culture'.[16]

In particular, it is in the figures of the 'courtesan', or prostitute, and the actress—Baudelaire's 'creatures of show'—that we find the crucial representations of the feminine in, and as, modernity. Concealing 'trickery and struggle' beneath 'surface finery', these figures epitomize the theatrical fakery and the exotic fantasy so central to commodity culture. It is noteworthy, therefore, that Elisabeth Barillé, in her semi-fictionalized biography *Anaïs Nin: Naked under the Mask*, describes Nin's self-constructions in exactly the terms of these quintessential representations of modern femininity: 'Hers was the ritual of an actress, of a courtesan, of a prostitute. Three species of women: one who lies, one who flatters, one who sells herself. Three temptations for Anaïs. Pleasure, treachery, fantasy.'[17]

Nin herself wrote, in a 1946 letter to Leo Lerman, who had requested a 'short autobiography': 'I am a writer. I would rather have been a courtesan' (*Journals*, IV, 200). This is, of course, a peculiar statement, one which seems to enact the duplicity of the courtesan it evokes: Nin was always extremely proud and jealous of the identity as 'writer' which she appears to be dismissing here. At the same time the statement does show the fascination of the courtesan for Nin, the 'temptation' of 'pleasure, treachery [and] fantasy' Barillé picks up on. Furthermore, Nin's identification with the courtesan and the actress, the mistresses of illusion and display, is allied with a strong interest in precisely the staginess and artificiality that

[15] Williams, *Dream Worlds*, 90, 91.

[16] *The Gender of Modernity*, 62.

[17] Elisabeth Barillé, *Anaïs Nin: Naked under the Mask* (London: Minerva, 1993), 43. Barillé's book could also perhaps be described, borrowing Brownstein's term, as a 'postmodern biography'. Barillé, a novelist, uses fictional interludes and reflections on abstractions such as 'Costume', 'Jazz', 'Voyeurism', to build up a portrait of Nin. In her 'Author's Note', she appears to acknowledge the link between this fictionalizing method and Nin's own self-fictionalizing: 'Anaïs Nin's words have inspired this portrait, albeit a fictional one, but woven from the very tissue of her work and her life' (n.p.).

is seen to characterize modern life and culture. In March 1935, Nin writes in her diary:

Note importance of fact that I don't care for good quality of materials, permanent values, real gems, real silver, gold, mahogany, solid woods, quality of dresses, stuffs—unimportant. Everything only for effect, as on the stage. Contented with false jewelry, lacquered woods, painted walls, imitation woods. Exactly like stage settings. Or stage costumes. Everything in [her house in] Louveciennes, on close inspection, shoddy, but beautiful. Interest in effect, in illusion. (14 March 1935 [*Fire*, 42])

Here, of course, illusion and theatricality are valued positively rather than negatively. Nietzsche, in contrast, attacks Wagner as reducing music to 'mere spectacle, theater, delusion'; he explicitly opposes the theatre, and the actor (and most of all the actress), to 'authenticity', at the same time noting the great popularity of what he is condemning: 'success with the masses no longer sides with those who are authentic—one has to be an actor to achieve that . . . [In] declining cultures, wherever the decision comes to rest with the masses, authenticity becomes superfluous, disadvantageous, a liability. Only the actor still arouses *great* enthusiasm.'[18] Andreas Huyssen comments: 'Wagner, the theater, the mass, woman—all become a web of signification outside of, and in opposition to, true art [and 'authenticity' more generally]: "In the theater one becomes people, herd, female, pharisee, voting cattle, patron, idiot—*Wagnerian*" '.[19] And yet Nietzsche's association of women with the theatre is not merely a misogynistic fantasy (though clearly he is using the association to misogynist ends). On the contrary, the nineteenth-century theatre was a particularly significant site for women, being (like the department store) one of the few public spaces in which women could (literally in this case) act.[20] The actress thus becomes the symbolic focus for questions of feminine display and sexuality, and for issues of surface and depth, 'authenticity' and 'illusion'.

'SHE WANTS TO ACT ONLY HERSELF'

Nin's preoccupation with the figure of the actress can be seen very early in her writing: in her diary in 1930 she is already recording her experiments

[18] Nietzsche, *The Case of Wagner*, cited in Andreas Huyssen, *After the Great Divide: Modernism, Mass Culture, and Postmodernism* (London: Macmillan, 1988), 51.

[19] Ibid.

[20] The crucial difference between the theatre and the department store as public spaces for women was one of class: respectable women shopped, less respectable women performed on the stage.

with stories about actresses (*Early Diary*, IV, 329). But her most sustained portrayals of the woman who is a professional actress, in fact a film star, are her focus on the character of Stella in a section of *Winter of Artifice*[21] and of Luise Rainer in the third volume of the *Journals.*

Stella, as her name suggests, is a 'star' with all a star's accoutrements—a 'movie star bed of white satin', a 'movie star apartment' (12, 26). But Nin uses her to portray above all the tensions and conflicts of identity for which the very notion of a 'star', and especially a female star, seems to provide a particular focus. Rachel Brownstein begins her book on the French stage actress Rachel with a meditation on the symbolic associations of the star:

> [stars] reflect, reveal and focus a problem that has preoccupied Western culture for at least two hundred years: the shape and depth of individual character, the outlines of the integral, coherent self, the relation between the substance of a self—sometimes called character—and appearances, self-presentations, temporary social roles.
>
> A star is someone whose roles shape her character and get conflated with it, whose personal life appears to be spectacular as we watch it get theatrically played out . . . Stars are signs of anxiety about identity . . . Simply by being herself, a star poses the question of whether and how coherent, integral identity hangs on performances and fictions.[22]

A star, then, highlights questions of the 'substance' or 'reality' of the self over against mere roles or performances. Stella is tormented by these very questions: Nin's story begins with her in a cinema or projection-room watching herself on screen, and being unable to accept her screen self as (part of) herself: 'Stella sat in a small, dark room and watched her own figure acting on the screen. Stella watched her "double" moving in the light, and she did not recognize her. She almost hated her. Her first reaction was one of revolt, of rejection. This image was not she. She repudiated it. It was a work of artifice, of lighting, of stage setting' (9).

Just as Stella appears 'doubled', so there is a double response here. The key word is 'repudiated'. In her discussion of the 'repudiation of femininity' in Freud's writings, Rachel Bowlby analyses the dynamics of repudiation as follows: '"repudiation", even aside from its Freudian uses, is

[21] It is important to be aware of the complex dating and publishing history of the stories that make up *Winter of Artifice* (summarized helpfully by Philip K. Jason in *Anaïs Nin*, 39). Although the first edition of the book appeared in 1939, under the title *The Winter of Artifice*, the 'Stella' story was not added until the Swallow Press edition of 1961; so that although it appears as part of one of Nin's earliest published works, it in fact dates from much later.

[22] Brownstein, *Tragic Muse*, pp. ix–x.

not, after all, just any old word. It is strong language, and seems to imply not just rejection or refusal, but also that what is rejected is somehow a part of the repudiator; that it is illegitimately cast off . . . There is the implication that what you repudiate really belongs to you.'[23] This is precisely the dynamic here: while Stella refuses the image, pushes it away, her feelings of hatred and revulsion reveal her own involvement with the figure on the screen. In fact, Stella is jealous: 'What Stella had seen on the screen, the figure of which she had been so instantaneously jealous, was the free Stella. What did not appear on the screen was the shadow of Stella, her demons, doubt and fear' (11). In this way Nin sets up the key issue she will examine through the figure of Stella, the film-star: although Stella denies that the screen persona is 'her', she is at the same time jealous of her own image, recognizing in it the self that she fails to be in everyday life.

Nin examines this dynamic in more detail in her diary portrayal of the Hollywood actress Luise Rainer, on whom the character of Stella is clearly based:[24] 'Luise is always saying that the Luise on the screen is not she. It is an image born of lighting, of artifice, enhanced by acting. She did not recognize or love the actress. Luise's image of herself and the image on the screen do not match. The woman on the screen is a stranger to her . . .' (*Journals*, III, 140). And yet, of course, the woman on the screen is *not* a stranger: although Luise sees her actress self as 'an illusion', she is jealous of her as a 'heightened self'. Nin, in the diary, sees Luise's screen self in exactly this way: 'The exalted figure on the stage is the woman she becomes in moments of self-confidence, confidence in the actress, but this confidence deserts her when she falls back into her personal life. She needs the costume, lights, decor, challenge of another personality' (145). She tries to persuade Luise that this screen self *is* part of her, is even the 'best' part of her: 'She could not understand how I related them [i.e. 'Luise's image of herself and the image on the screen'], how they fed one another, how together they did represent a complete Luise, one freed by acting, the other bound, one confident, the other filled with doubt' (140). Nin says to her: '"You split the two women when they could be

[23] Bowlby, *Still Crazy*, 145.

[24] While acknowledging that the Stella figure is in some sense clearly derived from or based on the diary portrayal of Luise Rainer, I would reject the implication that the diary portrait is therefore 'raw material' for the fictional character. Rather, Nin uses the portrayal of Luise much as she uses that of Stella: to focus the issues she is interested in, the actress's conflicts of identity, the questions of 'roles' and 'reality'. Her portrait of Luise is just as motivated and organized as is that of Stella. See Chapter 1 for my critique of the idea of the diary as 'raw material'.

unified. I say they are the same, but you create the difference between them"' (145); because, Luise replies, '"I don't want anyone falling in love with that other woman, I want them to love me for myself, not that heightened image"' (145).

The paradox here, as Nin observes, is that while Luise rejects her screen self as a 'fraud' (145), she chooses her roles only in relation to herself, to the identifications she can make: 'At the same time, when I find her reading scripts and plays, I see that she is looking for a character that she feels identified with, some affinity, some role which might be an extension of herself' (145). Nin puts this particularly well in her story of Stella: 'She rejects all the plays. Because they cannot contain her. She wants to walk into her own self, truly presented, truly revealed. She wants to act only herself' (*Winter*, 33). Underlying Stella/Luise's feeling of division or alienation, the perceived split between the acting self and the 'real' self, there is another feeling—that, somehow, it is *through acting* that she will truly realize her self: 'She is a woman who has lost herself and feels that she can recover it by acting this self' (33); 'The acting is simultaneously a dramatization of a divided self, and at the same time she seeks through it the magic unification, two women made one through a role' (*Journals*, III, 145); 'She is not reading plays as plays, but as roles which might deliver her from her own dramas' (153).

Nin seems, then, to be exploring the paradoxical idea of acting one's own self, realizing (in the fullest sense of that term) what one most truly is precisely through acting it out.[25] In one sense, the actor/actress is the one who most reveals the 'secret being' of a person. He or she reveals more, communicates more deeply, than anyone else: 'Nothing fascinates me more than the actress who makes visible, expressive, every mood and feeling, whose every gesture reveals, communicates, fascinates one' (122); 'The actor allows us such intimate glimpses of human beings in a state of love and openness . . . On the stage you are taken into the secret being of another and witness the exposure of a human being usually only uncovered in moments of love' (139). Yet this 'secret being', this heightened reality of the self, is only available through acting; in Brownstein's words, it 'hangs on performances and fictions'.

It is particularly interesting, then, that while Nin describes Luise's search for roles that are 'projections' or 'extensions' of herself, she men-

[25] See Chapter 5 for discussion of the (more radical) idea that any identity is constituted through an endless series of performances—is, in Judith Butler's term, a 'performative accomplishment'.

tions only one role by name, that of Rachel Félix: ' "Now you have found Rachel, which you want to do" ' (159).

'SOMEONE MAKING HERSELF UP'

Rachel Félix was born in 1821, the daughter of extremely poor French Jewish peddlers; when she died of tuberculosis in 1858 she was, in the words of one theatre historian, 'the most celebrated actress on earth'.[26] Having joined the Comédie-Française in 1838, she had her first major success in the role of Camille in Corneille's *Horace*, and went on almost single-handedly to restore the fortunes of the Comédie-Française and the popularity of classical French tragedy, the plays of Corneille and Racine, through her extraordinarily powerful performances of the great tragic heroines, most notably Racine's Phèdre. She toured Europe and America, was noted for her scandalous love life, and, after her early death, became, in John Stokes's words, 'an essential component in the mythic figure of the great performing woman'.[27] She appeared as the actress Vashti in Charlotte Brontë's *Villette* (1853); she is also the inspirational role model and artistic icon for James's Miriam Rooth, who declares that she wants to be 'the English Rachel'.[28] For Miriam, the Théâtre Français is the 'holy of holies', imbued with Rachel's spirit: 'I feel them here, all the great artists I shall never see. Think of Rachel—look at her grand portrait there!—and how she stood on these very boards'.[29] It is underneath this iconic portrait that Miriam stands—a physical, visual enactment of her allegiance—in her confrontation with Peter Sherringham, when he first asks her to give up acting and marry him.[30]

Rachel Brownstein's 'biography' of Rachel (she was always known simply by her first name) does not, however, aim to provide a factual record of Rachel's life and work. Brownstein states that she is 'interested, above all, in how Rachel and her life were embedded in legends. I want to map that fantastic forest, to suggest that the interlocking branches of fact and fiction there cannot be disentangled.'[31] Perhaps taking her cue from James himself and his portrait of Miriam Rooth, Brownstein argues that it is precisely through 'people's reflections of and on Rachel' that we can

[26] John Stokes, 'Rachel Félix', in Michael Booth, John Stokes, and Susan Bassnett, *Three Tragic Actresses: Siddons, Rachel, Ristori* (Cambridge: Cambridge Univ. Press, 1996), 115.

[27] Ibid. [28] James, *The Tragic Muse*, 181. [29] Ibid. 315. [30] Ibid. 327.

[31] Brownstein, *Tragic Muse*, 67–9.

best see her.[32] She analyses Rachel's symbolic valency—as actress, as sexually voracious woman, as exotic 'foreign' beauty. Brownstein notes the 'deeply and fundamentally contradictory' aspects of the nineteenth-century attitude towards actresses, seeing this as a limit case of attitudes towards women and 'the feminine' more generally:

> On the one hand actresses were condemned for pretending to be who they weren't—and weakening what characters they had by pretense. They were also rated for merely playing themselves. In the misogynist imagination, actresses are false—artful, artificial, duplicitous, like women in general—and on the other hand excitingly, transgressively true to the passions and the imagination. In a culture that confusedly conceived of female sexuality as an excess of either nature or artifice, they were taken to stand for Woman.[33]

Rachel, who at first was seen as 'chaste', later became associated (after news broke of some 'compromising' letters) with this excessive female sexuality; and this identification was bound up with the roles she played: 'The actress's growing reputation for greed and sexual excess bled easily into the images of murderous Roxane [the exotic mistress of a sultan in Racine's *Bajazet*] and incestuous Phèdre; as Rachel moved from role to role, it was as if to prove that one crime leads to another'.[34]

Rachel's role in relation to the nineteenth-century French preoccupation with national identity was also intriguing: her status as patriot, even national symbol, created through her dramatic on-stage recitations of the 'Marseillaise', could not but be complicated by her Jewishness—which she never tried to disavow, but, on the contrary, emphasized throughout her life and career. And this very Jewishness was central to her exotic, erotic appeal, through the operation of a certain kind of Orientalism: 'Rachel's popularity coincided with an aesthetic-erotic vogue for exotic women', a taste for 'Semitic feminine beauty'.[35] It could also be seen to exacerbate, perhaps, the actress's already liminal status: like the actress, the Jew in the fin-de-siècle period might be 'in', but would never quite be 'of', European society. Again, Miriam Rooth is described by Peter

[32] Brownstein, *Tragic Muse*, 27, 44. In his Preface, James notes his apparently paradoxical strategy of making Miriam the 'centre' of the book despite her only ever being seen through others' eyes: 'we have no direct exhibition of [Miriam's consciousness] whatever . . . we get at it all inferentially and inductively, seeing it only through a more or less bewildered interpretation of it by others' (The *Tragic Muse*, p. xvi). I shall go on to examine the 'bewildering' aspect of the actress in more detail below.

[33] Brownstein, *Tragic Muse*, 43.

[34] Ibid. 166.

[35] Ibid. 31. Both Mary Ann Doane and Gail Finney also note the Orientalist aspect inherent in the fin-de-siècle fascination with the exotic, sexual woman, the *femme fatale*; I shall return to this point later.

Sherringham as being 'of Rachel's tribe'; that is, she is 'more than half a Jewess'[36] (an affiliation with Rachel she is happy to claim); and there is, perhaps, an implied link betweeen the statelessness and rootlessness of the actress or the artist, and that of the Jew.[37]

As Brownstein argues, these processes of symbolic association, of myth-making, are not one-directional. If 'a star is someone whose roles shape her character and get conflated with it', that shaping or conflation is not simply something imposed from the 'outside': it is also a process in which the star herself is actively involved. Rachel, Brownstein suggests, 'seemed to flaunt the fact that she was a fiction and a fabrication, someone making herself up'.[38] On the other hand, we should avoid overstatement here. While Brownstein wishes to approach Rachel through her identity (or non-identity) as a 'star' and therefore a 'legendary' character, rejecting the idea of a factual reality 'beneath or beyond the layers of spectacle and symbol and stereotype',[39] she is also careful to make the point that Rachel did have a historical existence and agency, that she cannot be reduced to 'only a shimmer of language'.[40]

This point is important in thinking about the question of the actress's roles and her 'identity'—the question that concerns Nin in her portrayals of Stella/Luise—because it allows us to formulate the issue in a more nuanced way. If Rachel is 'making herself up' through the roles she enacts (and 'roles' here can encompass both her on-stage characters and the symbolic roles I have been discussing), these roles are not chosen at random. 'Rachel' is not merely an empty signifier, a blank that becomes filled by the role she plays. Rather, there is a negotiation. Certainly, she is in a sense created through the roles; as Brownstein argues, 'the heroines she played and the structure of the plays she starred in shaped her self and her life story'.[41] But she also 'makes herself up', creates, shapes, enacts, her self and her life *through* these roles. The role is not simply given, but is always interpreted—and this interpretation, even alteration or 'distortion', may be part of a self-enacting. John Stokes relates, for instance, that when Rachel played Jeanne d'Arc, she altered the text so that, in the trial scene, she was handed a French standard rather than a Bible—thus pointing up

[36] James, *The Tragic Muse*, 181, 51.

[37] Peter Sherringham 'guessed easily enough the dolorous type of exile of the two ladies, wanderers in search of Continental cheapness, inured to queer contacts and compromises' (ibid. 125). The language of 'exile' and 'wandering' here is suggestive of Miriam's ascribed Jewishness. Miriam herself describes her lack of interest in any national or ethnic identity: 'I'm of the family of the artists—*je me fiche* of any other!' (181).

[38] Brownstein, *Tragic Muse.*, p. xiii.

[39] Ibid. 27.

[40] Ibid., p. x.

[41] Ibid. 41.

the complexity of her situation as a French Jew playing a French Christian patriot-heroine.[42]

What we see here, then, is another example of the 'double-jointedness' identified in Chapter 1 in the context of (to use Susan Stanford Friedman's phrase) 'textual self-fashioning': acting, like the signature, like autobiography, is double-jointed, pulling in both directions at once, appropriating the role for the actress, expropriating the actress into the role. This seems to provide the best way to explicate the apparent paradox that Nin elaborates in relation to the actress—the problem that, while the acting self is seen as a fraud, a 'fiction', nonetheless it is through acting that the 'self' will truly be realized: 'She wants to walk into her own self, truly presented, truly revealed. She wants to act only herself.' The actress's identity does not lie in some 'real' self, removed from the sphere of acting, nor entirely in the roles she enacts on-screen, but in the negotiation between the 'fictional' and the 'historical' that she makes in her interpretations of roles as 'projections' or 'extensions' of her self.

There is a final twist to Luise Rainer's appropriation of, and expropriation by, the role of Rachel. In 1849, at the height of her fame, Rachel starred in a play written especially for her. Entitled *Adrienne Lecouvreur*, it was the story of the eighteenth-century tragic actress, the biggest star of her day, who led a turbulent personal life and died young in mysterious circumstances. Stars, Brownstein suggests, are 'translations, re-presentations' of other stars. In playing Adrienne, Rachel 're-presented' her own career as a performer;[43] she staged the myths and symbols surrounding her own identity as a legendary actress. She also, clearly, 'identified' with Adrienne: Ernest Legouvé, co-author, with Eugène Scribe, of *Adrienne Lecouvreur*, recounted in his memoirs 'how he came upon her rehearsing Adrienne's death scene alone in a darkened theater, tears rolling down her cheeks, and she told him that she was mourning her own death in Adrienne's'.[44] We may wonder whether Nin, when writing the story of Luise's identification with Rachel, knew about *Adrienne Lecouvreur*. In any case, it creates the vertiginous effect of a hall of mirrors. Rachel is the ideal choice of role for Luise, seeking to resolve the paradoxes of her own identity as actress precisely through acting them out. Not only is Rachel the perfect symbol of, and as, the actress: in her own stagings and interpretations, most of all in her playing the role of Adrienne, she too highlighted, and perhaps sought to resolve, the paradoxes of identity in exactly the same way as Luise (and Stella)—through acting.

[42] Stokes, 'Rachel Félix', 110. [43] Ibid. 105.
[44] Cited by Brownstein: *Tragic Muse*, 212.

'BEAUTIFUL, ACTUAL, FICTIVE, IMPOSSIBLE'

'To make up one's mind about an actress is, of course, the most troublesome of tasks.'[45] Thus Virginia Woolf, reviewing in 1911 a book about Rachel Félix with the title *Rachel: Her Stage Life and her Real Life.* The author of the book she is reviewing is—as his title suggests—intent on separating the actress's 'stage life' from her 'real life'; his argument is that Rachel was a tragic figure because her 'real' life, her 'own' life, was overshadowed by the 'unreal' life of her acting, her playing of roles. Woolf, on the other hand, is concerned precisely to question this distinction, to grapple with the issues of acting and identity, reality and illusion. Her (apparently casual) remark about the difficulty of 'making up one's mind' points to the problem raised by the figure of the actress, the epistemic unease—or, as Henry James puts it, bewilderment—she engenders.

This is one of the central themes explored by James through the figure of Miriam Rooth. Peter Sherringham, fascinated from the first by Miriam's 'variousness',[46] and unwittingly falling in love with her, finds himself suddenly confronted by a startling, even horrifying, *mise en abîme*:

> It came over [Peter] suddenly that so far from there being any question of her having the histrionic nature she simply had it in such perfection that she was always acting; that her existence was a series of parts assumed for the moment . . . Interested as he had ever been in the profession of which she was potentially an ornament, this idea startled him by its novelty and even lent, on the spot, a formidable, a really appalling character to Miriam Rooth. It struck him abruptly that a woman whose only being was to 'make believe', to make believe she had any and every being you might like and that would serve a purpose and produce a certain effect, and whose identity resided in the continuity of her personations, so that she had no moral privacy, as he phrased it to himself, but lived in a high wind of exhibition, of figuration—such a woman was a kind of monster in whom of necessity there would be nothing to 'be fond' of, because there would be nothing to take hold of.[47]

Peter's attitude towards this revelation shifts about through the book. At times he finds Miriam's 'labyrinthine' nature beautifully attractive: '"And do you think I haven't a character?" As he hesitated she pushed back her chair, rising rapidly. He looked up at her an instant—she

[45] Virginia Woolf, review of *Rachel: Her Stage Life and her Real Life*, by Francis Gribble (London: Chapman & Hall, 1911), in the *Times Literary Supplement*, 20 April 1911; repr. in *The Essays of Virginia Woolf*, I (ed. Andrew McNeillie; London: Hogarth Press, 1986), 351.

[46] James, *The Tragic Muse*, 143.

[47] Ibid. 167–8.

seemed so "plastic"; and then rising too answered: "Delightful being, you've a hundred!" '[48] At other times he is overwhelmed by 'the demon, the devil, the devourer and destroyer' aspect of Miriam.[49] In the end, Miriam must stand for unresolved and unresolvable contradictions: 'a beautiful, actual, fictive, impossible young woman of a past age [yet, in Gabriel Nash's vision, 'drawing forth the modernness of the age'], an undiscoverable country, who spoke in blank verse and overflowed with metaphor, who was exalted and heroic beyond all human convenience and who yet was irresistibly real'.[50]

For Nin, these questions of illusion and reality, surface and depth, had been raised most insistently by her encounter, in 1931, with a woman who was not a professional actress but, in Nin's eyes, 'an actress every moment': Henry Miller's wife June Mansfield. Already involved in a passionate affair with Miller, Nin became equally fascinated by Mansfield, who would appear as a central character in her journals and provided the model for Sabina, the *femme fatale* in Nin's fiction. The fascination of the *femme fatale* for Nin lay above all in her status as enigma, spinning endless tales around herself which, rather than presenting a clear self-portrait, 'confuse all the images' (*Spy*, 10), simultaneously provoking the desire for knowledge and blocking that knowledge. There is, in fact, in Nin's treatments of the *femme fatale* figure a striking emphasis on this epistemic dimension, rather than on the bodily or sexual dimension which we might expect to be dominant; and I shall go on to show how this is connected, for Nin, to issues of power, control, and authorship.

Nin's portrait of June[51] focuses immediately on the problematics of identity raised by her theatricality and role-playing. June's first appearance in *Henry and June* and in the *Journals*, and Sabina's in *House of Incest*, are presented in terms of an actress's first entrance on stage. Sabina appears, her face 'suspended in the darkness of the garden'; the darkness, the night, functions as a backcloth, 'a photograph unglued from its frame'

[48] James, *The Tragic Muse*, 187. [49] Ibid. 224.

[50] Ibid. 286; Nash's 'joyous, amused, amusing' vision of Miriam as quintessentially modern is on pp. 173–4. It should also be noted that what Miriam most fully and finally represents in James's novel is the artist—as Peter Sherringham, despite himself, has to recognize ('Wasn't she the artist to the tips of her tresses—the ambassadress never in the world . . . ?' [283]). James's novel thus represents a fuller development of Baudelaire's concession that, if the actress 'comes close to the courtesan, on the other [hand] she reaches up to the poet'; and indeed could be seen as a counter to the predominantly negative fin-de-siècle representation of the actress—if Miriam sometimes appears to Peter as a 'monster', she is also a genuine and triumphant artist.

[51] As with the case of Luise Rainer, so here my use of June's first name is intended to point up her status as a *character* in Nin's story.

(*House of Incest*, 180). In *Henry and June*, Nin describes June's entrance more dramatically: 'As she came towards me from the darkness of my garden into the light of the doorway I saw for the first time the most beautiful woman on earth' (14). In the *Journals*, the theatrical nature of this setting is made explicit in a retrospective description: 'June and I, arriving at the house, stand under the light over the front door, the light like a stage light which illumined her the first night I saw her' (*Journals*, I, 142).

June is 'an actress every moment', taking poses: 'she stood for a second halfway up the stairs where the light set her off against the turquoise green wall' (*Journals*, I, 26; *Henry and June*, 16). Nin sees her as the theatrical character pushed to the limit: 'Her role in life alone preoccupies her . . . I saw in her a caricature of the theatrical and dramatic personage. Costume, attitudes, talk. She is a superb actress. No more. I could not grasp her core' (*Henry and June*, 14). June, in fact, comes to stand for 'the theatre': 'She was the essence of the theatre itself, stirring the imagination, promising such an intensity and heightening of experience, such richness, and then failing to appear in person, giving instead a smoke-screen of compulsive talk about trivialities' (*Journals*, I, 27).

Nin sees June as representing her own fantasy of womanhood: ' "You're the only woman who ever answered the fantasies I had about what a woman should be" ', Nin tells her (*Journals*, I, 30; or, in *Henry and June*, ' "You are the only woman who ever answered the demands of my imagination" ' [16–17]). The fantasy June represents is that of no self, no 'core', no 'sincerity', as Nin tells her in a speech which is itself a fantasy:

> I wanted to run out and kiss her fantastic beauty and say: 'June, you have killed my sincerity too. I will never know again who I am, what I am, what I love, what I want. Your beauty has drowned me, the core of me . . . Deep down, I am not different from you. I dreamed you, I wished for your existence. You are the woman I want to be. I see in you that part of me which is you.' (*Journals*, I, 27–8)[52]

June's appeal resides in the fact that her character 'seems to have no definable form, no boundaries, no core'; she is merely an endless play of roles and illusions. She cannot be 'sincere' because the very notion of sincerity depends on a stable self (similarly, Miriam Rooth produces in Peter Sherringham 'the sense that if she was sincere it was the sincerity of execution, if she was genuine it was the genuineness of doing it well'[53]). June

[52] This dynamic of identification—seeing part of oneself, or a fantasy self, in the other—is central to Nin's depictions of relationships between women. I shall focus on this in more detail in Chapter 5.

[53] James, *The Tragic Muse*, 220.

is a locus for the erotics of multiplicity I ascribed to Nin in Chapter 2, the fantasy of the self as myriad, unconstrained, and non-conflictual. The importance of this fantasy for Nin is the liberatory potential it suggests for avoiding definitions, which she sees as equivalent to limitations, constraints: 'As soon as someone defines me, I do as June does: I seek escape from the confinements of definition' (*Journals*, I, 35). This evasion of definitions is repeatedly ascribed to Sabina in the novels: 'She was always trespassing boundaries, erasing identifications' (*Albatross*, 123). The confusions and vagueness of Sabina's endless stories are above all smoke-screens to prevent any clear points of identification or definition: 'At first she beckoned and lured one into her world; then, she blurred the passageways, confused all the images, as if to elude detection' (*Spy*, 10). Her multiple self-portraits are always blurred, so that there is no definition, and therefore no limit or boundary.

However, just as for Peter Sherringham, for Nin the fascination of the enigma also contains frustration and even fear. While June's evasiveness and fluidity exert a strong appeal for Nin, they also trouble, confuse, and frighten her: 'The extent of her falsity was terrifying, like an abyss. Fluidity. Elusiveness. Where was June? Who was June?' (*Journals*, I, 27).[54] While on the one hand she exults in June's destruction of sincerity and identity ('I will never again know who I am, what I am, what I love, what I want'), on the other hand, June's elusiveness provokes in her an almost violent desire for 'clarity', a desire to expose June and 'force' her into reality:

> June's elusiveness, her retreat into fantasy, suddenly enrage me, because they are mine . . . I want to force her into reality (as Henry does). I, who am sunk in dreams, in half-lived acts, I want to do violence to her . . . Her subtlety makes me desire frankness; the quicksands of her evasions make me, for the first time, demand clarity. At times I feel as she does, like taking flight from selves I do not know, and at other times I feel like Henry, like pursuing and exposing these selves to crude daylight. (*Journals*, I, 34)

Here we can see Nin setting up the issue of the epistemic difficulty represented by this figure of elusive femininity. We can also see (and I shall return to this point later) an interesting sliding of identifications on Nin's part: she oscillates in this passage between her identification with June,

[54] Ironically, Miriam Rooth uses the word 'abyss' to describe—admiringly—Mlle Voisin, the older actress she encounters on her visit to the Théâtre Français: 'She's strange, she's mysterious . . . She showed us nothing—nothing of her real self . . . she's so perfect . . . Her charming manner is . . . an abyss—it's the Wall of China' (*The Tragic Muse* 328–9). Miriam here, just like Nin, is seduced by and identifies with the enigma.

the position of femininity and enigma, and her identification with Henry, the position of masculinity, directness, and potential violence.

REVEALING AND CONCEALING: THE *FEMME FATALE*

While this notion of epistemic difficulty, a mysteriousness or evasiveness which defies the structures of knowledge, may be associated with 'woman' in general, both in Nin's texts and in the wider field of representations it is particularly bound up with certain kinds of woman or versions of femininity: the actress, as we have seen, and the *femme fatale*. Mary Ann Doane writes: 'The femme fatale is the figure of a certain discursive unease, a potential epistemological trauma . . . She harbors a threat which is not entirely legible, predictable, or manageable . . . a secret, something which must be aggressively revealed, unmasked, discovered.'[55]

Both Doane and Gail Finney analyse the characteristics and cultural significance of the 'fatal woman' as she was represented, almost obsessively, through the nineteenth century and into the twentieth. The nineteenth-century *femme fatale*, Finney writes, 'frequently takes the form of the *allumeuse* (literally, "a woman who ignites"), who excites men's desire without satisfying it. But the essential, defining quality of her nature, combining as it does beauty and death, is its two-sidedness.'[56] *Allumeuse* is, in fact, the perfect description of Nin's character Sabina: 'Sabina brought in her wake the sound and the imagery of fire engines as they tore through the streets of New York, alarming the heart with the violent gong of catastrophe. All dressed in red and silver, the tearing red and silver siren cutting a pathway through the flesh. The first time one looked at Sabina one felt: everything will burn!' (*Ladders*, 92; see also *Spy*, 7, 104–5)

In *House of Incest*, she is clearly associated with both beauty and death—her beauty is itself deadly: 'from the eyes a simoom wind shrivelled the leaves'; 'beneath the skin of her cheeks I saw ashes' (180, 183). Further, the motif of two-sidedness to which Finney draws attention is a repeated motif throughout *House of Incest* in the image of the two faces of woman, the division between night and day. Sabina and the narrator

[55] Mary Ann Doane, *Femmes Fatales: Feminism, Film Theory, Psychoanalysis* (New York and London: Routledge, 1991), 1.

[56] Gail Finney, *Women in Modern Drama: Freud, Feminism and European Theater at the Turn of the Century* (Ithaca, NY: Cornell Univ. Press, 1989), 52.

are the two sides of woman, opposites but indissolubly linked together: 'I am the other face of you. Our faces are soldered together by soft hair, soldered together, showing two profiles of the same soul . . . Only our faces must shine twofold—like day and night—always separated by space and the evolutions of time' (185–6).

The figure of the *femme fatale* represents the point of convergence of various key discourses of the late nineteenth and early twentieth centuries, including urban modernity, psychoanalysis, and the 'society of the spectacle'. Above all, the *femme fatale* is a focus for anxieties about both female sexuality and the stability of the self. The former anxiety was particularly bound up with the discourses and experiences of modern urbanization and consumerism (the 'streetwalker-princess' figure of 'La Parisienne'); the latter, with psychoanalysis. Thus, Doane argues, the *femme fatale* is 'a clear indication of the extent of the fears and anxieties prompted by shifts in the understanding of sexual difference in the late nineteenth century'; and she is 'an articulation of fears surrounding the loss of stability and centrality of the self, the "I", the ego'.[57] The *femme fatale* articulates these anxieties through her 'overrepresentation' of the body and the unconscious.[58] She is associated not with consciously controlled, ordered knowledge and reason but with 'deception, secretiveness, a kind of anti-knowledge'; and if this deceptiveness and 'anti-knowledge' are viewed as problematic (even traumatic), they may also be transvalued, situating the woman as 'privileged conduit to a—necessarily complex and even devious—truth'.[59] Thus 'woman' in general and the *femme fatale* in particular may come to represent the locus of a battle over illusion and reality, deception and truth, knowledge and 'anti-knowledge'. As we have seen, Nin sets up her portrait of June in the *Journals* in terms of just such a battle; as I shall go on to show, her 1961 story 'Sabina' (which is largely based on the text in the first volume of the *Journals*) is focused explicitly on this issue.

The deceptiveness of the *femme fatale* is represented particularly through the imagery of the *veil* and, relatedly, the striptease. The veil is inherently ambiguous in function: 'it simultaneously conceals and reveals, provoking the gaze'.[60] Functioning in this ambiguous way as a

[57] Doane, *Femmes Fatales*, 1.

[58] Cf. ibid. 2.

[59] Ibid. 3. The notion of women's privileged access to some realm of truth, meaning, or authenticity (cashed out, for example, in terms of 'closeness to nature' or 'connection with the unconscious') can sometimes be seen to underlie theories of a 'female' or 'feminine' language or writing. I discuss these theories in Chapter 4.

[60] 'Veiling over Desire: Close-Ups of the Woman', in *Femmes Fatales*, 49.

bodily/sexual tease, both revealing and concealing, the veil can then also function symbolically to figure the epistemic 'tease' represented by the *femme fatale*: the 'structure' of the veil, Doane argues, is 'clearly complicit with the tendency to specify the woman's position in relation to knowledge as that of the enigma'.[61] The same structure is found in the striptease, which also puts into play 'the dialectic of concealing and revealing'.[62]

It is also important to note here that the veil is traditionally associated with the East, indicating the Orientalism mentioned earlier. This aspect of the fin-de-siècle *femme fatale* can be seen particularly in the endless representations of the figure of Salome. This minor biblical figure[63] became—for the French Symbolists and Decadents in particular—the quintessential representation of the *femme fatale*, appearing in paintings, poems, opera, and of course Oscar Wilde's Symbolist play, first performed (in French) in 1893. Bram Dijkstra writes that '[in] the turn-of-the-century imagination, the figure of Salome epitomized the inherent perversity of women . . . Salome became the endlessly multiplied image of woman'.[64] With a certain relish, Nin associates herself with Salome in a series of diary entries in 1929 recounting a theatre director's attempt to persuade her to take the role in a production of Wilde's play: 'The two producers and the Director still want me for Salomé, because they have the idea that she was like me—young, innocent-looking, dreamy, and yet devilish!' (15 May 1929 [*Early Diary*, IV, 183]). In his 1924 novel *A Passage to India* E. M. Forster draws on the image of the enigmatic Eastern *femme fatale* to convey the epistemic threat that India represents to its colonizers and would-be conquerers:

How can the mind take hold of such a country? Generations of invaders have tried, but they remain in exile. The important towns they build are only retreats, their quarrels the malaise of men who cannot find their way home. India knows of their trouble. She knows of the whole world's trouble, to its uttermost depth. She calls 'Come' through her hundred mouths, through objects ridiculous and august. But come to what? She has never defined. She is not a promise, only an appeal.[65]

[61] Ibid. 54.

[62] '*Gilda*: Epistemology as Striptease', in ibid. 108.

[63] She is described only as 'the daughter of Herodias' in Matthew (14: 3–12) and Mark (6: 17–29), but named as Salome by Josephus (*Antiquities of the Jews* 18.5.4). The account of her dance and John's subsequent beheading does not appear in Luke or John.

[64] Dijkstra, *Idols of Perversity*, 384.

[65] E. M. Forster, *A Passage to India* (Harmondsworth: Penguin, 1985 [1924]), 148–9.

India itself (or 'herself') is personified here as seductive but eternally enigmatic Woman, luring the mind of the (male) 'invader' *en abîme* through her sex/speech, her 'hundred mouths'.

We can see this Orientalism at work in Nin's depictions of Sabina. Her 1961 story begins with her favourite image of the labyrinth, here explicitly associated both with Oriental cities and with Sabina, who is thereby herself symbolically linked to the Orient:

> Certain cities of the orient were designed to baffle the enemy by a tangle of intricate streets. For those concealed within the labyrinth its detours were a measure of safety; for the invaders it presented an image of fearful mystery.
>
> Sabina had chosen the labyrinth for safety. ('Sabina', 45)

Later, Sabina is explicitly compared to the veiled Eastern women: 'Sabina was like those veiled figures glimpsed turning the corner of a Moroccan street, wrapped from head to foot in white cotton, throwing to a stranger a single spark from fathomless eyes' (46). Here again the veiled Oriental woman seems to stand as a (male) fantasy of ever-elusive Woman: 'Was she the very woman one had been seeking? There was a compulsion to follow her' (46).[66] Similarly, 'the Arabs' represent evasiveness and mystery, providing a (symbolic) racial origin for Sabina:

> Sabina remembered reading that the Arabs did not respect the man who unveiled his thoughts. The intelligence of an Arab was measured by his capacity to elude direct questions. The questioner was always suspect. Sabina was of that race. Did she truly originate thousands of years ago from the people who veiled their faces and their thoughts? Where did she come from that she understood so well this racial dedication to mystery? (47)

(In *The Four-Chambered Heart*, however, Nin refers to Sabina's 'Semitic labyrinthian mind'; she walks 'with the poise of Biblical water carriers' (162). The Orientalist stereotyping is inherently vague: any 'eastern' race will do, it seems, to suggest veils, labyrinths, and mysteries.)

Sabina's easternness, though, is always figurative: her veils are linguistic rather than material. From her first major appearance in *Ladders to Fire*, through her subsequent appearances in *A Spy in the House of Love*, briefly in *Seduction of the Minotaur*, and finally in the 1961 story, Sabina is characterized through her *speech*, the endless stories she tells, or half-tells. Sabina talks 'profusely and continuously', but her stories are

[66] In *Mrs Dalloway* Virginia Woolf puts a strikingly similar fantasy into the mind of Peter Walsh, entertaining himself by following through the London streets an attractive young woman who 'seemed . . . to shed veil after veil, until she became the very woman he had always had in mind' (Virginia Woolf, *Mrs Dalloway* [London: Triad Grafton, 1976 (1925)], 59).

chaotic, unfinished, fragmentary, filled with 'indistinct incidents', 'hazy scenes' in which it is impossible to distinguish places and persons:

> A broken dream, with spaces, reversals, contradictions, galloping fantasies and sudden retractions. She would say: 'he lifted my skirt', or 'we had to take care of the wounds', or 'the policeman was waiting for me and I had to swallow the drug to save my friends', and then as if she had written this on a blackboard she took a huge sponge and effaced it all by a phrase which was meant to convey that perhaps this story had happened to someone else, or she may have read it, or heard it at a bar, and as soon as this was erased she began another story . . . (*Ladders*, 92–3; repeated almost verbatim at the beginning of *Spy*, 7–10, and again at the end, 104–9)

Subjects and objects are blurred; persons cannot be distinguished, but merge into each other: 'The faces and the figures of her personages appeared only half drawn, and when one just began to perceive them another face and figure were interposed, as in a dream' (*Ladders*, 93). Above all, it is Sabina herself who is hidden and blurred in these stories: while she appears to be revealing herself and her life history, in fact she is always keeping these pictures of herself out of focus, evading definition.

This emphasis on the epistemic and linguistic dimensions of the *femme fatale*—her status as enigma—is noteworthy because it contrasts with the emphasis on the body and on (excessive or perverse) sexuality which is central to most accounts of the *femme fatale*. For example, Cassandra Laity, in her analysis of H.D.'s use of the figure of the *femme fatale*, puts far more stress on the 'threatening materiality' associated with this figure, using terms such as 'visceral' to describe the 'exploded and explosive female bodies' she finds in H.D.'s work.[67] Certainly, Nin does characterize Sabina in terms of sexuality. In *Ladders to Fire* we are told that Jay (the Henry Miller character) 'hates' her because she is sexually free, 'the woman without fidelity, capable of all desecrations'; because 'he knew instinctively that she regarded him as he regarded woman: as a possible or impossible lover' (*Ladders*, 94, 95). *A Spy in the House of Love* traces Sabina's movement from one lover to another, her attempts to live out this sexual freedom without experiencing a disintegration of self. It is perhaps in the prose poem *House of Incest* that Nin approaches most closely the 'visceral' dimension of the *femme fatale*, with intensely imagistic descriptions of Sabina's deadly beauty and sexual power: 'She stared with

[67] Cassandra Laity, *H.D. and the Victorian Fin de Siècle: Gender, Modernism, Decadence* (Cambridge: Cambridge Univ. Press, 1996), 119, 125. Bram Dijkstra also discusses the association of 'woman' in general with an engulfing materiality: woman is 'lodged in the earth, needing the earth . . . the very personification of instinctive physical greed whose primary natural function [is] to try to catch, engulf and, if possible, absorb the male' (*Idols of Perversity*, 237).

such an ancient stare, heavy luxuriant centuries flickering in deep processions. From her nacreous skin perfumes spiralled like incense. Every gesture she made quickened the rhythm of the blood and aroused a beat chant like the beat of the heart of the desert, a chant which was the sound of her feet treading down into the blood the imprint of her face' (180).

Particularly in the later works, though, it is Sabina's enigmatic speech, her association with deception and 'anti-knowledge', that predominates. It is in her speech that Sabina enacts the dialectic of revealing and concealing that structures both the veil and the striptease; she represents above all a block to knowledge, a point of resistance to orderly structures of thought, Doane's 'potential epistemological trauma'. Doane's analysis of the *femme fatale*, in fact, fits Nin's texts so well precisely because, while both acknowledge the 'imbrication of knowledge and sexuality' in the figure of the fatal woman, both also tend to emphasize the epistemic rather than the sexual dimension.

This imbrication of issues of knowledge and sexuality in the figure of the woman is brought out particularly well in Nin's short story 'Sabina'. Here, once again, Jay is cast as Sabina's opponent, the one who is troubled by her elusiveness and mystery. Jay, with his 'love of facts', hates mystery and indirectness, wants to get to the bottom of everything, to find the reality behind the illusion; he has a 'passion for stripping, unveiling, exposing the truth' ('Sabina', 48). Paradoxically, and inevitably, just this hatred of mystery draws him to Sabina, the feminine mystery *par excellence*: 'They were drawn together by his need to expose illusion, her need to create it. A satanic pact. One must triumph: the realist or the mythmaker' (52). Once again, the woman becomes the site of a battle over knowledge: 'from the first day [Jay] was trapped by what he believed to be a duel between reality and illusion' (47).

The sexual dimension in this battle is implicit from the beginning of Nin's story, with the language of 'stripping' and 'unveiling' and the characterization of Jay as having 'the primitive urge of the invader' (47). But it is rendered explicit later in the text in an exchange between Jay and his confidante Djuna:

> 'I want the key, the key, the key to the lies. I thought that with passion I could break her open, break her elusiveness, find a naked woman who would give all of herself.'
>
> 'You make it sound like rape . . .' (58–9)

Here Jay's desire to break Sabina open epistemically, to find the 'truth' behind her mysteries, is figured as a sexual desire to 'break her open', to reveal her nakedness. The epistemic trauma Sabina represents for him, the 'trauma' of withheld or inaccessible (or possibly non-existent) truth, is also the 'trauma' of inaccessible sexuality, the frustration of the (male) spectator of the striptease artist: 'Her symbolic resistance to nakedness of thought and feeling became associated in his mind with the image of the strip tease, women exposing gradually areas of their bodies and vanishing when they were about to be seen completely' (52). What is noteworthy here is that the epistemic 'trauma'—the mystery—is the *primary* concern; what Jay wants *above all* is 'the key to the lies'.

In several places in this text, Nin seems clearly to valorize the 'feminine mystique' of Sabina, setting it against and denigrating a masculine directness and drive for knowledge. Jay is presented as clumsy and even violent in his attempts to 'penetrate' Sabina's mysteries; he represents a limited, one-dimensional masculine perspective which fails in the face of Sabina's elusiveness: 'He had believed only in what he saw, in one dimension, like a candid photographer, and he now found himself inside rows of mirrors with endless reflections and counter reflections' (46). Jay appears as a failed analyst, not subtle enough to understand Sabina's indirect discourse: 'Jay suspected that much was being hidden from him; it was hidden not by Sabina, but by his own purely external vision. Among the chaotic confessions, the rambling talks, the flow of fiction, he had not been able to detect the revelatory ones. Sabina escaped direct questions, but offered other clues' (51). Sabina's fluidity is set against Jay's crude and constraining drive for knowledge: 'Jay often attacked her, denigrated, disparaged. He wanted to fix her dispersed attention, to contain her chaos and her fluidity. He hated the multiple changes and transformations which were like so many unknown, foreign Sabinas to be pursued, tracked down, possessed. A distracting harem' (55).

This value-laden opposition might suggest a clear identification, on Nin's part, with the figure of feminine mystery over against the masculine drive for knowledge. And yet, as we have seen, Nin's identifications around this issue are more complex. In the *Journals* text she admits her own ambivalent response to June's evasions and mysteries, her identification with Henry's desire to 'expose' the truth—or, perhaps, to expose the fact that there is no 'truth' because, behind the veils and smokescreens, there is nothing 'there'.

In her story 'Sabina', Nin worries away at the question: *why* does the *femme fatale* present these mysteries and evasions? Once again it is Djuna who puts her finger on this as the important issue, while Jay searches blindly for the answer to the riddle of Sabina: 'He did not ask the correct question of the Sphinx. He did not say to Sabina what Djuna said to her later: "I am not concerned with the secrets, or the lies, or the mysteries. I am concerned with *what made them necessary*" ' (53). Nin suggests various possible answers to this question. In the statement at the beginning of the story that 'Sabina had chosen the labyrinth for safety', there is a clear implication that Sabina's elusiveness is a *defence*—against the dangers of definition, as I have already suggested; against the 'judgment' she fears from Jay (47) or from others; against 'distortion' ('She feared to see a distorted image of herself in him' (49)). This interpretation of elusiveness as defence is also found in *A Spy in the House of Love*, in a passage which reveals once again the imbrication of the epistemic and the sexual: 'Before he could speak and harm her with words while she lay naked and exposed, while he prepared a judgment, she was preparing her metamorphosis, so that whatever Sabina he struck down she could abandon like a disguise, shedding the self he had seized upon and say: "That was not me" ' (58).

Or again, Sabina's elusiveness is perhaps a feminine tactic, the deliberate creation of mystery in order to maintain a hold over the man: 'Sabina created mysteries as a natural flowering of her femininity. How else to hold his interest for a thousand nights?' (52). Here there is a clear allusion to Scheherezade, who told stories to save her life, and the lives of other women, from the despotic sultan. But it is Sabina's overwhelming need for reassurance in her own powers, her need to be loved (50), that drives her myth-making. The paradox here, then, is that if she creates mysteries as a 'natural flowering of her femininity', this femininity seems not to be 'natural' in the sense of any kind of independent drive or essence, but merely to revolve around the figure of the man. And Nin does in fact suggest that Sabina has no 'nature' of her own: 'No passion or desire springing from independent desires of her own, but from the desire to be loved' (50–1). A passage in *Children of the Albatross* makes the point more strongly: '[Sabina] eluded tabulations only to place herself more completely at the disposal of anyone's fantasy about her. She kept herself free of all identifications the better to obey some stranger's invention about her' (124).

There is, then, another side to the *femme fatale* in Nin's writing: she begins to appear not as the all-powerful, unfettered woman, but as a far more passive and dependent creature. Doane suggests that the *femme fatale* blurs the distinction between active and passive; she is 'an ambivalent figure because she is not the subject of power but its *carrier*'.[68] I would argue that it is precisely this ambivalence that Nin reads in the fig-

[68] *Femmes Fatales*, 2.

ure of the *femme fatale*, and which is particularly central to her portrait of June in the *Journals*. This issue of power is strongly bound up, for Nin, with questions of authorship and with the importance, as Diane Richard-Allerdyce puts it, of being 'capable of drawing one's own self-portrait'.[69]

June appears in the *Journals* as a powerful and fascinating figure; at the same time, Nin sees her as lacking power or control: 'She seemed at once destructive and helpless' (*Journals*, I, 33). Nin sees June as acting unconsciously, unable to direct her own power: 'If there is any calculation in her whose destiny is beyond her control, it comes only afterwards, when she becomes aware of her power and wonders how she can use it. I do not think her power is directed. Even she is baffled by it . . . her destructiveness is unconscious' (34, 39).

Ultimately, however, Nin believes that the power June lacks is the power to control her own representations, to 'draw her own self-portrait'. Although this appears to be exactly what June does—in her endless spinning of tales around herself, she seems constantly to make and remake 'portraits' of herself—Nin comes to believe that June's stories are, in fact, only reflections of what she and Henry want June to be. She suggests that June lacks independent existence; there is no 'core' behind or underneath the play of roles and illusions: 'She lives on reflections of herself in others' eyes . . . There is no June Mansfield. She knows it' (*Henry and June*, 15). The power that June lacks is the power that Nin attributes to herself and to Henry, grounded in their identity as *writers*: 'The same thing which makes Henry indestructible is what makes me indestructible. The core of us is an artist, a writer' (*Journals*, I, 76). June is 'the powerful, fictionalized character' (48); that is, she is powerful for Nin because Nin constructs her as the figure of her fantasy, the *femme fatale*. On this view, it is the writers, the ones giving out the roles and drawing the portraits, who really have the power. June is endlessly written and rewritten by both Miller and Nin, but she herself remains a beautiful 'empty box' with 'no ideas, no fantasies of her own' (55–6). Whereas, Nin thinks, she and Henry are 'indestructible', June is vulnerable; in fact, Henry has 'killed' her in his writing (141). Nin sees June's sense of self destroyed in the face of Henry's endless writings and rewritings of her: 'Now she stands before the bulk of Henry's writing and cannot tell whether she is a prostitute, a goddess, a criminal, a saint' (151). Nin tells June that she will 'rescue' her from Henry's literary 'ravages', by making a different portrait of her: ' "I will make a great character out of

[69] Richard-Allerdyce, *Remaking of Self*, 13.

you, June, I will make a portrait you will like"' (155). But, of course, this merely underscores June's dependence, and her difference from Henry and Nin: she is scripted, they are the scriptors. Nin goes on: 'Henry cannot impose a pattern on me, because I make my own. And I can make my own portrait too' (155).

In her depiction of this three-way drama, then, Nin attempts to nullify June's seductive power over her (grounded in her own identification with June, her recognition that they are both obsessive self-mythologizers) by invoking the superior power of the author, or rather (as Roland Barthes writes it) 'the Author', figure of authority and control.[70] As Richard-Allerdyce notes, Nin's identification with June, the 'actress every moment', breaks down over this issue of self-authoring: 'The difference between June and her, Nin writes, is that June remains unconscious of the role of self-construction through tale-telling, while Nin herself is self-consciously embracing the role of inventor creator.'[71] Richard-Allerdyce's overall argument is that, for Nin, the 'right to author her own life'[72] took on great importance as part of her lifelong attempt to recover from the emotional and possibly sexual abuse she experienced as a child from her father: 'Creating one's own pattern was an especially important idea for Nin, for on it would depend her ability to mourn her past trauma in fiction and to create herself anew in her own rather than in her father's image.'[73] Certainly, from a very early age Nin identified writing with control; in her diary in 1916, at the age of thirteen, she wrote: 'I am nothing but dust, made to be walked on. Only I am a little bit ambitious, and I who am dust, I want to spread myself on a lot of paper, turn into lots of sentences, lots of words so that I won't be walked on' (25 November 1916 [*Early Diary*, I, 145]).

[70] See Barthes, 'The Death of the Author', *passim.*

[71] Richard-Allerdyce, *Remaking of Self*, 177 n. 42.

[72] Ibid. 50.

[73] Ibid. 28. Noël Riley Fitch's biography of Nin, which came out in 1993, was structured around the plausible but unverifiable hypothesis that Nin was abused as a child by her father. Fitch argued that many of Nin's adult behaviour patterns, notably her promiscuity, her drive for control, and her highly problematic relations with 'father figures', fit the patterns typical of victims of childhood incest. Richard-Allerdyce's study focuses on the effects of trauma in Nin's work and her attempts to overcome this trauma in and through her writing: 'We do not know whether Nin was sexually abused by her father as a child . . . What we do know is that Nin's lifelong writings show the effects of severe traumatization around the issue of the paternal, and she suffered throughout her life from these effects' (*Remaking of Self*, 42). According to the 'unexpurgated' diary volume *Incest*, Nin and her father engaged in a passionate (and consensual) sexual relationship in the summer of 1933. Even if this account represents a fantasy on Nin's part rather than recounting 'real events', it clearly suggests (in tandem with her obsessive returns, both in her life and in her texts, to the 'issue of the paternal') what Richard-Allerdyce describes as a lack of normal boundaries in the father–daughter relationship.

With her invocation of the power of the Author, then, Nin moves from an identification with June to an identification with Henry ('the same thing which makes Henry indestructible is what makes me indestructible'): she arrogates to herself the traditionally masculine position, the position of the artist rather than of the muse.[74] Writing is the way, or the place, in which to regain mastery of one's story, oneself. The irony here, though, is that for Nin writing is also the territory onto which the battle to seduce, to spin veils around oneself, is shifted; the *femme fatale* returns, or, perhaps, was there from the beginning.

'COURTING THE WORLD': WRITING AND SEDUCTION

In a sharply revealing passage in the sixth volume of the *Journals*, dated 'Fall 1957', Nin writes:

> Every act related to my writing was connected in me with an act of charm, seduction of my father. Every act was accompanied by guilt and retraction. Every act was doomed. I was doomed by the enormity of my sin (the wish to charm my father) to be punished, to fail.
>
> Every act from selling a book, accepting a dollar, involving others, was charged with direct sexual associations: courting the world. In my dreams I did not publish *Under a Glass Bell* but I bought a vulgar parrot-green dress, a whorish dress. In my dreams at night I did not achieve a work of art and present the world with it, but I lay naked on a bed (with an invisible lover) and all the world could see me. (*Journals*, VI, 109)

Here Nin admits the extent to which, for her, writing is charged with a thoroughgoing and painful sexualization (focused once again around a guilt-ridden sexual association with her father). The process of writing, producing her story, offering it to the world, is felt as an attempted seduction—or, more strongly, as whoring. But it is also felt as a painful and

[74] Barthes writes: 'The Author is thought to *nourish* the book, which is to say that he exists before it, thinks, suffers, lives for it, is in the same relation of antecedence to his work as a father to his child' ('The Death of the Author', 145). It is difficult to say whether Barthes is here suggesting a critique of the masculinization of 'the Author' or simply reproducing it. (It is worth noting that in the 'moral rights' clause of a publishing contract, the author—male or female—is obliged to assert his or her 'moral right of paternity in the work'.) On the subject of muse and artist, Nin portrays the following exchange between herself and June: '"[Gabriele] D'Annunzio," June said, "was only [Eleonora] Duse's mediocre penman. Even some of his plays were born of Duse and would never have been written if she had not existed." . . . "But," I agreed bitterly, "Duse is dead, and D'Annunzio has done the writing, and he is famous and not Duse."' (*Journals*, I, 43)

humiliating exposure: in putting her texts on view, she puts herself on view as a sexual and shameful spectacle (the 'invisible lover', following so closely on the guilty admission of the previous paragraph, might indeed suggest the 'unspeakable' act of incest or incestuous abuse). We can see in this passage, then, an understanding on Nin's part that the dynamic of seduction—simultaneous movement towards revealing and towards concealing—might be at work in her writing.

Precisely this dynamic, in fact, has been noted, particularly in relation to the edited *Journals*, by several critics and commentators on Nin's work. Julia Casterton, in a 1982 article, focuses on the 'delusion', central to the reading of confessional texts such as diaries, of intimate access to the writer: 'we imagine it is she [Nin] we are reaching through her narratives (as though the narratives themselves were webs, enticing yet distorting vision)'.[75] The image here is implicitly that of veils ('webs'), recalling Doane's analysis: like the veil, the stories Nin spins around herself both provoke the gaze, the desire for knowledge ('enticing'), and frustrate it ('distorting'). Casterton argues that while Nin (as we have seen in Chapter 1) 'emphasizes the immediacy, honesty, accuracy of her confessional skills', she is 'ingenuously denying the artifice of the diary, its *simultaneous secrecy and exposure*'.[76]

Other critics make the point more explicitly. Fitch, in the introduction to her biography, writes that Nin 'hide[s] from her reader behind a million words, enticing, yet camouflaging herself with a labyrinth of mirrors. A literary striptease.'[77] And Nancy Scholar, in a section entitled 'Autobiography as Seduction', argues that Nin's mythic self-construction and 'revelations' in the diaries must be seen as an extended striptease, directed ultimately at the seduction of the father, and more generally at the seduction of all her readers, who may be taken as standing in for the father: 'In exposing her psyche . . . to the reader, Nin performs the same striptease her father demanded of her, only in literary form. From the inception of her journal, in fact, Nin associated writing with charming

[75] Maxine Molyneux and Julia Casterton, 'Looking Again at Anaïs Nin', *Minnesota Review* 18 (1982), 93. This article has a particularly interesting structure: it consists of a transcription of an interview with Nin recorded by Molyneux in 1970, framed by an introduction and commentary by Casterton dating from 1982. Casterton, in the introduction, explicitly sets up the article as both a retrospective, critical examination of the interview text and an attempt to get to grips with Nin's problematic, 'uneasy' status in relation to women's writing and feminist analysis. The article is noteworthy since it is one of very few critical attempts to historicize Nin in this way, and perhaps the only example I have encountered of feminists self-consciously looking back at Nin's place in an earlier feminist context.

[76] 'Looking Again', 94, my emphasis.

[77] Fitch, *Anaïs*, 5.

and seducing, since the diary began as a way of winning back the father's love.'[78] The striptease, the seduction, operates, as we have seen, through revelation and concealment: 'the writer invites and excites her readers with intimate suggestions, and then vanishes behind her mask . . . Nin draws us into the labyrinth of her life-book, leading us on with a seductive wave of her scarf, but the closer we get to her down these winding passageways, the further she seems.'[79] Scholar neatly returns us here to the image of the Orient, the labyrinthine cities of the east which, as we have seen, are used to figure Sabina's elusiveness and mystery, and which Nin associated with her own life: in 'Through the Streets of My Own Labyrinth', she describes 'the ancient city of Fez, which was so much like my own life, with its tortuous streets, its silences, secrecies, its labyrinths and its covered faces' (*Under a Glass Bell*, 71).[80]

The *femme fatale*, then, returns not only as a figure within Nin's texts but also in the *structure* of those texts, especially her diary texts. Like Sabina, like June, Nin is 'impelled by a great confessional fever' (*Ladders*, 93), a desire to tell stories, to create a sense of intimacy, to court and entice; but, again like Sabina, she remains hidden behind her veils, 'throwing to a stranger a single spark from fathomless eyes' ('Sabina', 46). This is why, I would argue, Nin's portrayals of June and Sabina focus so much on story-telling, rather than on the body or sexuality itself, as the sphere of mystery and seduction; why, for Jay in the 1961 story, Sabina's status as a 'sphinx', an epistemic tease, takes priority over—while being clearly bound up with—her status as a prick-tease, a sexual frustration. In her repeated returns to Sabina's 'profuse' talk, her spiralling, indistinct stories, Nin presents an image of her own writing, especially her diary texts. This renders ironic, then, her attempts to invoke the power of the writer over against the *femme fatale*, to set herself, as the author, firmly in control of this teasing figure and reduce it to a fantasy at her disposal. As the passage cited at the beginning of this section acknowledges, and as is suggested by her emphasis on June's and Sabina's 'stories', it is in writing above all that we can see Nin compulsively enacting the seductions and myth-making of the *femme fatale*.

78 Scholar, *Anaïs Nin*, 38.

79 Ibid. 40.

80 Her experience of Fez (on a visit in April 1936) as 'the image of [her] inner self' (*Fire*, 239; see also *Journals*, II, 80) inspired the title and structuring idea of her *roman fleuve*, *Cities of the Interior* (made up of the five novels from *Ladders to Fire* through to *Seduction of the Minotaur*). Taken as a whole, the *Cities* text to some extent repeats the 'labyrinthine' structure, with its narrative loops, repetitions, and lack of closure.

4

'Revolution in Writing': Gender, Modernism, and the Aesthetics of the Ideal Language

One of the most consistent features of the reception of Nin's work—from reviews dating from the 1940s through to feminist critical appraisals of the 1980s and 1990s—has been a focus on the interrelations of artistic creativity and gender; more specifically, of creativity and femininity. Edmund Wilson, reviewing *Under a Glass Bell* in the *New Yorker* in 1944, described Nin's stories as taking place in 'a special world, a world of feminine perception and fancy'.[1] Lawrence Durrell, in his 1958 Preface to *Children of the Albatross*, wrote: 'I have always thought of [Nin] as belonging to the great subjective-feminine tradition (Virginia Woolf, Djuna Barnes, Anna Kavan) which has tried to give us a poetic notation of the female artist's world'.[2] More broadly, critical considerations of Nin in relation to gender and art look in two directions: backwards, to the slightly earlier context of modernist women writers such as Woolf and Richardson and their attempts to formulate a new 'feminine' aesthetic; and forwards, to the predominantly French feminist theory of the 1970s which focused on the idea of a feminine language, an *écriture féminine*. Nin—whose writing career stretched from the Paris of the late 1920s and 1930s to the America of the 1970s—is thus interestingly positioned in relation to the history of the debate around gender and artistic creativity, or more particularly gender and *language*.

We can see in the above quotation from Lawrence Durrell the linking of Nin back to Woolf; Wilson also makes this connection in his review, stating that Nin's stories 'belong to a peculiar genre sometimes cultivated

[1] Edmund Wilson, review of *Under a Glass Bell*, *New Yorker*, 1 April 1944; reprinted in Robert Zaller (ed.), *A Casebook on Anaïs Nin* (New York: Meridian, 1974), 3.

[2] Lawrence Durrell, Preface to *Children of the Albatross*, 1958; reprinted in Zaller (ed.), *Casebook*, 2.

by the late Virginia Woolf'.[3] In a 1989 article, Sharon Spencer referred to Nin as 'the third woman writing in English . . . to have committed to paper the need for a feminine theory and practice of literature', the first two being Richardson and Woolf.[4] And Ellen Friedman, writing in 1991, made the same comparison: 'Like Dorothy Richardson and Virginia Woolf, Nin felt that the traditional fictional forms could not accommodate a woman's consciousness or the deep structures of her experience'.[5] Looking in the other direction, Nin is seen as a 'forerunner' of French feminist ideas on women and writing, 'presaging' or 'anticipating' these ideas. So, for instance, Spencer states that Nin's feminine writing 'preceded by 40 years the theories of contemporary French writers such as Annie Leclerc and Hélène Cixous';[6] Ellen Friedman suggests that '[Nin's] description of womb writing anticipates the language of those current feminists who call on women to "write the female body" ';[7] and Margret Andersen writes that 'a comparison of Nin's statements on woman's writings with those of Annie Leclerc shows Nin as a forerunner of modern French thought on this subject'.[8]

We can see that, in fact, the French feminist work on language and sexual difference, to the extent that it was made available in English and appropriated by Anglophone feminist critics,[9] provided a new way for the latter to 'think back' through a twentieth-century 'tradition' of experimental women writers, focusing on the link between the drive—central to the modernist project—towards radical, ground-breaking aesthetic forms, and the attempt to inscribe 'the feminine' into language and culture, from which it is thought to have been repressed.

[3] Wilson, review, 3.

[4] Sharon Spencer, 'The Music of the Womb: Anaïs Nin's "Feminine" Writing', in Ellen G. Friedman and Miriam Fuchs (eds.), *Breaking the Sequence: Women's Experimental Fiction* (Princeton: Princeton Univ. Press, 1989), 165.

[5] Ellen G. Friedman, 'Anaïs Nin', in Lea Baechler, A. Walton Litz, and Elaine Showalter (eds.), *Modern American Women Writers* (New York: Charles Scribner's Sons, 1991), 347.

[6] Spencer, 'The Music of the Womb', 171.

[7] Friedman, 'Anaïs Nin', 347.

[8] Margret Andersen, 'Critical Approaches to Anaïs Nin', *Canadian Review of American Studies* 10/2 (1979), 263.

[9] The key event here was the publication in 1980 of the anthology *New French Feminisms*, edited by Elaine Marks and Isabelle de Courtivron (Hemel Hempstead: Harvester Wheatsheaf); most of the anthologized texts dated from the mid- to late 1970s (for instance, Luce Irigaray's *Speculum: de l'autre femme* [1974], Hélène Cixous and Catherine Clément's *La jeune née* [1975] and Irigaray's *Ce sexe qui n'en est pas un* [1977]). It is also important to be aware that, like any cross-cultural appropriation, this was a selective appropriation, producing for Anglophone feminists a 'canon' of texts (including those cited above) that have come to represent 'French feminism'.

This is particularly clear, for instance, in the preface and introduction to Ellen Friedman and Miriam Fuchs' 1989 collection *Breaking the Sequence*, a book whose avowed task is 'to introduce and explore the rich tradition of women's experimental fiction in [the twentieth] century'.[10] To the extent that they see their project as 'archaeological and compensatory', part of 'the recovery and foregrounding of women writers',[11] Friedman and Fuchs' approach is firmly in line with what had always been the central methodology of Anglo-American feminist literary criticism. But the influence of French criticism can be clearly seen in their claim that 'in the case of twentieth-century experimental writers, the woman in the text is also an effect of the textual practice of breaking patriarchal fictional forms; the radical forms—nonlinear, nonhierarchical, and decentering—are, in themselves, a way of writing the feminine'.[12] Here we can see the way in which Friedman and Fuchs seek to combine the French theoretical focus on *écriture féminine*, the inscription of the feminine through radical linguistic forms, with the Anglo-American project of 'excavating' muted traditions of women writers.

Arguing that French feminists, despite theorizing a 'feminine literature', have exemplified this with reference to the work of *male* modernist writers, while male theorists of modernism have created a canon of male experimental writers and devalued or ignored women writers who attempted similar things in their work, Friedman and Fuchs seek to establish the tradition of women's experimental writing as the 'missing link' between modernism and feminism. This is also a strongly politicized link, operating through the equation of formal radicalism with socio-political radicalism, a refusal of hegemonic structures: 'experimental literature and feminism share not only a profound quarrel with established, patriarchal forms, but also a sense of identification with what has been muted by these forms'.[13] Turning this around, 'what has been muted' by patriarchal forms (both literary and socio-cultural) can be identified as 'the feminine':

In exploding dominant forms, women experimental writers not only assail the social structure, but also produce an alternate fictional space, a space in which the feminine, marginalized in traditional fiction and patriarchal culture, can be expressed. Thus, the rupturing of traditional forms becomes a political act, and the feminine narrative resulting from such rupture is allied with the feminist project.[14]

[10] Friedman and Fuchs (eds.), *Breaking the Sequence*, xi. [11] Ibid.
[12] Ibid. 3. [13] Ibid., p. xii. [14] Ibid. 4.

In the same year that Friedman and Fuchs' book came out, 1989, Rita Felski's *Beyond Feminist Aesthetics* was published, containing a robust attack on the idea of 'feminine' writing. Felski argued against both the notion of formally experimental writing as inherently politically radical or 'subversive', and the classification of such writing (or of any other style of writing) as 'feminine', or feminist, per se. Against what she saw as these sweeping claims, Felski argued for a thoroughgoing process of *recontextualization* of texts and their authors. This would apply to the politicizing of texts or writing practices, whether authored by women or men: the political value of a text or a style of writing (its status as 'subversive' or 'conservative') must be seen in the context of its specific historical-cultural location and the conditions of its production and reception. It would also apply to the gendering of texts or writing practices. If we are interested in exploring the issue of women's writing as 'feminine' or 'feminist'—the interplay of politics, aesthetics, and gender—we should, Felski argued, recontextualize this writing by 'relating the diverse forms of women's writing to the cultural and ideological processes shaping the effects and potential limits of literary production at historically specific contexts'.[15] Following Felski, Lisa Rado (in her introduction to the 1994 collection *Rereading Modernism*) formulated the goal for feminist criticism as a focus on 'the relationship between gender and poetic production for a given author at a given historical moment'.[16]

Felski's call for recontextualization is an important corrective to the over-generalized equation of 'experimental', 'radical', and 'feminine' writing, just as Rado's call to focus on specific authors is a useful corrective to the poststructuralist tendency to do away altogether with 'the author' as the producer of a text, reducing subjectivity entirely to the play of language *within* the text (though it is equally important to avoid the opposite extreme of reducing the text to a simple expression of an omnipotent authorial self). What Felski does not focus on, however, is the belief in the radical potential of experimental writing, and the self-conscious drive towards the creation of a 'feminine' writing practice, as *themselves* open to recontextualization and historicizing. The former (what Peter Nicholls calls the 'translation of politics into style'[17]) can be seen as the central credo of modernism; the latter can be ascribed, in different ways, to many twentieth-century women writers, arguably including Richardson, Woolf, and Nin.

[15] *Beyond Feminist Aesthetics*, 28. [16] Rado (ed.), *Rereading Modernism*, 12.
[17] Peter Nicholls, *Modernisms: A Literary Guide* (London: Macmillan, 1995), p. vii.

Rather than dismissing the intertwined issues of a 'feminine' writing practice and the self-conscious modernist drive for 'radical' new aesthetic forms, grounded in the perceived link between politics and aesthetics, we should apply Felski's call for contextualization precisely to these issues and their historical interrelations. In this chapter, I shall attempt to trace these intertwined concerns through the work of Nin, examining her various formulations of an 'ideal' language or aesthetic practice. I shall look firstly at her aesthetics in the context of her self-conscious modernism, relating her ideas on a 'new' language and the synthesis of artistic forms to those of other contemporary writers and avant-gardes. In the second part of the chapter I shall go on to consider her ideas in relation to issues of gender and aesthetics, specifically questions around female creativity and *écriture féminine.* I shall try in particular to demonstrate the *shifts* in Nin's ideas across different times and different contexts, the tensions as well as the links among her ideas about femininity, creativity, and radical art.

I. MODERNISM AND A 'NEW LANGUAGE'

Starting points: Lawrence and *transition*

When she was editing her diaries for publication in the 1960s, Nin chose to begin with 1931, seeing this as the formative moment of her career as a writer: Henry Miller became both her lover and her literary mentor/rival, and her book on D. H. Lawrence was accepted for publication. However, it was in 1930 that she made what were to be her crucial literary discoveries. During the period spanned by what was eventually published as the fourth volume of the *Early Diary* (1927–31), Nin had been trying to formulate her literary aims and desperately seeking a context in which to situate herself as a writer.[18] In November 1929, she set down in the diary

[18] Despite having been in Paris since the end of 1924, Nin was relatively isolated from the artistic and literary scene. As Shari Benstock suggests in *Women of the Left Bank*, the networks of women artists, writers, and sponsors tended to form around predominantly lesbian circles; heterosexual women in partnerships with men tended to be less independent of conventional societal structures (see Benstock's Preface, p. x). This was certainly true of Nin as the young and attractive wife of an up-and-coming banker: in her early diaries (prior to her relationship with Henry Miller) she frequently reports her frustration at having to play the role of charming hostess to her husband's business clients, and the constraints on her activities because of her social position. Further, Nin was somewhat younger than many of the writers and artists based in Paris at the time; in 1927 she was only just beginning to write stories and experiment with different styles.

her literary ambition: 'to write clearly of impenetrable, nameless, and usually indescribable things; to give form to evanescent, subtle and fluid thoughts' (*Early Diary*, IV, 231). A month later, on Christmas Eve, she describes her first encounter with 'a strange and wonderful book', D. H. Lawrence's *Women in Love*, which she sees as 'concerned only with the description of feelings, sensations, conscious and unconscious'. To achieve this, she writes, Lawrence 'had to torment and transform ordinary language; words are twisted and mishandled, sometimes beyond recognition'. The result is both extraordinarily powerful and radically perceptive: 'he has an occult power over human life and sees deeper than almost anyone I know' (*Early Diary*, IV, 267).

This literary encounter was to be of vital importance for Nin in relation to her sense of what she was trying to do in writing and her attempt to situate herself in a wider context.[19] Four months later, in April 1930, she writes: 'Lawrence has . . . given me a world to live in, a world where I fit. Over and over again, in his descriptions of women I find myself. In his treatment of language, in the poetic intensity of his prose, I find courage for my own writing. I find, at last, a kind of home' (*Early Diary*, IV, 294). In the same month, Nin began to plan her own study of Lawrence's writing. She sent the essay to her agent in June, and in August it was accepted for publication by the magazine *Canadian Forum* (*Early Diary*, IV, 326). The article appeared in the magazine, under the pen name 'Melisendra', in October 1930 (353). In January 1931, after rashly telling Paris-based editor Edward Titus that she had written a book on Lawrence, which he immediately asked to see, she would spend a frantic two weeks expanding the article into the book that appeared in 1932 as *D. H. Lawrence: An Unprofessional Study*, her first major published work.

In the same month that her article appeared, October 1930, Nin records for the first time 'devouring' the magazine *transition* (353); and this was to be of equal importance to her, the complement to her discovery of Lawrence. Reading *transition* revealed to Nin the wider literary context she had been seeking, expanded the 'world' Lawrence had given her. This world even had a name: *modernism*. On 24 November 1930, Nin wrote: 'Reading the last number of *transition* has been tremendous for

[19] In *The Novel of the Future*, Nin wrote: 'Defending and explaining D. H. Lawrence then gave me my own orientation. I was planning my course' (117). This point is made both by Hinz and by Richard-Allerdyce, who suggests that 'Nin's use of Lawrence was more an anticipation of her own later novels' characterizations and themes than it was a study of Lawrence's use of the unconscious' (*Remaking of Self*, 22; see also Hinz, *The Mirror and the Garden*, 15–32).

me. I read all these things after I have done my work and then find an affinity with modernism which elates me' (*Early Diary*, IV, 358). While joyfully embracing this affinity, however, Nin was keen to maintain her sense that this was based on a shared vision; being 'modernist' was *not* a matter of following a trend: 'If now I am more conscious of my modernism, at least my work remains *natural*, because modernism came to me through vision and is not . . . an acquired tendency' (358).[20] At the end of the year, she summed up the vital significance of her twin discoveries for her ambitions as a writer and her sense of her own place in relation to the wider literary world:

> The tremendous, immeasurable importance of *transition* for me. This was the island I had been steadily sailing to—dreaming of—but I was not so very certain of its existence. I thought I would have to build it up alone. No. Here is my group, my ideas, my feelings against banal forms . . . Now I read Jung, Jolas, like a famished man; here are the minds I love, here are the ideas I have obscurely, vaguely felt. I know now what my instincts were leading me into . . . Here at last is depth as I understand it, vision and intellect working in unity. Lawrence and *transition*. What a year for me! (26 December 1930 [*Early Diary*, IV, 370–1])

The ideas to which *transition* was dedicated were, indeed, the very ideas Nin was feeling her way towards, those that would remain central to her work and her aesthetic credo: the magazine was a perfect 'home' for her. Published in Paris from 1927 to 1930, and in The Hague from 1932 to 1938, *transition* was founded and edited by Eugène Jolas, former literary editor on the Paris edition of the *Chicago Tribune*. Although Nin would not meet Jolas until the late 1930s, she felt an affinity with him from the start because of his multilingualism. Born in the US, Jolas had grown up in Lorraine with a French father and German mother; caught, like Nin, between languages, he called his unpublished autobiography 'Man from Babel'.[21] The shifting editorial group at *transition*, mainly American expatriates, included Jolas's wife Maria, *Tribune* journalists Elliot Paul and Robert Sage, Kay Boyle, Harry Crosby, and Stuart Gilbert, a friend of James Joyce and closely involved with the publication of his

[20] See also the following exchange in *A Woman Speaks*, 200: 'Q.: "I would like to hear you discuss some of the more practical aspects of plotting, planning and structuring novels, the process you go through." A.N.: "I always answer that by saying that I was *born modern*." '

[21] Noël Riley Fitch, 'Introduction', in *In transition: A Paris Anthology: Writing and Art from* transition *Magazine 1927–30* (London: Secker & Warburg, 1990), 12. Deirdre Bair puts a rather negative gloss on this point, suggesting that Nin's enthusiasm for Jolas lay in the fact that he, like her, 'was frequently accused of garbling all three of his languages' and of publishing 'only submissions from writers who did the same' (*Anaïs Nin*, 96).

work in Paris. Despite her enthusiasm for *transition*, Nin was only peripherally connected with this group (although later, back in the US after the outbreak of war, she did become friends with both Kay Boyle and Harry Crosby's widow Caresse); her closest contact among them was Stuart Gilbert, who wrote a Foreword for *House of Incest*[22] and also read some of the diaries Nin was attempting to find a publisher for. Nin shared her discovery of *transition* with Henry Miller; both of them would eventually publish fragments of their work in the magazine.[23]

Best known for publishing eighteen instalments of Joyce's 'Work in Progress', sections of what was to become *Finnegans Wake*, *transition* also published a wide variety of experimental prose, poetry, and visual art, as well as manifestos and critical pieces, including an article by Jung entitled 'Psychology and Poetry'. The magazine was revolutionary and polemical in tone, with an explicit aesthetic agenda: '*transition* saw it as its task to declare war on traditional literature and herald the source of creation in the irrational, unconscious world of dreams, calling for a new language to express that creation'.[24]

This preoccupation with style and form as ideologically significant, and the concomitant obsession with manifestos and self-conscious aesthetic theorizing, can be seen to lie at the heart of the modernist and avant-garde agenda, from the Symbolists onwards. Peter Nicholls traces this back to the corruption and commercialism of the Second Empire and the response to it by Baudelaire's artistic generation: as political institutions and 'bourgeois society' as a whole began to be seen, by artists and intellectuals, as degraded, corrupt, and 'philistine', so the sphere of art became correspondingly valorized, jealously held apart from the sociopolitical realm of the bourgeoisie. Aesthetics replaced politics as the terrain of radicalism: 'the ground of opposition', Nicholls argues, 'shifted from political rhetoric and polemic to literary "style"'.[25] With this shift came a new consciousness of language as a *medium*; a consciousness that Raymond Williams explains in the context of the new importance, in the late nineteenth century, of the metropolis and the new forms of experience and perception engendered by metropolitan life. Immigration to the city, away from traditional (geographical and cultural) communities and structures, created an experience of distancing and defamiliarization, resulting, Williams argues, in a quite particular experience of and

[22] Reprinted in Zaller (ed.), *Casebook*, 1.

[23] A five-page fragment of Nin's *House of Incest*, and Miller's 'The Cosmological Eye', appeared in issue 27, April–May 1938.

[24] Fitch, 'Introduction', *In transition*, 13.

[25] Nicholls, *Modernisms*, 11.

attitude towards language: 'Thus language was perceived quite differently. It was no longer, in the old sense, customary and naturalized, but in many ways arbitrary and conventional. To the immigrants especially, with their new second common language, language was more evident as a medium—a medium that could be shaped and reshaped—than as a social custom.'[26] Language becomes a malleable medium, something that may be worked with, like clay or paint, rather than simply being the invisible, because customary and familiar, means of everyday communication. Here we can see the origins of the self-conscious drive (so central, in various guises, to the Symbolists and to the later modernists and avant-gardes) towards a form or usage of language that makes a radical break with the 'everyday' language, seen as corrupted or deadened by its instrumental functions within a degenerate, commercialized culture.

In the 'Proclamation' published in the June 1929 issue of *transition* (signed by, among others, Kay Boyle, Harry and Caresse Crosby, and Stuart Gilbert), the editorial group declared themselves 'tired of the spectacle of short stories, novels, poems and plays still under the hegemony of the banal word, monotonous syntax, static psychology, descriptive naturalism'. There followed a twelve-point 'declaration', beginning with the claim that 'the revolution in the English language is an accomplished fact', and going on to assert the right of the 'literary creator' to experiment and take liberties with language in order to achieve this new form of expression (much as Nin had noted Lawrence's 'tormenting', 'twisting', and 'mishandling' of 'ordinary language'): 'The imagination in search of a fabulous world is autonomous and unconfined . . . The literary creator has the right to disintegrate the primal matter of words imposed on him by text-books and dictionaries . . . He has the right to use words of his own fashioning and to disregard existing grammatical and syntactical laws.' Citing Rimbaud, the Proclamation declares that its aims for language 'can be achieved only through the rhythmic "hallucination of the word" '.[27]

An earlier manifesto published in the third issue of *transition*, June 1927, is particularly resonant in relation to Nin's own formulations. Entitled 'Suggestions for a New Magic', the piece pinpoints American literary realism as the aesthetic enemy: 'Realism in America has reached its point of saturation. We are no longer interested in the photography of

[26] Raymond Williams, 'Metropolitan Perceptions and the Emergence of Modernism', in *The Politics of Modernism: Against the New Conformists* (ed. Tony Pinkney; London: Verso, 1989), 46.

[27] 'Proclamation', June 1929; *In transition*, 19.

events, in the mere silhouetting of facts, in the presentation of misery, in the anecdotic boredom of verse.'[28] In search of 'a new magic' in language, writers need 'new words, new abstractions, new hieroglyphics, new symbols, new myths'.[29] In its coupling of the insistent 'new' with seemingly archaic forms—hieroglyphics, symbols, myths—this passage points up both the editors' interesting attitude towards their own modernity, and the crucial sources of the language they are seeking. *transition*, they state, 'will attempt to present the quintessence of the modern spirit in evolution', will attempt to express the experience of living in 'this chaotic age'.[30] Yet, they suggest, the deepest revelation of this modern experience, the 'modern spirit', will come not through a superficial modernism, 'literature that wilfully attempts to be of the age', but through 'a perception of eternal values', contact with a deeper source of experience: 'we prefer to skyscraper spirituality, the immense lyricism and madness of illogic'.[31] The crucial point is the *source* of the writing:

> We are not interested in literature that wilfully attempts to be of the age. Unless there be a perception of eternal values, there can be no new magic. The point of departure is unimportant. The poet may use the rhythm of his age, if he be so inclined, and thus tell us, with accelerated intensity, the Arabian Nights' adventures of his brain. But let him not forget that *only the dream is essential*.[32]

This passage coincides strikingly with Nin's own formulations of the 'revolution in writing'. In *The Novel of the Future*, she suggests that, with the separation of poetry and prose, and the separation of conscious and unconscious, 'writing lost its magical power' (165). The task is to reinvest language with this power, to create the 'new magic'. The way to achieve this, for Nin, is through the reintegration of poetry and prose, conscious and unconscious; above all, that is, through the reinstatement of 'the realm of the dream' (*Novel*, 12). This does not lead to isolation, a private language of neurosis, but rather to Jolas's new-old language of symbols: 'The dream then, instead of being something apart from reality, a private world of fantasy or imagination, is actually an essential part of our reality which can be shared and communicated by imagery' (*Novel*, 23).

[28] 'Suggestions for a New Magic', June 1927; *In transition*, 23.
[29] 'Suggestions for a New Magic', 23–4. [30] Ibid. 23, 24. [31] Ibid. 23.
[32] Ibid., my emphasis.

The dream realm

Nin recognized the importance of the 'dream realm' to the 'revolution in the English language' declared by *transition*. In April 1931, having recently begun to study the work of Jung, she wrote: 'Jung defines the nondirected thinking of our epoch: "We no longer compel our thoughts along a definite track, but let them float, sink and mount according to their own gravity." It seems to me that this is how the moderns have approached the dream realm. It is the basis of Proust, Joyce, and Jolas's efforts in *transition*' (*Early Diary*, IV, 418). She refers frequently to her own efforts in this direction, the problem of finding a language adequate to conveying the subtleties of dreams: 'there remains only to be written the revelation of the deeper dreams, which slip out, always, between over-definite words' (20 April 1931 [*Early Diary*, IV, 420]). Later, by the time she was working on what became *House of Incest*, and involved in a literary (as well as sexual) partnership with Henry Miller, she had become more confident: 'Talking on the dream, I am always fertile and voluble. It is my favourite realm, and I am so familiar with its technical aspects' (October 1933 [*Journals*, I, 277]); 'the dream realm is becoming my speciality' (February 1934 [322]).

Both the reference to Jung and the mention of the 'technical aspects' of dreams point towards the crucial role of psychoanalysis in the context of this focus on dreams. Here Nin found a central point of convergence with the Surrealists; as she was later to write in *The Novel of the Future*, 'André Breton was one of the first literary writers to accept Freud as one of the great forces in helping man rediscover the meaning and vitality of words and in giving importance to dreams and the subconscious' (15). In the first 'Manifesto of Surrealism', published in 1924, Breton specifically acknowledged the pioneering importance of Freud's work on the dream: 'Freud very rightly brought his critical faculties to bear upon the dream. It is, in fact, inadmissable that this considerable portion of psychic activity . . . has still today been so grossly neglected.'[33] Freud, Breton argued, was helping to bring about a new resurgence of the dream realm, the realm of imagination and 'the marvellous':

> Under the pretense of civilization and progress, we have managed to banish from the mind everything that may rightly or wrongly be termed superstition, or fancy . . . a part of our mental world which we pretended not to be concerned with any

[33] André Breton, 'Manifesto of Surrealism' [1924], in *Manifestoes of Surrealism* (Ann Arbor: Univ. of Michigan Press, 1969), 10–11.

longer—and in my opinion by far the most important part—has been brought back to light. For this we must give thanks to the discoveries of Sigmund Freud . . . The imagination is perhaps on the point of reasserting itself, of reclaiming its rights.[34]

Although Breton prioritizes the neglected realm of the unconscious (even suggesting that we might see the *waking* state as a 'phenomenon of interference'[35]), his emphasis is on the *synthesis*, the connecting, of the two realms, as is clear from his definition of 'surreality' and statement of his literary credo: 'I believe in the future resolution of these two states, dream and reality, which are seemingly so contradictory, into a kind of absolute reality, a *surreality*, if one may so speak. It is in quest of this surreality that I am going.'[36]

This emphasis on the connection of the two realms is shared by Nin, especially in *The Novel of the Future*. We may see, in fact, a gradual shift of emphasis, from the early focus on the dream realm in itself ('the dream realm is becoming my speciality') to the focus on the artist's task of bridging, even 'fusing', conscious and unconscious, 'physical reality' and 'psychological reality': 'What the psychoanalysts stress, the relation between dream and our conscious acts, is what the poets already know. The poets walk this bridge with ease, from conscious to unconscious, physical reality to psychological reality. Their profession is to fuse them so that they may function harmoniously.'[37] Hence the importance, for Nin, of the phrase which she takes from Jung and which she uses as the title of the first chapter of *The Novel of the Future*: 'proceed from the dream outward'.[38]

[34] Ibid. 10.

[35] Ibid. 12.

[36] Ibid. 14.

[37] *Novel*, 5. It is noteworthy that whereas Nin in her earlier writings tends, like Breton in the above quotation, to reserve the term 'reality' for the 'outer', physical sphere, or for the realm of conscious thought, she later comes to see the distinction between 'reality and the dream' in terms of different forms or levels of 'reality' (hence the statement cited above, that the dream is 'an essential part of our reality').

[38] Evelyn Hinz also uses a shortened form of this phrase ('Proceed from the Dream') as the title of Chapter V of *A Woman Speaks*, in which she collects Nin's lecture and seminar discussions of the dream. Here there is a particular focus on the role of the dream as an instigating wish or image which serves as a guide for the creation of a life or a particular experience (Nin gives the example of her dream of a boat leading to her life on the houseboat [119])—hence, the movement from the dream 'outward'. Nin does also stress the equally important role of the dream as instigator or governing image for writing: 'So the dream can be the beginning of a poem, it can be the beginning of a novel, it can be the beginning of a plot, a search' (122). It is worth noting here that many critics have understood Nin's fiction-writing career as a whole to follow the pattern suggested by this key phrase, 'proceed from the dream outward', moving from the intensity and hermeticism of *House of Incest*, to the dream-imagery of *Under a Glass Bell*, to the novels with their

Evelyn Hinz, in *The Mirror and the Garden*, understands Nin's new critical emphasis on the interconnection of conscious and unconscious as a deliberate corrective to her earlier stress on the unconscious alone, and argues in particular that, in *The Novel of the Future*, Nin puts more stress on artistic control and method in creating this new synthesizing language.[39] This is important because, while Nin and Breton put equal stress on the dream or the unconscious as the source for writing, their ideal writing practices are in fact quite different. Nin does not advocate, or claim to practise, Breton's 'automatic writing' (though Elisabeth Roudinesco suggests that, in fact, automatic writing was for the Surrealists themselves more important as a 'slogan', 'a kind of residue or effective phantom', than as an actual practice[40]). Rather, her interest is in the writer's ability to bring the dream, and the unconscious, into language 'not by a literal transcription of the unconscious, but by shaping his perceptions through the medium of the symbol'.[41] This relates to Nin's statement, cited above, on the 'technical aspects' of dreams. She takes from Freud's writings on the 'dream-work' the idea that dreams, far from being simply random and unstructured, operate according to certain specific principles: symbolization, condensation, displacement.[42] In a discussion with Miller on dream-writing, for instance, she stresses the need for condensation: 'we agreed [that] there must be a telescoping, a condensation in words. (Psychoanalysis describes the great condensation in dreams)' (*Journals*, I, 317). The language of the dream is above all the language of symbolism; and it is the language of *images* rather than words (*A Woman Speaks*, 120). The task for the 'poetic writer' is to transport the symbolism, the strange patterns of condensation and displacement, and the imagistic quality of dreams into language. Writing should become, in fact, a 'directed dream' (*Novel*, 32)—a term that indicates the need for input from both conscious and unconscious, both a use of the symbolizations and structures of the dream and an overlying artistic control. Nin gives perhaps her best account of this in a question-and-answer session

attempted combination of psychic reality and external reality. Critics are notably divided as to which end of the spectrum they consider more successful. Personally, I would argue that Nin's best writing is contained in *House of Incest* and *Under a Glass Bell*; I agree with Nancy Scholar's assessment (*Anaïs Nin*, 98) that the 'condensed format' of short stories or short prose poems best suited Nin's strengths as a writer.

[39] See Hinz, *The Mirror and the Garden*, 86.

[40] Roudinesco, *Jacques Lacan & Co.*, 25, 26.

[41] Hinz, *The Mirror and the Garden*, 87.

[42] See in particular Chapter VI, 'The Dream-Work', in *Interpretation of Dreams*, in which Freud discusses the specific processes of dream construction.

transcribed in *A Woman Speaks.* She states that 'the two processes are necessary, letting the unconscious flow but then knowing how to select what is significant, important, or meaningful'; she goes on to describe the process of letting the pattern emerge from the unconscious and then editing accordingly: 'when you follow the unconscious, the unconscious forms patterns . . . So when you finish writing a spontaneous poem or a spontaneous novel you see a pattern. It emerges at the end. You don't see it at the beginning but at the end. There it is. So then you can edit with integrity to maintain this pattern, this thing that came through' (201, 202).

Nin's stress on the imagistic quality of the dream-'language' also indicates why she, in common with many other contemporary writers, seized (as I shall go on to show) on the new medium of *film* as supremely fitted for portraying the dream and the interactions of conscious and unconscious.

Although Nin does accurately take over Freud's ideas about the dream-work and the main structuring principles of dreams, her broader notion of the unconscious, as she employs the idea in relation to the ideal artistic practice, is not strictly Freudian. In this Nin may be close to other contemporary writers and artists, again including the Surrealists. Raymond Williams suggests that, with the enthusiastic taking up of psychoanalytic ideas by avant-garde writers and artists, the concept of 'the unconscious' came to function as something of a catch-all, representing among other things the modern version of the very old idea of artistic creation through *inspiration.* We can trace the 'itinerary' of the idea of inspiration, Williams writes, 'from metaphysical notions of literal possession by gods or spirits in the moment of true utterance, through the conventional personifications of inspiring muses of great predecessors, ancestor poets, into the Romantic version of creative access to the new all-purpose personification of Nature, and finally—or is it finally?—to creative access to "the unconscious"'.[43]

What drops out of view here, of course, is Freud's notion of repression, his central idea that unconscious psychic contents *are* 'unconscious' (i.e., not present to conscious awareness) because they are inimical to the ego (mainly because of their sexual content) and have been 'censored' or repressed, only able to present themselves to consciousness in distorted or compromised form. This idea was at the heart of Jung's disagreement with Freud: while Jung (like Rank) saw Freud as overly

[43] 'Language and the Avant-Garde', in *The Politics of Modernism*, 72.

focused on sexuality and its central role in repression and the formation of the unconscious, Freud saw Jung as deliberately trying to eliminate what he prudishly saw as 'objectionable' in psychoanalysis and, especially, as unable to face the 'sexualizing' of religion, ethics, and art. Freud saw these as manifestations of the sublimation of libido, but for Jung, he claimed, they 'had to be something "higher" from the start'.[44] Certainly, Jung emphasized the role, in artistic creation, of the *collective* rather than the *personal* unconscious. While his notion of the 'personal unconscious' is broadly similar to Freud's idea,[45] his notion of the 'collective unconscious' refers to an innate 'potentiality' of primordial images, or archetypes, which are 'the psychic residua of innumerable experiences [i.e. phylogenetically] of the same type'.[46] It is these archetypes, or symbols, that are vital to artistic creation: 'The creative process . . . consists in the unconscious activation of an archetypal image, and in elaborating and shaping this image into the finished work'.[47]

As we have seen, Nin usually cites Freud as the most important pioneer in relation to dreams and the unconscious. Nonetheless, her descriptions of 'the unconscious' and uses of the idea may be seen to have more in common with Jung's, particularly in the emphasis on the unconscious as a rich source of imagery and the concomitant de-emphasis on the 'negative' understanding of the unconscious in terms of psychic conflict.[48] A passage in *A Woman Speaks* shows a strongly Jungian understanding of the unconscious (though Nin here uses the vague term 'psyche') and its role in creativity: 'The psyche is the soul, which, as Jung and other psychologists have pointed out, exists collectively and individually, and is revealed in dreams. That is why we have to learn symbolism—to understand what happens within us. The psyche is a dual sort of current in our lives; it's from there that the richness comes, the whole tie with the universal world, and the whole potential for creation' (124).

We can also see here, I think, the underlying influence of Emerson, who had, as Jeffrey Steele argues, 'readily assimilated the new [nineteenth-century] psychological vocabulary of the "unconscious" to express his

[44] Freud, 'On the History of the Psychoanalytic Movement', 122.

[45] He defines it as 'the sum total of all those psychic processes and contents which are capable of becoming conscious and often do, but are then suppressed because of their incompatibility and kept subliminal'; C. G. Jung, 'On the Relation of Analytical Psychology to Poetry' (1922), in *The Collected Works of C. G. Jung*, XV (London: Routledge & Kegan Paul, 1966), 80.

[46] 'On the Relation of Analytical Psychology to Poetry', 81. [47] Ibid. 82.

[48] See Chapter 2 for my discussion of Nin's de-emphasis of psychic conflict in the context of the women's liberation movement.

awareness of the need for new creation'.[49] This was a creation that (echoing the trajectory of 'inspiration' sketched by Williams) had the forces of 'the psyche', rather than God, at its source. Steele argues, in fact, that we can trace a line of thought from the German Romantics' interest in the 'vital creative force' within the artist, through Emerson, to Jung, with his emphasis on 'individuation' as a process of conscious interpretation of the 'archetypal energies' and symbols projected by the unconscious. This trajectory, I would argue, is an important conceptual background for Nin. More broadly, as Williams suggests, pre-psychoanalytic, Romantic ideas about unconscious creative forces, as well as Freud's writings, inform the modernist concern with a language that finds its sources and structuring principles in 'the unconscious'. While the avant-garde artistic communities were enthusiastic in their appropriation of psychoanalytic ideas, then, they were also notably selective, focusing above all on the unconscious as the source of symbols, images, and patterns, the 'new magic' called for by *transition* and by Nin.

Sensory language and the synthesis of art forms

If Nin found in *transition* and Surrealism the wider context for her early interest in the attempt to bring dreams into language, she found in Lawrence the attempt to bring the *sensory* realm, the realm of the body, into language. As Diane Richard-Allerdyce stresses, Nin's early focus on Lawrence's 'physical' language, 'the "texture" of his writing',[50] was an important foundation for her whole writing career. Her admiration for Lawrence's radical attempt to 'see with the soul and the body' (*D. H. Lawrence*, 1) was also a starting-point for her own attempts to define and practise a poetic prose that 'writes the body'—that brings into language the bodily forces of rhythm, movement, and desire, what Julia Kristeva theorizes as the *semiotic* modality.[51] Relatedly, Nin's analysis of Lawrence's 'synthesis' of different art forms within language connects to the wider modernist preoccupation with such a synthesis of forms and sensory affects.

Nin argued in her 'unprofessional study' of Lawrence's work that his overriding concern was with the attempt to integrate the 'multiple

[49] Steele, 'Interpreting the Self', 86. [50] Richard-Allerdyce, *Remaking of Self*, 22.

[51] See Julia Kristeva, *Revolution in Poetic Language* (trans. Margaret Waller, with introduction by Leon S. Roudiez; New York: Columbia Univ. Press, 1984 [1974]), *passim*. Kristeva's title, of course, reveals again the belief in the radical, 'revolutionary' potential of art and aesthetics characteristic of both the early twentieth-century avant-garde movements and French poststructuralism of the 1970s.

planes' of human experience: his notion of 'blood-consciousness' links subconscious life to the impulses of the body, and must itself be put into connection with the 'upper plane' of consciousness and rationality (*D. H. Lawrence*, 4, 5). To enter Lawrence's world, to understand what he tried to do in his writing, it is necessary to take the same approach: 'The world D. H. Lawrence created cannot be entered through the exercise of one faculty alone: there must be a threefold desire of intellect, of imagination, and of physical feeling, because he erected his world on a fusion of concepts, on a philosophy that was against division, on a plea for whole vision: "to see with the soul and the body"' (1).

In her chapter entitled 'Language—Style—Symbolism', Nin analyses in more detail the way in which Lawrence tried to achieve this in language, the 'tormenting' and transformation of 'ordinary' language she had noted in her diary after reading *Women in Love*. She begins by stating that 'Lawrence's language makes a physical impression' (71). It has movement (he 'tormented words to catch the mobility of things' (73)) and, above all, rhythm: there are 'repetitions like choruses, words that are meant to suggest more than their own determinate, formal significance'; 'the words almost cease to have a meaning: they have a cadence, a flow' (73). Language becomes musical, a pattern of sound and rhythm. But it also becomes painterly: Lawrence is 'a painter' not only literally, but also in his writing, which has a 'quality of *color*' (75). He tries to convey taste and texture in writing, linking language and the body through the senses: 'his most abstract thought is always deep reaching [because] it passes through the channels of the senses' (78). Nin sums up Lawrence's use of language as follows:

> Lawrence attempted some very difficult things with writing. For him it was an instrument of unlimited possibilities; he would give it the *bulgingness of sculpture*, the feeling of heavy material fulness . . . He would give it the nuances of paint: thus his effort to convey shades of color with words that had never been used for color. He would give it the rhythm of movement, of dancing: thus his wayward, formless, floating, word-shattering descriptions. He would give it sound, musicality, cadence: thus words sometimes used less for their sense than for their sound. It was a daring thing to do. Sometimes he failed. But it was certainly the crevice in the wall, and opened a new world to us. (78–9)

Nin's argument is that Lawrence tries to bring into writing the forms and affective qualities of other arts: music, dance, painting, sculpture. He tries, above all, to achieve in language the sensory affects of these other arts, through a particular concentration on the *material*, physical qualities of language: sound and rhythm. In this way, words 'suggest' more than their 'determinate, formal significance'; they 'almost cease to have a meaning'. Nin's qualification is important here. Lawrence's language, although 'twisted' and 'tormented',[52] never loses its meaning entirely: rather, in this sensory language, the determinate 'meaning' of words becomes only one aspect of their affective ability—we apprehend the language not just intellectually but also physically, sensually, as we might apprehend music or dance.

This notion of a synthesis of art forms and their affects is both central to Nin's later developments of her ideas about an ideal poetic language[53] and, more widely, an important (but not uncontested) strand of modernist and avant-garde thinking as a whole. Williams states that 'a key element in both Modernism and the avant-garde was a deliberate running-together, cross-fertilization, even integration of what had hitherto been seen as different arts', and cites 'the aspiration to develop language towards the condition of music, or towards the immediacy and presence of visual imagery or performance'.[54] The Symbolists, in particular, with their emphasis on a poetic language of 'intuition, mystery, [and] suggestiveness',[55] aspired to the creation of a language that could approximate the condition of music. More specifically, they took as their model first the music of Wagner and then that of Debussy, breaking away from classical forms towards a more free-flowing and fluid effect.

Many commentators on Nin's work have noted her love of Debussy and fascination with his music. The point I want to make here is the importance for Nin of Debussy's music as a model of *modern* musical form. In her diary in April 1931, after attending a performance of Beethoven and Berlioz, she analyses her preference for Debussy and her aspiration to bring the qualities of his music into her writing:

I didn't care for Beethoven's *Pastoral* or Berlioz's *Fantastique*. Both too literal and descriptive. Prefer suggestive music like Debussy's and Falla's—something more subtle, more indirect. Gilbert [Chase, her cousin] told me modern music will go

[52] Nin's descriptions of Lawrence 'twisting', 'tormenting', and 'shattering' language interestingly anticipate Kristeva's emphasis on the violence with which the semiotic 'irrupts' within the symbolic, 'pulverizing' and 'tearing [it] open' (*Revolution*, 51, 56, 62). They also recall the *transition* writers' statement in the 1929 'Proclamation' that 'the literary creator has the right to disintegrate the primal matter of words' (*In transition*, 19).

[53] See e.g. *A Woman Speaks*, 177–8: 'As a writer I wanted simply to take all the various expressions of art into writing, for I believed that each art must nourish the other, each one can add to the other . . . In every form of art there is something that I wanted to include, and I wanted writing, poetic writing, to include them all.' See also *Novel*, 89: 'Jazz, collages, mobiles, animation in films, the combination of several arts have all indicated ways of renewal for the novel form'.

[54] 'Language and the Avant-Garde', 70.

[55] Nicholls, *Modernisms*, 25.

one way or the other: toward more suggestivity or back to classical impersonality, like Bach. So now I know why I dislike Bach . . . I would give twenty years of my precious life to be able to write as Debussy composed, to be able to give that profound, intangible, wordless sensation. I suppose Lawrence achieved that . . . [Music] goes directly *through* our senses, whereas only a certain kind of writing will go through our senses, and it is this penetration I seek. (17 April 1931 [*Early Diary*, IV, 417–18])

Here, as well as the association already noted of the ideal language with *sensory* affect, we find the valorization of a modern 'suggestivity' and 'indirectness' over against the 'impersonality' of classical forms. More generally, the modernist interest in the 'cross-fertilization' of the arts (Nin uses the similar term 'cross-pollination' [*Novel*, 164]) involves an emphasis on the *modernity* of the forms being invoked, a desire to find aesthetic forms somehow appropriate to the times, and a rejection of 'antiquated', outmoded forms or styles.

In *The Novel of the Future* (as the title suggests), Nin puts particular emphasis on this need for aesthetic forms appropriate to the times we live in. Indeed, the book is an interesting (if sometimes slightly bizarre) attempt by Nin to update her own aesthetic preoccupations and models to fit the context she is now writing for: America in 1968. (As such, it inadvertently reveals how the attempt to make a radical break, to 'make it new', in Ezra Pound's memorable phrase, is an endlessly repeated gesture, part of an ongoing cycle.[56]) Thus, while she cites Symbolism, Surrealism, and psychoanalysis as the chief contexts of and influences on her development as a writer, and sets her writing firmly in the predominantly French tradition of 'poetic novelists' such as Giraudoux, Jouve, and Proust, she also attempts to argue that, although American literature (and culture more generally) was dominated through the 1940s and 1950s by 'social realism' and politics, with a corresponding rejection of Surrealism and 'poetic prose', the cultural shift of the 1960s has brought a closer parallel to the original concerns of the modernists: 'The purpose of this book is to study the development and techniques of the poetic novel. I will try to evaluate some of the writers who have integrated poetry and prose . . . It is a grouping, a relating of such writers to trends now acceptable and recognized under other names, "expanded consciousness", or if you prefer, "psychedelic", with emphasis on *psyche*' (*Novel*, 3–4).

[56] It is also ironic that this gesture depends on precisely the logic (the *dernier cri* constantly replacing the *démodé*) that drives commodity culture—to which, of course, avant-garde artists always see themselves as opposed.

One of the most obvious cases of this updating (and Americanizing) is precisely in Nin's use of musical models for writing: she no longer focuses on Debussy as her exemplar of modern musical form, but on jazz. This is a shift that is clearly traceable through her diaries of the 1940s and onwards, and in *Seduction of the Minotaur* (1961), where jazz features significantly. Jazz is important for Nin in several respects. As a quintessentially American art form, it represents a link—one of the few links Nin can see—between the American context and the French avant-garde tradition. 'Jazz writing', she suggests, will be the American counterpart to what the Surrealists, the *transition* 'revolutionaries', were trying to do: 'jazz is the only American expression or manifestation of life rhythms, emotion, the senses and surrealism. Its equivalent in writing is to me the future of American writing . . . Jazz or jazz writing expresses the lyrical, the tempo, the pulsation of heightened living. It is the equivalent of surrealism in France' (Winter 1956–57 [*Journals*, VI, 75]).[57]

In the diaries, Nin's exploration of jazz and its potential as a model for writing is linked to her friendship with the American writer James Leo Herlihy: 'I say "rhythm" and it means as much to him as it does to me: contemporary rhythms. He is the first who tried to describe my way of writing in terms of jazz: I state a phrase and then restate it in another key, reaching out for still another, like the horn player. Jim's understanding of improvisation. There is a jazz rhythm in my writing and Jim of the future heard it' (Autumn 1952 [*Journals*, V, 96]).

With its use of improvisation around a theme, producing associative patterns rather than the formal compositions of classical music, jazz is structurally analogous to the unconscious realm that Nin is aiming to bring into writing: '[The unconscious] is first of all ruled by flow, as life itself. It has, like life, a capricious lifeline and a different way of arranging its patterns. It might be compared with jazz. It is unwritten music in the sense that it is constantly improvising. It is ruled by free association.'[58]

[57] Of course, throughout the twentieth century jazz underwent its own continuous process of reinvention and changing with the times. In 1959, two years after Nin's comments here, Miles Davis's seminal album *Kind of Blue* would herald another major shift within jazz; modal jazz, with its emphasis less on melody and more on improvisation within a 'mode' or specific set of notes, would perhaps exemplify particularly well Nin's comments about patterned improvisation.

[58] *Novel*, 27. Nin's description of the 'capricious lifeline' of the unconscious recalls Virginia Woolf's description, in *Orlando*, of Memory as the 'capricious seamstress' of the psyche, in which we find 'a perfect ragbag of odds and ends . . . lightly stitched together by a single thread'; *Orlando: A Biography* (London: Virago, 1993 [1928]), 46. Nin had certainly read and admired *Orlando* in 1929; see *Early Diary*, IV, 200.

However, the importance of *rhythm* in jazz is equally crucial, since it is rhythm that engages the body and the senses. As I have shown, Nin focuses on Lawrence's use of sound and rhythm, his attempt to create a language with the movement of music or dance, and it is perhaps rhythm above all that becomes central to Nin's own attempt to create a physical and sensory language, to write the body through, as Richard-Allerdyce puts it, 'the embodiment of desire in language'.[59] In the wider modernist context, too, rhythm in language had been a particular point of controversy. Cassandra Laity notes that Ezra Pound objected precisely to Swinburne's focus on rhythm: Pound, Laity writes, 'disparages Swinburne's excess of the "rhythm-building faculty" at the expense of the "word-selecting, word-castigating faculty" '.[60]

This preoccupation with rhythm as the inscription of the body, and especially of desire, can be seen at many levels throughout Nin's writing. In the central (italicized) passage of *Winter of Artifice*, describing the frustrated climax of the passion between father and daughter, Nin employs the conceit of an orchestra, '*the orchestra of their desire*' (*Winter*, 84). There is an imagistic fusion of body and musical instrument: '*the violins shaking their hair and she passing the violin bow gently between her legs, drawing music out of her body*' (84); music represents the forbidden desire flowing between father and daughter: '*music in the tongue, in the fingers*' (85). The ultimate failure of the attempted connection is expressed in the daughter's questions, '*Can we live in rhythm, my father? Can we feel in rhythm, my father? Can we think in rhythm, my father?*' (87). Similarly, in *Ladders to Fire*, the failure of both Lillian and Djuna to connect with others is expressed in terms of rhythm: 'there were in Lillian and Djuna rhythms which left them suspended in utter solitude' (*Ladders*, 18). In a later passage, Lillian's 'violence', the chaotic forcefulness that characterizes her throughout the novel sequence, is again expressed in terms of a 'broken rhythm' (45). Significantly, in the final novel *Seduction of the Minotaur*, Lillian achieves psychic and physical harmony in Golconda, where 'music was an unbroken chain' (*Seduction*, 57). She is employed at the local nightclub as a jazz pianist, and jazz functions throughout the

[59] *Remaking of Self*, 159. Cf. also Kristeva's emphasis on the rhythmic nature of the semiotic: the *chora* is 'analogous only to vocal or kinetic rhythm' (*Revolution*, 26).

[60] Laity, *H.D.*, 100. Laity sees a clearly gendered dimension to this debate: 'Swinburne's attention to sound over meaning is cited by both Pound and Eliot as detrimental to the concrete objectives of modernism and by extension to modernism's masculine agenda' (99). In the second part of the chapter I shall discuss the important link between the 'materiality' of language and 'the feminine'.

book as a figure for the rhythms and improvisations of both body and unconscious:

Jazz was the music of the body. The breath came through aluminium and copper tubes, it was the body's breath, and the strings' wails and moans were echoes of the body's music. It was the body's vibrations which rippled from the fingers. And the mystery of the withheld theme known to the musicians alone was like the mystery of our secret life. We give to others only peripheral improvisations. The plots and themes of the music like the plots and themes of our life never alchemized into words, existed only in a state of music, stirring or numbing, exalting or despairing, but never named. (*Seduction*, 20)

But, of course, Nin did want to 'alchemize' music into words, and jazz became an important model for her ideal language, providing, as I have shown, both a structural parallel to the associative patterns of the unconscious and the all-important link to the body through rhythm (and importantly, jazz rhythms are 'contemporary' rhythms): 'Rhythm is inseparable from life, from the senses, from a sensory way of perceiving and feeling life . . . The importance of rhythm in my estimation is a measure of the difference between a live book and a dead one' (*Novel*, 90).

Film: 'the perfect medium'

Nin's stress on the *imagistic* nature of dreams, and the idea that the 'language of the unconscious' is a language of images, led her to seize enthusiastically on film as the medium more suited than any other to portraying dreams and the interactions of conscious and unconscious realms. Relatedly, she saw film as providing another model, perhaps the most significant of all, for writing.

It is perhaps surprising that commentators on Nin's work have paid far less attention to her interest in film as an aesthetic model than to her interest in music. For instance, while Oliver Evans calls Nin 'a pioneer in the application of cinematic effects to prose fiction', he does not discuss this any further; and while Sharon Spencer stresses the importance of music, dance, and painting for Nin's concept of 'symphonic writing', she does not mention film, despite stating that 'Nin portrays her characters again and again in a series of "shots"'.[61] Yet Nin's interest in film is particularly significant in terms of placing her within the wider context of modernist concerns with new aesthetic forms, and in relation to the

[61] Oliver Evans, *Anaïs Nin* (Crosscurrents Modern Critiques; Carbondale, Ill: Southern Illinois Univ. Press, 1968), 194; Spencer, *Collage of Dreams*, 23.

frequently ambivalent attitudes of modernists towards new technology. In her interest in film as a new art form Nin was very close to the positions of other writers, notably Virginia Woolf and H.D. Further, film itself may be seen as in many ways the quintessentially modern(ist) medium. Raymond Williams suggests that film not only utilized the new 'metropolitan' forms of perception but was 'an art form created, in all important respects, by these perceptions'; recalling Woolf's image of the 'chaos of the streets' as 'a scene awaiting a new art to be transfixed'.[62] Film became an obvious focal point for the ideological battles over different notions or aspects of 'modernity': while H.D. and Nin (in common with, for instance, Woolf and Dorothy Richardson) valorize film as the modern synthesis of conscious and unconscious, dream and action, it is also fundamentally imbricated in the 'degraded' modernity of the spectacle, the 'image' in the contexts of advertising and commercialization; and it is, of course, bound up with the (masculine) modernity of technology. Film thus seems to embody particularly strikingly the tensions we might see within the desire for an ideal aesthetic practice that is simultaneously both 'magical' and 'modern'.

From very early in her writing career, Nin was excited by the potential she saw in the cinema, the possibilities inherent in film as a new art form. In December 1927, after seeing Fritz Lang's *Metropolis*, she wrote: 'I felt last night that it is only in *film* that reality and unreality, poetry and science, can be fully achieved and communicated' (*Early Diary*, IV, 38). She maintained this belief in the revelatory potential of film throughout her life, although feeling that it had rarely been exploited to the full. In a 1972 review of *A Safe Place*, written and directed by Henry Jaglom, she wrote:

> From the early beginnings of the motion picture film, Antonin Artaud said that only films would be able to depict dreams, fantasies, the surrealist aspect of our experience. But very soon they veered away from that magic power and turned to one-dimensional stories. Very few made attempts to penetrate the deeper layers of our way of experiencing life. Yet [film] was the perfect medium for capturing our inner life. ('Henry Jaglom: Magician of the Film', in *Sensitive Man*, 86)

This has a double importance for Nin: not only is film valuable in itself as the 'perfect medium for capturing our inner life', it is—like music—valuable as a model for writing. The 'magical power' that writing has lost is the very power Nin attributes here to film. Her analysis of the ways to restore this 'magical power' to writing centrally involves filmic qualities;

[62] Williams, 'Metropolitan Perceptions', 46; Virginia Woolf, 'The Cinema' (1926), in *The Crowded Dance of Modern Life* (ed. Rachel Bowlby; Harmondsworth: Penguin, 1993), 58.

and her various writings on film as an art form reveal more fully the ways in which she believes film can capture our 'inner life'. Here we find striking parallels to the claims of other contemporary writers for the potential of this new art form, both in itself and in relation to writing.

Virginia Woolf's article 'The Cinema' appeared in 1926, the year before Nin saw *Metropolis.* Woolf argued for the enormous potential in films—though so far, she suggested, unfulfilled—as a new form of expression for thought and feeling, above all for the emotional aspects of our psychic experience which seem to defy effective expression in words. The key to the cinema's potential lies in its use of the visual image, and the suggestive power of abstraction. The cinema can go beyond the static images of painting, uniquely able to combine abstract imagery with movement and sequence, opening up to us a new 'language' of thought and emotion; in the potential of the cinema lies the answer to Woolf's rhetorical questions: 'Is there, we ask, some secret language which we feel and see, but never speak, and if so, could this be made visible to the eye?'[63]

Woolf also hints at the areas of our experience in which we already come close to this 'language' of images: in the cinema, she suggests, 'the dream architecture of arches and battlements, of cascades falling and fountains rising, which sometimes visits us in sleep or shapes itself in half-darkened rooms, could be realized before our waking eyes. No fantasy could be too far-fetched or insubstantial.'[64] The film, then, could portray our dreams, the fantastic sequences of images that arise from the unconscious in sleep; or, perhaps, in the 'half-darkened rooms' of psychoanalysis. The latter image is itself anticipated in Woolf's 1919 essay 'Modern Fiction', and serves to link her argument here about the new form of expression in film with her discussion there of new forms in writing which 'attempt to come closer to life', to 'resemble the vision in our minds'.[65] 'For the moderns', Woolf argues, 'the point of interest . . . lies very likely in the dark places of psychology', and this produces a change of emphasis in writing: 'The emphasis is laid upon such unexpected places that at first it seems as if there were no emphasis at all; and then, as the eyes accustom themselves to twilight and discern the shapes of things in a room we see how complete the story is, how profound.'[66]

[63] Woolf, 'The Cinema', 57.
[64] Ibid. 58.
[65] Virginia Woolf, 'Modern Fiction' (1919), in *The Crowded Dance of Modern Life*, 9, 8.
[66] Ibid. 10–11.

Earlier in her essay, Woolf suggests the potential ability of the cinema to make use of other art forms: 'So many arts seemed to stand by ready to offer their help'.[67] She goes on to argue that, in fact, cinema's appropriation of literature, seemingly the art form most suited to film adaptation, has been merely trite and reductive. And yet, when cinema realizes its potential for rendering visible dream, fantasy, and emotion, the resulting art form *will* be in some sense a synthesis—it will make use of elements from other arts, yet will go beyond them: 'Something abstract, something which moves with controlled and conscious art, something which calls for the very slightest help from words or music to make itself intelligible, yet justly uses them subserviently—of such movements and abstractions the films may, in time to come, be composed'.[68]

In 1930, four years after Woolf's essay was published, H.D. wrote 'The *Borderline* Pamphlet', accompanying the release of the film *Borderline*, written and directed by Kenneth Macpherson, in which both H.D. and Bryher acted, alongside Paul and Eslanda Robeson. For our purposes here, the essay is most interesting not for H.D.'s specific reflections on *Borderline* but for her discussion of 'modern screen art' or 'film art', of which this film is an example.[69] Like Woolf, and, as I shall show in more detail, like Nin, H.D. sees film art as a synthesis of elements or qualities from other art forms: 'the film, rightly presented, is not a matter of one effect but many, nor of any one art but many'.[70] This is revealed in the structure of H.D.'s essay, which moves in its numbered sections through the different art forms brought together in the film—painting, sculpture, music, drama. Having begun with a reference to Leonardo da Vinci, H.D. builds a picture, through her discussions of film's pictorial, sculptural, musical, and dramatic qualities, of film art as a 'renaissance' art, and of the creative director as a modern renaissance artist: 'He may not himself, personally, draw, paint, sculpt, yet instinctively, in his outlook, he must maintain sympathy with all these art-facets and with music, drama, and every form of writing. For in the film alone to-day, may these allied arts be welded.'[71]

In the penultimate section of the essay, H.D. writes: '*Borderline* is a dream and perhaps when we say that we have said everything. The film is the art of dream portrayal and perhaps when we say that we have achieved the definition, the synthesis toward which we have been striving. Film is art of another dimension, including not only all art but

[67] 'The Cinema', 55.
[68] Ibid. 57.
[69] H.D., 'The *Borderline* Pamphlet', in Scott (ed.), *The Gender of Modernism*, 112.
[70] Ibid. 117.
[71] Ibid. 115.

including all life.'[72] Film art is the 'synthesis'—of all the arts, of 'dimensions', of art and life—*because* it is 'the art of dream portrayal'. The 'achievement of a nightmare and a dream', H.D. goes on to claim, is the 'greatest' achievement.[73] To be more exact, the achievement is in the synthesis of the 'dimensions' of dream and of life or action, 'the welding of the psychic or super-normal to the things of precise every-day existence'.[74] Film art, H.D. claims, is 'the modern attempt to synchronize thought and action, the inner turmoil and the outer, the static physical passivity and the acute psychic activity'.[75]

Both Woolf and H.D., then, see in film the same possibility that Nin sees for 'capturing our inner life'. In Woolf's focus on sequences of imagery we also find a link to Nin's concentration on the *image* as the central factor connecting film and dream. The importance of this idea for Nin comes through particularly clearly in her discussion, in the fifth volume of her *Journals*, of Ian Hugo's films of Venice.[76] Nin declares: 'We are living in the age of the image' (136). This statement brings together several important issues. First, it has clear *technological* connotations, alluding to the specifically twentieth-century use of ever more sophisticated means for producing and reproducing images ('we can register more perfectly with cameras the external image', 136). The cinema is obviously one of the most significant arenas for these new imaging techniques. But if the twentieth century is the age of visual technology, it is also, for Nin, the age of psychoanalysis;[77] and psychoanalysis, in its stress on the unconscious wish represented pictorially through dreams, may be seen as stressing the role of the image in the psychic realm.[78] So, in her discussion of Hugo's film, Nin emphasizes the cinematic technique of 'layered sequences of images, superimpositions', a process of 'improvisation' (as she had emphasized in relation to jazz). This technique enables the film to 'capture' or 'reflect' our psychic life because it mirrors the patterns of thought and feeling:

[72] Ibid. 121 [73] Ibid. 124. [74] Ibid.

[75] Ibid. 123, emending 'other' in Scott's text to 'outer' as the parallelism seems to require.

[76] 'Ian Hugo' was the pseudonym used by Nin's husband Hugh Guiler when he became an engraver and experimental film-maker.

[77] Nin frequently speaks of psychoanalysis as providing, in some sense, a world-view for the twentieth century; for instance, in *The Novel of the Future*, she writes: '[psychoanalysis] has altered the consciousness of our time, influenced us even against our knowledge. It has penetrated, infiltrated, affected all our thinking, arts, and living' (88). In *A Woman Speaks*, she describes psychoanalysis as 'part of our modern awareness' (133).

[78] In Chapter 2, I discuss Nin's focus on the wish-image, and the unconscious 'language of images', as guides for creating one's life.

The freedom of improvisation expressed in Ian Hugo's films corresponds to our emotional life, which is continuously projecting and retaining on our inner screen previous images . . . He also seeks to capture how our thoughts jump from scene to scene in an *apparently* unrelated way, to better match the structure of our emotional life, which is fluid, symphonic, and composed on several levels at once . . . By following such improvisations, assembling images according to the design of our emotions, we also enter this region below consciousness. (*Journals*, V, 136–7)

The image, then, and the possibility of combinations of images, superimpositions and improvisatory sequences, are the crucial factors in cinema's superior ability to portray our 'inner life', Woolf's 'dream architecture'. Hence, as Nin writes in *The Novel of the Future*, 'It was not the writers but the film-makers who opened the way to the language of images which is the language of the unconscious' (97). In fact, cinematic techniques and terminology provide the perfect language to *describe* the patterns of the unconscious and thought more generally, as we can clearly see from Nin's references, above, to our 'inner screen' and our thoughts 'jump[ing] from scene to scene'. Again, she writes in *The Novel of the Future*: 'I have only discarded the novel's explicit and direct statement in order to match the way we truly see and feel, in images resembling film sequences' (27). In a similar way, Freud had earlier seized on contemporary photographic techniques as providing the perfect metaphors for the operations of the dream-work.[79] Comparison with filmic techniques, Nin argues, ought to enable us to understand more clearly how our minds work: 'when film-makers talk of superimposition of images, everyone understands. One film exposed over another. Double exposure. When I speak of this happening constantly in our unconscious, it sounds abstract and mysterious'—but, she implies, it is no more mysterious than what happens in the cinema (*Novel*, 125). By the same token, then, the film is above all 'the art of dream portrayal'; there is a perfect fit.

In *The Novel of the Future*, Nin focuses on the use of filmic qualities and techniques in the attempt to create a poetic prose language that can depict both 'inner' and 'outer' reality, H.D.'s synthesis of dimensions. She argues that the literary establishment has been slow to recognize the potential of such techniques when transferred to writing: 'In films we accepted abrupt transitions, jump cutting, fadeouts, flashbacks, fluid dream sequences, superimpositions' (171). Writing has lost its 'magical

[79] 'The face that I saw in the dream was at once my friend R.'s and my uncle's. It was like one of Galton's composite photographs' (*Interpretation of Dreams*, 219–20).

power', Nin suggests, because of the separation of 'dimensions' and exclusive focus on the external realm of 'social realism': 'There has been a chasm between poetry and prose in which writing lost its magical power, a chasm between art and science, and a chasm between the conscious and the unconscious' (165). If Breton was correct to see in Freud's stress on dreams and the unconscious the means of restoring 'meaning and vitality' to language, the powerful techniques of the film provide the best means of incorporating the unconscious realm into writing. In *A Woman Speaks*, in answer to the question '"Do you think the film is going to influence the novel?"', Nin replies: '"I think there is a mutual influence . . . the novel will come closer to the film . . . the films have brought us back to the importance of the image and the study of dreams . . . the dream and the film resemble each other very strongly' (*A Woman Speaks*, 198–9).

H.D. makes a strikingly similar argument in the *Borderline* pamphlet. She suggests that 'words' have somehow lost their magic: 'words, as such, have become weathered . . . Words are all alike now, the words even one feels of a foreign language have lost "virtue".'[80] The film can revitalize our sense of language by putting words into images: 'We take so for granted the use of the term for instance, "flying upstairs", that we do not realize how apt and arresting that phrase really is, until the camera again shows us that, actually, in vision or in retrospection or in anticipation, we "fly" upstairs'. So, paradoxically, through the use of *images* rather than words, the film can restore to language its lost 'virtue': 'The film brings words back . . . Words become again "winged" indeed. We "fly" upstairs with Lulu.'[81] The film, then, may be seen as a kind of modern 'picture-writing'; and, H.D. suggests, 'we will perhaps begin [to] "write" our novels and plays in "pictures"'.[82] We can read this statement as making a double claim: it suggests both that film, because it is imagistic, is the perfect medium for expressing what has hitherto been jadedly expressed in writing (a language that has 'lost virtue'); and that writing itself could be revivified by adopting the pictorial, imagistic techniques of the film. We find here, then, a very strong parallel to Nin's double argument for film

[80] '*Borderline* Pamphlet', 120. This is a good example of the common modernist critique of the debased 'contemporary condition' of language, as analysed by Williams in 'Language and the Avant-Garde'.

[81] '*Borderline* Pamphlet', 120. She is referring to Pabst's film *Pandora's Box*.

[82] Ibid. References to picture-writing or hieroglyphics are central throughout H.D.'s work. Cf. also the use of the phrase 'new hieroglyphics' in the *transition* editorial 'Suggestions for a New Magic', 23–4.

both as an expressive medium in itself and as a model for an ideal form of writing.

Although film is for Woolf, Nin, and H.D. above all the medium of dream portrayal, and although its expressive ability may be described in quasi-mystical terms as a 'magical' power, all three writers stress to varying degrees the *technological* aspects of film art. This gives film a particularly significant—and ambivalent—place in the context of the attempt to envisage a form of aesthetic expression that is appropriate to the time, 'modern' or 'new'. I have already noted the technological aspect of Nin's phrase 'the age of the image', and her interest in the use of specific techniques of film-making, such as jump cutting and double exposures, in order to create particular effects. For Woolf, the 'enormous technical proficiency'[83] of the cinema seems rather double-edged: she implies that the technology of the cinema has, so far, been in advance of the creative ability of film-makers, so that cinema's true potential ('what the cinema might do if it were left to its own devices'[84]) has only been revealed in accidental glimpses. Despite these shortcomings, though, it is the technology of the cinema, of a different order from that of other arts, that gives it its unique expressive potential: 'The most fantastic contrasts could be flashed before us with a speed which the writer can only toil after in vain'.[85]

The most sustained and most interesting focus on the technology and modernity of film, though, is found in H.D.'s *Borderline* pamphlet. H.D. describes film as a modern-day renaissance art, and the director (in this case Macpherson) as a modern-day 'Leonardo'. She writes: 'Juxtaposition of "Leonardo" with "modern screen art" is neither as inept nor as ironical as it may seem at first glance. This name connotes mechanical efficiency, modernity and curiosity allied with pure creative impulse. The film *per se*, is a curious welding of mechanical and creative instincts.'[86] The 'modernity' of the cinema is here understood in terms of the drive for 'mechanical efficiency' and technological ingenuity associated with the modern period in the broadest sense—hence H.D. is not 'inept' in linking the cinema with renaissance Italy. However, the cinema is also implicated in another kind of 'modernity': 'Yet you may ask, granted that, what has Leonardo, demi-god of accepted intellectuality, to do with this gutter-offshoot of modernity? What has that steel blade to do with harem beauties in bathing costumes and with sugar and spice and

[83] 'The Cinema', 58. [84] Ibid. 56. [85] Ibid. 58.
[86] '*Borderline* Pamphlet', 112.

everything that is nice and must, *must*, MUST remain in the commercially constituted realm of so-called cinematography?'[87] Here H.D. suggests modernity as the realm of commercialism and visual commodification, glamour and advertising—another implicit context for Nin's phrase 'the age of the image'. Obviously, H.D. (like Nin) wants to make a separation between the commercial world of 'so-called cinematography' and what she calls, stressing again the paradoxical juxtaposition, 'the new mechanical-creative film art'.[88] Nonetheless, it remains the case that even 'art' cinema, as a twentieth-century visual technology, is bound up in complex ways with the cultural focus on 'the image'.

H.D. focuses in detail on the techniques of film-making, the lighting effects, the precise preparations for each shot, the complexities of 'the proper focus, lense [sic], distance, stop and rate of "turning" '.[89] Her emphasis on the technology of the cinema gives weight to her analysis of film as the 'miracle' of the relationship between the 'ultra-modern' and the 'ultra-classic', the alliance of 'beauty' with 'sheer grit and technical efficiency'. This alliance makes film art the perfect art of the time: 'There is beauty, there has always been beauty. The problem in every art period is to present that beauty in a form allied to its environment and its time.'[90]

Most interesting of all, perhaps, is H.D.'s use of strikingly masculine imagery to convey this 'ultra-modern' aspect of film art. The film director, H.D. writes, 'must be mechanic, must be artist, must be man, must be warrior'.[91] Watching Macpherson at work, she says, is '[l]ike watching a young gunner alone with his machine gun'.[92] In fact, the 'young gunner' takes on the characteristics of his gun, becomes identified with it, a hybrid of man and machine: 'He stands, after any human being would drop dead of fatigue, casually with his elegant Debrie, machine man with it . . . Kenneth Macpherson, at work, is a hard-boiled mechanic, as if he himself were all camera, bone and sinew and steel-glint of rapacious grey eyes.'[93] It is possible, of course, to read these descriptions on a simple biographical level as referring to H.D.'s own erotic attachment to Macpherson.[94] But far more interesting is the fact that H.D., many of whose writings focus on the devastating psychological effects (usually on female characters) of war and masculine identification with the values of

87 '*Borderline* Pamphlet', 112–13. 88 Ibid. 113.

89 Ibid. 114. H.D., always an idiosyncratic speller, writes 'lense' for 'lens' throughout.

90 Ibid. 114. 91 Ibid. 115. 92 Ibid. 113. 93 Ibid. 114.

94 They had begun an affair in 1926; in 1927 Macpherson entered into a marriage of convenience with Bryher and the three lived together, with H.D.'s daughter Perdita.

war,[95] is here closer to the Futurists in her use of images of an eroticized, heroic masculinity and her fantasy of the 'ultra-modern' technology of the cinema as an 'elegant' fusion of man and machine. The 'beauty' of modernity here appears as masculine in its hard-edged outlines: '[Macpherson] reaches forward . . . toward the lean skyscraper beauty of ultra-modernity'.[96]

While Nin never uses such strikingly masculine imagery in relation either to film technology or to modernity more generally, there is in *The Novel of the Future* an emphasis on modern form as characterized above all by clean, uncluttered lines and by speed. Here we find a technological cast, similar to that in H.D.'s essay, to Nin's general argument that artistic form should be appropriate to the age we live in. Thus, for instance, she notes the 'paradox' that 'people accepted abstract painting in their homes and studied the abstractions of science, but in the jet age read novels which corresponded to the horse and buggy' (*Novel*, 3). She argues that the accelerated pace of modern living must be matched by an acceleration and a paring down in writing: 'emotionally, as well as scientifically, our words are going to travel more lightly and swiftly, and for this we have to rid ourselves of excess baggage. The more accelerated our life becomes, the more we have to learn to select only the essential' (*Novel*, 26–7). The novel, just like our houses and means of transport, must be designed to fit the age of 'the jet plane, quicker living, lighter living' (*Novel*, 195).

Despite her focus on the realm of 'magic' and the dream, then, Nin's attitude towards technologized modernity is, like H.D.'s, interestingly ambivalent rather than straightforwardly hostile. For Nin, the speed and technology of modernity were associated particularly with New York. On returning to Paris after spending several months in New York in 1935, Nin wrote: 'I'm suffering deeply because I miss the electric rhythm of New York . . . I was drunk on liberty and sensation and bigness and space and dynamism. Paris is a vegetable patch. Where are my wings, my airplanes, my ships, trains, and the luminousness of New York?' (5 July 1935 [*Fire*, 101]). A passage from January 1936, anticipating another trip to America,

[95] See e.g. *Bid Me To Live* (London: Virago, 1984 [1960]) in which the collapse of Julia Ashton's relationship with her husband Rafe is inextricably bound up, on many levels, with his participation in the First World War. In her long poem *Helen in Egypt* (1961), H.D. transposes the problem to the setting of the Trojan War.

[96] '*Borderline* Pamphlet', 116. There is an interesting echo here of the term 'skyscraper spirituality' used in the *transition* piece 'Suggestions for a New Magic' (see above): whereas the *transition* writers use the skyscraper as an emblem of a modernity understood negatively, H.D. uses the same image positively.

expresses particularly well the ambivalence suggested above, revealing both an awareness of the awesome destructive powers of modernity and an eroticized fascination with them: 'I feel ready for a new rhythm, the rhythm of New York. I will take care of those whose lives are broken, who were crushed in the machine. But I am not the victim of that machine. I stand outside and I can enjoy the enormous, fantastic heartbeats of it, and the noise' (4 January 1936 [*Fire*, 185]). Here we see, just as in H.D.'s description of the film director, modernity envisaged as a sort of hybrid, a machine with 'enormous, fantastic heartbeats'. In this emphasis on the 'machine', the electric rhythm, and dynamism of modernity—and then the transfer of these qualities of speed, rhythm and clean lines to the ideal of modern writing—Nin, like H.D., comes surprisingly close to the preoccupations of the Futurists.

II. CREATIVITY AND FEMININITY

This quasi-Futurism is, of course, only one strand within Nin's thinking about modernist aesthetics and the new art forms. However, it does serve as a warning note in relation to the question of the 'gendering' of these aesthetic forms and practices, suggesting that we may not be able to make a straightforward equation between 'revolutionary', experimental writing and art forms, as advocated and practised by modernist women, and an inscription of 'the feminine' into art and culture. In Nin's case, it is also interesting to note that none of her 'manifestos' for the ideal poetic language—the 1968 *Novel of the Future* and the earlier essays 'Realism and Reality' (1946), 'On Writing' (1947), and 'The Writer and the Symbols' (1959)—focuses to any great extent on gender, either the gender of the writer or the ascription of gendered characteristics to the writing itself.

Yet Nin certainly was concerned, throughout her career, with the interactions of gender and language (or creativity more generally), and especially with the specificity of *women's* creativity and the role of 'the feminine' in creation. Diane Richard-Allerdyce, arguing for Nin's importance as a modernist and feminist writer, states that 'Nin's nearly lifelong effort to define writing in terms of gender places her within a tradition of *l'écriture féminine*'.[97] Richard-Allerdyce does not define just what she means by this reference to a 'tradition', but the framework of her approach is clearly that of French poststructuralist feminist theory,

[97] Richard-Allerdyce, *Remaking of Self*, 12.

with its focus on the inscription of 'the feminine' as what has been repressed from language and culture, and on bringing into language both the 'immense resources of the unconscious'[98] and, especially, the *body*.

We can trace the historical importance of these links between 'the feminine', the body, and the unconscious in modernist aesthetics. In her study of D. H. Lawrence's use of language, Nin focused on his attempt to achieve the sensory affects of other arts, such as music, painting, and sculpture, through an emphasis on the material, phonic properties of language—the use of sound and rhythm. Here, Nin was in fact addressing a debate that was both central to the development of modernist aesthetics and already strongly gendered. In his 1901 essay 'Women and Language', Remy de Gourmont linked 'woman' with oral rather than written language, the materiality of 'primitive chattering' rather than the abstractions of 'verbal innovation': 'Woman . . . had . . . from the earliest times, no doubt, retained the most musical, the most rhythmical parts of speech—some combination of phrases resembling those melopeias repeated insatiably by Negroes. Man created. Woman learned by heart . . . The first song-book was woman's memory.'[99] Not only is 'woman's' language the material language of song, she is herself, in her bodily form, a kind of language:

> Even when she is silent, a woman continues to speak—often with a sincerity which her words lack. Even when she is motionless she continues to speak, and she is often more eloquent then than with words or with gestures. The form of her body makes her breathing a language. The rhythm of her bosom betrays the state of her soul and the degree of her emotion . . . The whole woman speaks. She is language incarnate.[100]

De Gourmont disingenuously extols 'woman', the conserver of songs and tales, teacher of infants and muse to 'poets', as 'the mistresss of civilization',[101] while excluding women (along with 'Negroes', male or female) from the realms of literary and cultural creation. The connection he makes between the material properties of language and the female body would provide, as Peter Nicholls comments, 'a sort of deep structure for the subsequent waves of modernism'.[102] In the more overtly

[98] Hélène Cixous, 'The Laugh of the Medusa' (original French edn. 1975), repr. in Marks and de Courtivron (eds.), *New French Feminisms*, 250.

[99] Remy de Gourmont, 'Women and Language', in *Decadence and Other Essays on the Culture of Ideas* (trans. William Bradley; New York: Harcourt, Brace, 1921), 123, 124–5.

[100] Ibid. 128–9.

[101] 'In all societies, so long as she is young and beautiful, woman, even when a slave, is the mistress of civilization' (ibid. 136).

[102] Nicholls, *Modernisms*, 61–2.

misogynistic aesthetics of T. S. Eliot, Ezra Pound, and Wyndham Lewis, the emphasis is on control, on giving shape and outline to shapelessness and chaos; in his 1923 review of *Ulysses*, Eliot praised Joyce's 'mythic method' as a 'way of controlling, of ordering, of giving a shape and a significance to the immense panorama of futility and anarchy which is contemporary history'.[103] The implicit genderedness of this 'shaping' becomes notoriously explicit in Pound's bizarre Postscript to de Gourmont's *Natural Philosophy of Love*, which he translated in 1921: 'man really the phallus or spermatazoide charging, head-on, the female chaos. Integration of the male in the male organ. Even oneself has felt it, driving any new idea into the great passive vulva of London'.[104] This 'female chaos', archetypally, is both material—the realm of the 'mass', of the 'sluggish matter'[105] that Joyce's Stephen Daedalus must transcend—and mystical or intuitive, the uncontrollable realm of desire and the unconscious. The rejection of this subjective-feminine 'chaos' is inscribed at the aesthetic level as the rejection of the 'materiality' of language: for Eliot, Nicholls argues, 'a decadent language is one which has somehow become "bodily", a condition which prevents "objectivity" and which is quickly marked as "feminine" '; Cassandra Laity makes the same point in relation to Pound.[106] Similarly, for Stephen Daedalus in Joyce's *Portrait*, women's language is 'soft' and associated with their bodily presence: 'it was only amid softworded phrases or rosesoft stuffs that he dared to conceive of the soul or body of a woman moving with tender life'.[107] This unavoidably recalls the 'soft language' of the goat-like devils in Stephen's vision of his personal hell, who (like the demonic counterparts of the susurrating rosesoft women) 'swish' around him in circles, 'to enclose, to enclose'.[108]

But compare de Gourmont ('The whole woman speaks. She is language incarnate') with Hélène Cixous in 'The Laugh of the Medusa' (1976):

[103] T. S. Eliot, 'Ulysses, Order, and Myth', *The Dial*, 70/5 (Nov. 1923), 483.

[104] Ezra Pound, 'Translator's Postscript' to Remy de Gourmont, *The Natural Philosophy of Love* (1921), repr. in Ezra Pound, *Pavannes and Divagations* (London: Peter Owen, 1960), 204.

[105] James Joyce, *Portrait of the Artist as a Young Man* (1916), in *The Essential James Joyce* (London: Triad Grafton, 1977), 301. For a discussion of the modernist association of 'the feminine' and 'the mass', see Huyssen, 'Mass Culture as Woman: Modernism's Other', in *After the Great Divide*.

[106] *Modernisms*, 195; for Laity's point about Pound, see n. 60, above.

[107] Joyce, *Portrait*, 291.

[108] Ibid. 277.

> Listen to a woman speak at a public gathering . . . She doesn't 'speak', she throws her trembling body forward; she lets go of herself, she flies; all of her passes into her voice, and it's with her body that she vitally supports the 'logic' of her speech. Her flesh speaks true. She lays herself bare. In fact, she physically materializes what she's thinking; she signifies it with her body. In a certain way she *inscribes* what she's saying . . .[109]

In this text, Cixous famously exhorts women, 'Write your self. Your body must be heard'.[110] Circling back in this uncanny similarity to de Gourmont, the 1970s feminist theorizing of the idea of feminine language did not reject but *transvalued* the archetypal associations of the feminine with both the intuitive (or unconscious) and the material or bodily. In particular, the French feminist work grounded in linguistic and psychoanalytic theory focused on the body, the unconscious, and 'the feminine' as the repressed of language and the symbolic order, and therefore on the radical potential of the disruption of these systems through what Cixous describes as 'a *new insurgent* writing',[111] a writing practice which may thus be described both as *écriture féminine* and as 'writing the body'. In examining Nin's ideas about language and femininity, women's creation, and writing the body, we are thus in a sense following a double thread: while Nin's thinking about these issues shifted and changed, across time and across different contexts, so too has the complex of ideas *woman–language–body* followed a twisting and in some ways strangely circular path, from de Gourmont's nostalgic prehistory, to the high modernist horror of 'female chaos', to the feminist celebration of women's 'linguistic flesh'.[112]

Woman's creation: 'on being the womb'

The focal point of reference for most discussions of Nin's theory of women's writing or 'feminine' writing is the series of forcefully polemical passages in volume II of the *Journals*, from 1937, in which Nin expounds the need for, and the characteristics of, 'the art of woman'.[113] Interestingly, this attempt to define for herself an artistic credo did not arise primarily out of the aesthetic concerns she had formulated in her

109 Cixous, 'Laugh of the Medusa', 251. 110 Ibid. 250. 111 Ibid.

112 This term is taken from Chantal Chawaf's 1976 article 'La chair linguistique', trans. and repr. in Marks and de Courtivron (eds.), *New French Feminisms*, 177–8.

113 Sharon Spencer, for instance, uses part of this text as a structuring epigraph for her essay 'The Music of the Womb', 161; Margret Andersen focuses on the same passages in her article 'Critical Approaches to Anaïs Nin'.

work on Lawrence—though we can clearly see Nin, in that study, using Lawrence's writing as a model for what would become her own artistic ideals. Rather, her ideas here about 'woman's creation' arose from the conflict she felt between diary writing and fiction writing—a conflict that, crucially, she perceived as gendered.

In February 1937, Nin writes: 'I must continue the diary because it is a feminine activity, it is a personal and personified creation, the opposite of the masculine alchemy. I want to remain on the untransmuted, untransformed, untransposed plane. This alchemy called creation, or fiction, has become for me as dangerous as the machine' (*Journals*, II, 181). This passage is interesting because it contains, as well as the crucial description of the diary as both a feminine and a personal form of creation, several ideas and associations that are at odds with ideas expressed by Nin elsewhere. First, we can note the negative connotations here of 'the machine', with its suggestions of a depersonalized, masculine modernity. The machine clearly represents a threat here, whereas in the passages about New York cited above, Nin seemed to exult both in the strength of the machine and in her own ability to 'enjoy' its power. Perhaps more significant is her claim that she wants to remain 'on the untransmuted, untransformed, untransposed plane'. We see here the negative use of the very terms that she will later describe as the 'magic words', the formulas for the change, movement, and creativity that she sees as so vital (see *A Woman Speaks*, 172). Equally, the metaphor of alchemy, used here negatively, is frequently invoked by Nin in her later writings as a positive image of art.[114]

In this passage, there is a clear polarization, and corresponding value judgement: the personal, feminine creation of diary-writing, with which Nin associates herself, is opposed to the depersonalizing, masculine realm of 'creation, or fiction', which she feels threatened by. Again, in an earlier passage, from June 1935, she writes: 'We all write about the same people, but so differently. I am always true to life, as a woman is. Henry [Miller], [Michael] Fraenkel, and [Fred] Perlès invent, fictionalize'—the idea of 'fictionalizing' here carrying an implication of *distorting* (*Journals*, II, 49). It is this notion of the diary as a personal and feminine form of creation that underlies Nin's statements, in volume II of the *Journals*, on woman's creativity and language: she notes that it was 'the big talk [with Henry Miller and Lawrence Durrell] about or against the diary' that produced her reflections on feminine creativity (*Journals*, II, 262). In

[114] See e.g. *Novel*, 40: 'creation is an *alchemy*'. On p. 157, she describes Proust as an alchemist.

opposition to Miller and Durrell, whom Nin represents as arguing that, to become an artist, she must 'make the leap outside of the womb' (242), Nin presents a manifesto for woman's artistic creativity as essentially personal, connected to the body, nature, and the unconscious. Her key image is that of the womb, both a synecdoche for the (female) body and, as Spencer notes, 'a metaphor for the woman's approach to art':[115]

woman's creation, far from being like man's, must be exactly like her creation of children, that is it must come out of her own blood, englobed by her womb, nourished with her own milk. It must be a human creation, of flesh, it must be different from man's abstractions . . . the woman artist has to fuse creation and life in her own way, or in her own womb if you prefer. She has to create something different from man. Man created a world cut off from nature. Woman has to create within the mystery, storms, terrors, the infernos of sex, the battle against abstractions and art . . . The art of woman must be born in the womb-cells of the mind . . . Woman must not fabricate. She must descend into the real womb and expose its secrets and its labyrinths . . . But woman is not nature only. She is the mermaid with her fish-tail dipped in the unconscious. Her creation will be to make articulate this obscure world which dominates man, which he denies being dominated by, but which asserts its domination in destructive proofs of its presence, madness. (*Journals*, II, 242–4)

We can see here the ambivalence towards the notion of 'art' discussed in Chapter 1. On the one hand, 'art' has negative connotations of artificiality and 'abstraction', the masculine rejection of the 'human' and 'personal' which Nin sees as false and hypocritical. On the other hand, Nin *is* concerned with woman's *artistic*, literary, creation, despite her hyperbolic language which appears to make this creation literally physical ('exactly like her creation of children'). She wants to see the diary as a literary work which nonetheless remains 'human' and personal, and which is therefore an essentially *feminine* form.

In this context, it is interesting to look at the responses of the male writers—Miller, Durrell, and Robert Duncan—who equally saw Nin's diary as an essentially feminine literary enterprise. 'You have done it,' Nin cites Durrell as saying, 'the real female writing' (*Journals*, II, 263). In 1941 she reproduces a letter from Robert Duncan in which he praises the diary as 'the woman's creation', associated with 'life itself':

The very process of the diary is that of life itself, not devouring but nourishing, not transformed by art but passing through your body, your senses . . . Joyce has made the man's creation . . . In this diary you may achieve the woman's creation,

[115] Spencer, *Collage of Dreams*, 109.

the flow, the river which becomes monumental. It will be the form which is within life itself, the woman's creation which is generation. It is your life itself which will become monumental. The writing is only a record . . . (cited in *Journals*, III, 98)

Here we see even more clearly the opposition of 'man's creation' as artistic transformation and 'woman's creation' as bodily, 'generation' rather than 'art'. But here, although Duncan is ostensibly praising the diary as a written work, the writing in fact drops out of the picture, becoming 'only a record'. The diary becomes important not as a new, feminine literary form but as the 'record' of a life.

Perhaps the best known, and probably the most extravagant, paean to Nin's diary is Henry Miller's essay 'Un Être Étoilique', first published in the *Criterion* in 1937 (and discussed at length by George Orwell in his essay on Miller, 'Inside the Whale'[116]). Towards the end of the essay, Miller focuses on the diary specifically as a 'female' text: it is, he says, 'the first female writing I have ever seen: it rearranges the world in terms of female honesty'[117]—thus making again the link, so important to Nin at this stage, of woman's writing with a kind of personal 'truth' or 'honesty' distinct from the dangerous distortions of 'fiction'.[118] He goes on, in an extraordinary passage, to attempt to describe the salient features of this 'female writing':

The result is a language which is ultra-modern and yet which bears no resemblance to any of the masculine experimental processes with which we are familiar. It is precise, abstract, cloudy and unseizable. There are larval thoughts not yet divorced from their dream content, thoughts which seem to slowly crystallize before your eyes, always precise but never tangible, never once arrested so as to be grasped by the mind. It is the opium world of women's physiological being, a sort of cinematic show put on inside the genitourinary tract. There is not an ounce of man-made culture in it; everything related to the head is cut off.[119]

Here, in one bizarre sentence, Miller manages to combine associations to the dream realm, the (sexual) body, and even the cinema. Interestingly, he insists that this language, although quite different from

[116] Orwell does not, however, discuss the essay in relation to Nin, but purely in terms of Miller himself; it is, he remarks, 'one of those revealing passages in which a writer tells you a great deal about himself while talking about somebody else' ('Inside the Whale' [1940], in *Inside the Whale and Other Essays* [Harmondsworth: Penguin, 1957], 42).

[117] Henry Miller, 'Un Être Étoilique' (1937), reprinted in Zaller (ed.), *Casebook*, 21.

[118] As I shall show, she would later refine this naïve idea of 'personal truth' into a focus on the transpersonal realm, a truth which could be captured in fiction.

[119] Miller, 'Un Être Étoilique', 21–2.

'familiar' forms of experimental writing, is 'ultra-modern'; a claim grounded, I would suggest, in the association with the unconscious and the drive to explore and describe the realm of 'larval thoughts'. Miller goes on (in equally extravagant terms) to make the now-familiar distinction between this new female language and the realm of 'art', seen as masculine or male: 'The contrast between this language and that of man's [sic] is forcible; the whole of man's art begins to appear like a frozen edelweiss under a glass bell reposing on a mantelpiece in the deserted home of a lunatic'.[120] In contrast to female language, man's art appears lifeless ('frozen') and pointless.

Miller's descriptions of what he calls Nin's 'extraordinary unicellular language of the female' emphasize again the association with the *bodily* which is so predominant in Nin's diary passages on 'woman's creation'. Both Miller here and Nin in the diary do appear to be talking about a 'female' language in the strong sense of a *woman's* language, grounded in a woman's bodily experience of being-in-the-world. Several further passages from the 1937 diary suggest the importance for Nin, and for her conception of her own writing, of her sense of herself as a woman and, specifically, of the imagery of the womb through which this is focused:[121]

> Writing as a woman. I am becoming more and more aware of this. All that happens in the real womb . . . The diary ended in Fez, in a city, in a street, in a labyrinth for me, because that was the city which looked most deeply like the womb, with its Arabian Nights gentleness, tranquillity and mystery. My self, woman, womb, with grilled windows, veiled eyes. Tortuous streets, secret cells, labyrinths and more labyrinths. (*Journals*, II, 192)

> Waiting in the café, I write these words: 'On *being* the womb.' And it unleashes a tremendous feminine universe. I am completely divorced from man's world of ideas. I swim in nature. On *being* the womb . . . englobing. (*Journals*, II, 196)

Nin's emphasis here on the female body in connection with a woman's language raises the question which has proved the most problematic for Anglo-American feminist critics in relation to ideas of *écriture féminine*: how to understand the notion of 'writing the body', of bringing the (female) body into language. For instance, Ann Rosalind Jones, in a 1981 essay, criticized French feminist ideas of *écriture féminine* and *féminité* as

120 Miller, 'Un Être Étoilique', 22.

121 H.D., in her 1919 essay 'Notes on Thought and Vision', also uses womb imagery in relation to women's perceptions and creativity; she writes that 'the brain and the womb are both centres of consciousness, equally important' (*Notes on Thought and Vision & The Wise Sappho* [San Francisco: City Lights, 1982], 21).

essentialist, idealist, and of dubious political or pragmatic worth (though she conceded a certain 'polemical energy' to such ideas if taken as 'a utopian ideal, an energizing myth'[122]). Jones concluded that 'We [i.e. women] are more likely to write, and to read each other's writing, if we begin by working against the concrete difficulties and the prejudices surrounding women's writing than if we simplify and idealize the process by locating writing as a spontaneous outpouring from the body.'[123]

Clearly, the perception of 'writing the body' as somehow involving a 'spontaneous outpouring'—as though women's writing were literally a flow of milk, blood, or vaginal juices—ensures that the idea appears preposterous even as an 'energizing myth'. It is for this reason, I would suggest, that Diane Richard-Allerdyce, despite her commitment to Nin's importance in terms of *écriture féminine*, is at some pains to distinguish Nin's theory from 'its most essentialist counterparts', by which she implies theories that naïvely invoke 'women's physiology and bodily instincts'.[124] However, Richard-Allerdyce emphasizes throughout her study the importance to Nin's aesthetics of bodily—particularly sensory and rhythmical—dimensions of language, and the shifting connections, for Nin, between 'writing the body' and femininity. Despite her apparent desire to avoid (on Nin's behalf) the accusation of 'essentialism', she also concedes that 'in [Nin's] early work, feminine creativity hinges on the idea of a link between the corporality of language and a woman's relation to her own body'.[125] I would agree that it is in the passages cited above from the late 1930s that we find the strongest link, in Nin's aesthetics, between writing and *woman's* body or physical being-in-the-world. In what way, then, do we interpret this link; and, particularly, how do we understand Nin's use of the key image of the womb?

Luce Irigaray's notion of morphology is helpful here. In 'This Sex which is Not One', Irigaray's central image is that of the two vaginal lips 'which embrace continually'.[126] Irigaray uses this image to develop an account of 'the multiple nature of female desire and language' and to explain, in terms of *form*, the problematic place of woman in a 'phallomorphic' culture (represented very clearly, I would suggest, by Ezra

[122] Ann Rosalind Jones, 'Writing the Body: Towards an Understanding of *l'Écriture Féminine*', in Elaine Showalter (ed.), *The New Feminist Criticism: Essays on Women, Literature and Theory* (London: Virago, 1986), 372.

[123] Ibid. 373.

[124] Richard-Allerdyce, *Remaking of Self*, 12; see also 24; 174 n. 25; 196 n. 14.

[125] Ibid. 196 n. 14.

[126] Luce Irigaray, 'This Sex which is Not One' (1977), repr. in Marks and de Courtivron (eds.), *New French Feminisms*, 100.

Pound's misogynistic emphasis on defending what Irigaray here calls 'the *one* of form' against the formlessness of 'chaos' and 'matter'):

> The value accorded to the only definable form excludes the form involved in female autoeroticism. The *one* of form, the individual sex, proper name, literal meaning—supersedes, by spreading apart and dividing, this touching of *at least two* (lips) which keeps woman in contact with herself, although it would be impossible to distinguish exactly what 'parts' are touching each other. Whence the mystery that she represents in a culture that claims to enumerate everything, cipher everything by units, inventory everything by individualities. *She is neither one nor two.*[127]

Unsurprisingly, Irigaray's use of the image of vaginal lips has been criticized as a mystificatory and essentialist invocation of the body. As Margaret Whitford argues, however, Irigaray is here invoking a connection between the *morphology*—the symbolized or imagined form—of the body and that of language and culture. The morphology of the body stands in the same relation to the empirical, anatomical reality of the body as does the hysterical symptom: 'It must not be assumed here that the body here is the empirical body; symbolism (or representation) is selective . . . the relationship to anatomy is metaphorical, somewhat schematic'.[128] In other words, Irigaray analyses the 'female imaginary' in terms of a woman's metaphoricized relation to her body, focusing on the key image of the two lips constantly 'retouching'.

Nin's use of the womb image, with its 'englobing' and 'labyrinthine' aspects, is similarly morphological—as is suggested by her use of the phrase 'the womb-cells of the mind'. The 'real womb', as she puts it, is simultaneously physical, mythical, and metaphorical, able to serve as the imagistic focus for Nin's conceptions of her own creativity and femaleness. The image of the womb forms the central point in a network of key ideas, the associative links which are central to much of Nin's writing. The morphology of a woman's body becomes the basis for a series, or rather a circle, of metaphorical connections: Nin uses the womb image to link the ideas of woman, labyrinth, the eastern city, the veil, and—crucially—the diary. As I noted in Chapter 3, Nin sees the city of Fez as an image of her own life: Fez is both 'labyrinthine', and 'the city which looked most deeply like the womb'. The diary, of course, is Nin's

[127] Irigaray, 'This Sex', 101.

[128] Margaret Whitford, *Luce Irigaray: Philosophy in the Feminine* (London: Routledge, 1991), 58–9.

personal labyrinth ('I was eleven years old when I walked into the labyrinth of my diary' ['The Labyrinth', 66]), and the associative circle is complete when we note that the original title for 'The Labyrinth' was 'The Paper Womb'.[129] Her forceful polemic on 'woman's creation', a 'female writing', is thus strongly connected to the diary via the image of the womb, with its (imagined) labyrinthine nature and its ability to 'englobe'. As I shall go on to show, the notion of 'englobing' was to remain central to Nin's ideas about feminine writing as they later developed and moved away from the sole concentration on the diary. Here, though, it is important in its ability to suggest the (fantasized) nature of the diary as all-encompassing; Sharon Spencer makes the same point when she suggests that Nin's perception of the diary as a feminine form was grounded in its 'maternal' ability to enclose and protect: 'because in the diary experience was protected against loss, this writing was feminine, i.e. maternal'.[130]

Woman versus artist

Nin's vision at this point of 'woman's creation', though undoubtedly possessing polemical energy, and suggesting the importance of the body in language, is limited by its status as the positive pole of a rigid opposition that links 'art' or 'fiction' with a masculinity seen as dehumanized and dehumanizing. If the diary, as an ostensibly personal, true-to-life, and all-encompassing form, is linked to the maternal, nonetheless the maternal represents for Nin the opposite pole to the *creative*, which is feared as distorting, 'abstract', and masculine. There is, therefore, a double opposition: the opposition of diary and fiction or 'art' is paralleled by that of the woman, or the maternal, and the artist or creator. In the diaries, Nin frequently refers to her association of woman with the maternal, seen as a self-abnegating, even masochistic position which precludes the focus on self necessary for creativity: 'the masochism of woman is different from that of man. Hers comes from her maternal instinct. A mother . . . suffers, gives, feeds. A woman is taught not to think of herself, to be selfless, to serve, help. This masochism is almost natural to woman . . . It is my maternal instinct which places me in danger'

[129] It was published under this title in the Dec. 1937–Jan. 1938 issue of *The Booster*, a magazine of which Henry Miller's friend Fred Perlès had been given the editorship and which he and Miller turned into a short-lived 'house magazine' for their group of friends and writers, including Nin. See Fitch, *Anaïs*, 209–10.

[130] Spencer, *Collage of Dreams*, 103.

(*Journals*, I, 173). This description of the 'danger' of the maternal instinct recalls Nin's description, cited above, of fiction having become for her 'as dangerous as the machine'. Having set up a rigid opposition between impersonal masculine creativity and selfless maternal femininity, Nin feels herself to be in danger from both.

Nin focuses particularly on her conflict between the 'woman' and the 'artist' in the context of her analysis with Otto Rank in 1933–4. She portrays him as reinforcing this opposition: '"When the neurotic woman gets cured, she becomes a woman. When the neurotic man gets cured, he becomes an artist. Let us see whether the woman or the artist will win out"' (*Journals*, I, 301). Woman is 'too close to life, too human', unable to 'destroy': 'Rank believes that to create it is necessary to destroy. Woman cannot destroy. He believes that may be why she has rarely been a great artist' (*Journals*, I, 319; II, 36). These passages are important less as (putative) statements of Otto Rank's views than as indications of Nin's own construction of the conflicts,[131] providing the relevant background to her opposition, in 1937, of 'woman's creation' and 'man's art'.

As Richard-Allerdyce states, then, 'Nin's efforts to achieve integration of two "selves"—the creative and maternal—were also related to a need to reconcile the two forms of writing that she still considered in opposition—diary and fiction'.[132] Richard-Allerdyce traces the process of this resolution through Nin's accounts of her analysis with the Jungian Martha Jaeger in 1942–3. At the beginning of the analysis, Nin writes: 'This is a new drama. The father is absent from this drama. This one is the drama of the mother, of woman . . . the woman in relation to herself—her conflict between selfishness and individuality . . . There are depths I have not yet entered, which I struggled to express when I argued against Henry and Durrell and wrote about woman in creation' (*Journals*, III, 240–1).

Nin portrays Jaeger as focusing on her masochistic concept of the maternal ('you became the all-mother, giving out endlessly' [240]), and

[131] As I argued in Chapter 2, I agree with Sharon Spencer ('Delivering the Woman Artist') that Nin, to the end of her life, considered herself greatly indebted to Rank and particularly to his emphasis on creativity and the creative will. Even in her accounts of the analysis itself, she makes the point strongly that Rank, unlike her previous analyst René Allendy, *does* recognize the importance to her of her writing and creativity: 'He does not separate me from my work. On the contrary. He seizes me through my work' (*Incest*, 297; also *Journals*, I, 296). I would therefore argue that the statements Nin 'quotes' apparently opposing 'woman' and 'artist' are far more important in terms of her own struggle with these ideas than as transcriptions of what Rank supposedly said.

[132] Richard-Allerdyce, *Remaking of Self*, 69.

therefore as enabling her to make the link between her negative view of woman-as-mother and her 'guilt for creating', which produced a hostility to the idea of creativity, distorted into the idea of 'aggression' or 'destruction':

> I did not want to steal man's creation, his thunder. Creation and femininity seemed incompatible. The *aggressive* act of creation. 'Not aggressive,' said Jaeger, '*active*'. (259)

> The creator's guilt in me has to do with my femininity, my subjection to man. Also with my maternal self in conflict with my creative self. A negative form of creation. (260)

The resolution of what Nin calls 'the maternal complex, the guilt before creation' (264) thus involves two interrelated strands: moving away from a view of womanhood, or femininity, as essentially masochistic and selfless, and moving away from a view of creativity as aggressive or destructive—and masculine. In a passage from 1943, Nin suggests her new ability to make a positive link between femininity and creativity: 'I represent, for other women too, the one who wanted to create with, by, and through her femininity . . . It is the creative self which will rescue me . . . the displacement is taking place harmoniously and I am entering a larger realm' (264). The 'larger realm', I would suggest, is a realm of artistic creativity that can move beyond the sphere of the diary while remaining, in some sense, 'feminine'.

In the 1947 essay 'On Writing', Nin can speak of 'the power of art', a power that—citing D. H. Lawrence—she links to symbolization and its ability to connect with the deepest levels of human perception and experience: '"the power of the symbol is to arouse the deep, emotional, dynamic, primitive self"' ('On Writing', in *Mystic*, 40). This power is also sensory: 'art is our relation to the senses' (41). Writing in 1968, in *The Novel of the Future*, Nin refers to the opposition she constructed between diary and fiction firmly in the past tense: 'The duality between fiction and diary writing seemed for a long time to be an insoluble conflict'; 'I was wary of invention' (*Novel*, 107; 156). In a 1974 lecture entitled 'The New Woman', she suggests that as well as needing 'intimacy and a deep knowledge of a few human beings', the personal realm, we also need 'mythology and fiction', the realm of art ('The New Woman', in *Sensitive Man*, 16).

The importance of art, its transformative abilities and 'magical' powers, is a central theme in *A Woman Speaks*. In several passages, Nin discusses the conflict she had felt between diary and fiction, and the resolution of this conflict through the realization of the importance of art in *transforming* the emotional or psychological 'truth' of the personal realm into the transpersonal realm of the symbolic, the mythic:

> for the novel not to die—for writing not to die—we had to return to the sources of life, which meant biography, which meant basing all happenings on truth, but not forgetting that art would then transform this truth into poetry.
>
> We have two distinct needs. One is a human need to be intimate with experience, to be very close to experience, to be as directly related to events as possible . . . Then there's a second need in human nature which is to create something that has more permanence, which is the myth of our lives, the symbolic, spiritual significance of our lives. And this we can only do with a word that I know you don't like to use but which is *art*, which is literature . . . We need the documentary; we need the psychological story; we need the knowledge of our daily life, the inner journey, which the diary can accomplish; but we also need the fiction because the fiction is the myth. (*A Woman Speaks*, 179)

As I have already argued, we may disagree with Nin's construction of the diary as 'documentary'. The important point here, though, is the positive role Nin now ascribes to the 'alchemy' of art, of 'fiction', her recognition of the need to move beyond the 'entirely personal'. Rather than viewing art as the distortion of a (fantasized) realm of pure 'truth', she now sees it in terms of a necessary symbolizing or mythologizing of experience, though grounded in what she calls 'emotional truth' or 'emotional [or psychological] reality' (*A Woman Speaks*, 145).

The movement away from seeing art as masculine and dehumanized, the positive linkage of creativity and femininity, can be traced in an interesting diary passage from 1959, in which Nin discusses the work of Marguerite Young, whose enormous novel *Miss MacIntosh, My Darling* made a powerful impact on her. She writes:

> Long ago Otto Rank, who had written so much about the artist, stated that woman had not created imaginative works such as *Don Quixote* or *Ulysses* because she feared to cut the umbilical cord, to separate from the human and the personal. I had this fear. Out of it was born the diary. Marguerite solved this by developing a cellular structure, an unbroken cellular development, a vast mesh which would capture everything rather than separate, divide. She *englobed*. The female need to nourish, to encompass, to hold, commune with, was fulfilled in the spider-like web . . . So she had no need to cut the umbilical cord and seek abstraction. (*Journals*, VI, 215–16)

Here, once again, we find the idea of 'englobing', associated with the womb and (as Spencer states) with the perceived female/maternal need 'to encompass, to hold'. However, this image of 'englobing' is here, crucially, being applied to a woman's work of *fiction*. Marguerite Young, Nin suggests, has created a work of fiction that nonetheless 'captures everything'; in her 1968 review of the book Nin describes it as 'a complete universe . . . a search for reality through a maze of illusions and fantasy and dreams . . . a submarine world, geographically situated in the unconscious and in the night'.[133] Nin's use of the image of 'englobing' now serves to connect the idea of female writing not with a work perceived as removed from the sphere of art and fiction, but with a form of fiction characterized by its 'cellular' or 'web-like' structure and its ability to include the 'submarine' realms of the unconscious, fantasy and dream.

At this point we seem to have come much closer to the ideal language of poetic prose discussed in the first part of this chapter, a synthetic language that links conscious and unconscious, and that 'writes the body' by bringing rhythm and texture into language—bringing back, that is, what has been repressed not only from writing but from our culture and experience as a whole. As Richard-Allerdyce puts it, Nin's 'quest for a synchronic moment in art took her theories of creativity beyond the polarization of gender where they had started, while maintaining [the] emphasis on the physical texture of language so central to her first critical study' (her study of Lawrence).[134] I have traced this movement away from the gendered opposition of diary and fiction, 'woman's creation' and 'masculine alchemy', towards a positive understanding of the 'magical power' of art and specifically of a language grounded in the patterns and rhythms of desire, the body, and the unconscious. But I have also noted the persistence of the links between the body, the unconscious and the *feminine*, from the masculinist modernism of Pound, Eliot, and Lewis to the polemical celebration of *féminité* in French feminist thought. If Nin's formulations of the ideal poetic language stress the importance of writing the body and the unconscious, to what extent do they also stress 'the feminine' as part of this linguistic return of the repressed?

Écriture féminine?

Richard-Allerdyce claims that *The Novel of the Future* 'centers around [Nin's] ideas about the relation of the feminine to a synchronic moment in art'.[135] I would argue that, in fact, this is not the case. My point is not

[133] Review of *Miss MacIntosh, My Darling*, first published in *Open City* (Los Angeles, May 1968), reprinted in *Sensitive Man*, 72.

[134] *Remaking of Self*, 164.

[135] Ibid. 175 n. 31.

that Nin does not make, and explore, this connection; rather it is that Richard-Allerdyce is here misrepresenting the *focus* of *The Novel of the Future*, which does not 'centre' on the place of the feminine or on issues of gender at all. Certainly, Nin does refer to gender issues. She suggests a connection between a 'feminine awareness' and the desire to create an 'organic'[136] form of art that links and encompasses (mind and body, conscious and unconscious) rather than separating; in what is clearly (following her earlier comments about Marguerite Young's work) a rhetorical question, she asks: 'Was it a feminine tendency, to relate, unite, connect, organically, cellularly, while the masculine mind wanted to separate, to become independent?' (*Novel*, 75). She also makes a connection between a feminine sensibility and that of 'the artist' generally, thus suggesting that a male artist (or creative thinker) operates by means of a feminine mode of perception: 'The man who proceeds like a woman, in leaps, is the artist, the creative scientist, and the inventor' (*Novel*, 39); 'woman imitated man's intellectualizations and rationalizations and did not trust her way of perceiving which was related to the artist' (75).

However, Nin does not structure the book around these connections, but leaves them, to a perhaps surprising degree, in the background. *The Novel of the Future* is a polemical book; but it is not, in terms of Nin's own focusing of the issues, a polemic for an *écriture féminine*. It is, as Richard-Allerdyce rightly states, a call for a 'synchronic moment in art', and more particularly it is a study of a form of writing that can reintegrate the sundered aspects of our experience, reincorporating body, senses, and unconscious patterns into language. Nin calls for a writing of the body to overturn what she sees as a long-standing repression and oppression:

The Calvinist puritanism of speech [associated with the American school of 'social realism', the 'action novelist'] weighed heavily also on color, rhythm, musicality of language . . . This constriction caused a whole trend of gray, lifeless novels, pedestrian and without effectiveness, for our senses participate in our reception of words, and our senses were undernourished . . . Poetry is not an aesthetic luxury; it is our relation to the senses. (*Novel*, 94–5)

Here Nin's rhetoric is strikingly close to, for instance, that of French writer Chantal Chawaf in her 1976 essay 'Linguistic Flesh':

Isn't the final goal of writing to articulate the body? For me the sensual juxtaposition of words has one function: to liberate a living paste, to liberate matter.

[136] Interestingly, Marguerite Duras also uses the word 'organic' to describe 'feminine writing'; see excerpt from 1975 interview in Marks and de Courtivron (eds.), *New French Feminisms*, 174.

> Language through writing has moved away from its original sources: the body and the earth. Too often GOD was written instead of LIFE. Classicism and rationalism have mutilated the verbal paganism of the Middle Ages and the Renaissance. Linguistic flesh has been puritanically repressed . . . In order to reconnect the book with the body and with pleasure, we must disintellectualize writing. The corporality of language stirs up our sensuality, wakes it up, pulls it away from indifferent inertia . . .[137]

Chawaf goes on to make the link with the feminine, repressed along with the body and re-emerging through (the writing of) the body: 'If a music of femininity is arising out of its own oppression, it materializes through the rediscovered body'.[138] But Nin's polemic in *The Novel of the Future* is not primarily constructed in terms of gender and does not specifically call for a 'feminine writing'. Rather, the key figure is 'the artist', 'the poet'. Richard-Allerdyce's comment on volume VII of the *Journals* applies equally to *The Novel of the Future*: 'For the most part . . . Nin ceases to use terminology denoting gender to describe differences in artistic tone and uses terms such as the "modern" writer and the writer of the future, which she opposes to "traditional" artists'[139]—or indeed to 'non-artists'. The polemical drive of *The Novel of the Future* is not primarily towards a language that will liberate women through an inscription of the feminine, but towards a language that will restore to writing its 'magical power' through a 'new synthesis' of the dimensions of human experience.

However, if we turn to the lectures and seminars transcribed in *A Woman Speaks*, we do find much more focus on the relation between language and art and an inscription of the feminine. This shift of focus is strongly bound up with the particular context in which these texts were produced and received: the majority date from 1972–3 and were addresses given at events focusing explicitly on women, the arts, and the new feminism.[140] Nin speaks here from her position as a high-profile (if controversial) figure in the women's movement in the USA, following the publication of her diaries; more particularly, she speaks as a woman writer perceived as emphasizing (both in her writing and in her public persona) the feminine and the personal, and as focusing on the creative and the psychological rather than the political and sociological dimensions of 'liberation'. Clearly, questions surrounding the specificity of women's writing and artistic creativity more generally were central to this

[137] Chawaf, 'Linguistic Flesh', 177. [138] Ibid. 178. [139] *Remaking of Self*, 160.

[140] See *A Woman Speaks*, pp. xvii–xviii for details; titles include 'Women and Writing', 'The Emerging Woman', 'Adventurous Women', and 'Magic Women'.

context, giving Nin the setting and the impetus to foreground these issues, to focus her ideas differently than she had done in *The Novel of the Future*.

We find here, then, a considerable stress on the contemporary need for women to articulate their feelings and experiences: 'We need you to write, we need you to speak, we need this revelation of woman who is not only trying to be revealed to herself but needs to be revealed to others' (*A Woman Speaks*, 76). In this exhortation to women to write, and in the notion of this writing as an articulation of woman not only to man but to herself, a form of self-reclamation, Nin is very close to Cixous, who in 'The Laugh of the Medusa' repeatedly exhorts women: 'Write! Writing is for you, you are for you.'[141] Writing, for Cixous, will 'return' woman to herself:

> By writing her self, woman will return to the body which has been more than confiscated from her . . . Write your self. Your body must be heard . . .
>
> To write. An act which will not only 'realize' the decensored relation of woman to her sexuality, to her womanly being, giving her access to her native strength; it will give her back her goods, her pleasures, her organs, her immense bodily territories which have been kept under seal . . .[142]

Where Cixous suggests that 'womanly being' has been kept 'under seal', Nin uses the image of the veil. She locates the call for women's self-articulation firmly in relation to the contemporary moment, the moment of women's liberation:

> This is a tremendous moment for women which we are witnessing, because, in spite of their not realizing it, our women have been as veiled as in the Orient. They have veiled their thoughts through a long traditional sense of secrecy about their feelings; they have not been articulate. They have written as men, they have painted as men, and we did not really know what they felt. But now *we* have come to the moment of unveiling of women which is just as critical as the unveiling of Oriental women. We are unveiling our thoughts, we are unveiling our feelings, and for that we need extremely expressive, articulate women who will at least know themselves, know what they are trying to tell others, know who they are.[143]

Language is crucial to this 'unveiling'. Nin suggests that 'the feminine point of view has been much more difficult to express than the masculine',

[141] Cixous, 'Laugh of the Medusa', 246. [142] Ibid. 250.

[143] *A Woman Speaks*, 75; this text dates from 1973. It is interesting to note the unmitigatedly negative connotations here of the veil; cf. my discussion in Chapter 3 of Nin's fascination with the seductive figure of the veiled woman, and my analysis in Chapter 5 of her own staging of this image in the photograph she had taken for Otto Rank (Fig. 2).

because women 'have operated on a combination of instinct, emotion, intellect, and observation, a synthesis which we call intuition'; women experience 'a diffused awareness . . . they are sensory, they feel things with their whole bodies' (76, 77). The articulation of this synthetic awareness and experience, Nin argues, 'requires a much more complex language and expression' (77). Like Cixous, she issues a call to the pen: 'I would like to see women creating their own language . . . trying really to find a language for their feelings, a language for those things which come from the unconscious, which are instinctive' (75).

Here we can see Nin making a much stronger link between a synthetic mode of awareness, incorporating the bodily and instinctual/unconscious realms, and the specifically *feminine.* Her description of women's 'diffused awareness' is very similar to Irigaray's description in 'This Sex': '[woman] experiences pleasure almost everywhere . . . the geography of her pleasure is much more diversified, more multiple in its differences, more complex, more subtle, than is imagined'.[144] For both Irigaray and Nin, this diffused and complex awareness—more particularly, *desire*—requires a different, more complex, language than that which is adequate to express man's (supposedly) more one-dimensional, phallomorphic desire and mode of awareness. Irigaray writes: 'Woman's desire most likely does not speak the same language as man's desire'.[145] Nin, in the well-known Preface to *Delta of Venus,* writes: 'I had a feeling that Pandora's box contained the mysteries of woman's sensuality, so different from man's and for which man's language was inadequate'.[146]

In making this series of links between desire, language, and the feminine, Nin comes much closer to the French feminist arguments and manifestos: writing the body (and the unconscious) becomes the writing of the feminine, through its placement in an explicit context of feminist polemic. It is, of course, relevant that Nin's texts reproduced in *A Woman Speaks* are approximately contemporary with the publication of the key texts of the French writers I have been discussing: Irigaray published *Speculum: de l'autre femme* in 1974 and *Ce sexe qui n'en est pas un* in 1977, Cixous 'Le rire de la méduse' in 1975. But it is also important to note the very considerable differences within what we might broadly see as the context of second-wave feminism. The work of Cixous and Irigaray was grounded in the French theoretical context of structuralism and

[144] Irigaray, 'This Sex', 103.
[145] Ibid. 101.
[146] *Delta of Venus*, 14. The Preface was written in 1976, but Nin is quoting her own diary from 1941 (see *Journals*, III, 100).

Lacanian psychoanalysis—what Rachel Bowlby calls 'those textual revolutionaries of the Parisian 60s'.[147] Nin—while herself deeply influenced by a predominantly French literary and cultural tradition focused on psychoanalysis, Surrealism, and experimental art—was, in the 1970s, writing and speaking in the context of an American feminist movement much more focused on political and sociological change. In comparing Nin's ideas on writing the feminine with those of contemporary French theorists, then, we should bear in mind these contextual differences as well as the similarities. Precisely one of the most interesting aspects of Nin's 1970s call for women to 'creat[e] their own language' is that, with all its parallels—in both content and polemical stance—to the French manifestos for an *écriture féminine*, this call was being issued in a very different setting.[148]

We should also note that, even in the more overtly woman-centred context of *A Woman Speaks*, we find an attempt to stress the potentially universal reach of the ideal language and its ability to connect women and men. Nin defends her mentor, Lawrence (damned by Kate Millett in *Sexual Politics* alongside Henry Miller and Norman Mailer—the unholy trinity of sexual 'counter-revolutionaries') as the 'pioneer' in this creative endeavour: 'we do owe him a tremendous debt for his effort to find a language . . . which was not the language of ideas . . . but the language for feelings, instincts, emotions and intuitions' (78). The language of the unconscious is, Nin suggests, both feminine and universal: 'the dreams of men and women are the same, the unconscious is universal . . . *there* the things stem from feeling and instinct and have not gone through the rationalization process, and therefore this is a *feminine* point of view' (77). Again, as we saw in *The Novel of the Future*, she suggests that there is an affinity between the feminine mode of perception and that of 'the artist', female *or* male: 'the artist is the one who accepts this feminine, intuitive side and stays close to the unconscious' (89). In the focus on the unconscious and on a language through which to express it, then, Nin sees a means of bringing the sexes closer together, though closer to the pole of 'femininity': 'the study of the unconscious is the thing that really

[147] Rachel Bowlby, 'The Feminine Female', *Social Text* 7 (1983), 54.

[148] By the early 1980s, of course, ideas and practices of *écriture féminine* had clearly influenced American feminist criticism; Rachel Blau DuPlessis's 1981 piece 'For the Etruscans', reprinted in Elaine Showalter's 1985 collection *The New Feminist Criticism*, is a good example. In her introduction, Showalter cagily noted that 'whether these [French feminist] revolutionary critical styles alone can ever have revolutionary social impact is a question much debated by more empirical and activist American feminists' (9).

brings us [i.e. women and men] together, because in the unconscious man behaves far more as the woman always has' (97). She even suggests that the specific focus on women's writing and creativity should be viewed as what we might call strategic essentialism, an emphasis that will ultimately cease to be necessary:

> I'm sorry that we have to go through this phase of working as women and saying 'women writers', because this brings us back again to those distinctions. I wish we didn't have any distinctions. But we're still working with them, and until . . . we're treated as among the best artists, that distinction has to be made. I'm sorry it has to be done that way, but I think it's only a phase. (90)

Here Nin acknowledges the cultural and historical situatedness of her own focus, and the broader feminist focus, on the specificity of women's art and creativity. Clearly, she does take on the archetypal association of woman, or the feminine, with both the body and the unconscious; for Nin, this connection is strongly positive, connecting the feminine to the realm 'where all the richness lies', the Surrealists' realm of 'the marvellous'. But in her emphasis on 'the artist', Nin also emphasizes the potential universality of this realm. If women have, as she suggests, remained closer to the unconscious and to the sensory, nonetheless these realms are equally available to men, and have indeed been the home of 'the poets' to whom, throughout her writings, she confesses herself indebted—Rimbaud, Proust, Breton, Michaux, and Lawrence, as well as Djuna Barnes, Anna Kavan, and Marguerite Young.

In tracing Nin's explorations of the issues surrounding women and creativity, and the role of gender in her formulations of the ideal poetic language, we need to be aware of the different strands within Nin's thinking and the changes in the content and the focus of her ideas over time and in different contexts. This is particularly important precisely because many of Nin's formulations are so rhetorically striking and do lend themselves so well to a feminist appropriation, which may, however, elide some significant points. For instance, both Sharon Spencer and Margret Andersen focus on Nin's use of womb imagery in relation to women's writing. But neither Spencer nor Andersen notes—as Richard-Allerdyce does—that Nin's original articulation of 'the language of the womb' was closely bound up with the gendered *conflict* that she perceived, at that time, between diary writing and fiction writing, and between maternal femininity and artistic creativity.[149] Again, Spencer's

[149] As I have noted, though, Spencer does discuss this conflict in *Collage of Dreams*.

linking of Nin's womb imagery with her musical model for writing skates over the different, sometimes problematic, ways in which Nin's ideas on gender and writing interrelate at different points.

However, maintaining an awareness of these differences is not to underestimate either Nin's commitment to exploring the interactions of femininity and creativity, or the power and polemical energy of her writing on the issue. Nin's sense of herself as representative of other women's efforts at self-articulation comes through clearly in a diary passage from 1943 which also contains one of her most striking formulations of the link between the feminine and the musical language of the senses: 'I feel them seeking to speak through me, these women who have taken longer to speak than men because what stirred in them were states which are not articulate in the language of man, but perhaps in the language of music if this music could be frozen in the air to catch the words it forms' (*Journals*, III, 255).

5

'I am the Other Face of You': Fantasies and Femininity

In *House of Incest*, Nin's first published work of fiction and the text which she saw as containing the seeds of all her later writing, we find the image of two women become one, 'soldered together' in a fantasy of identification: 'For an hour you will be me; that is, the other half of yourself. The half you lost' (185). Sabina and the narrator are two faces of the same woman, revolving like day and night, like a planet—'the "two-faced herm" that makes beauty and death one':[1]

> I AM THE OTHER FACE OF YOU
>
> Our faces are soldered together by soft hair, soldered together, showing two profiles of the same soul . . . Only our faces must shine twofold—like day and night—always separated by space and the evolutions of time. (185–6)

In the first part of this chapter I want to trace the recurrence, through Nin's writing, of phantasmatic identifications between women—the ways in which, over and over again, one woman comes to stand as another's fantasy of self or of femininity. As I shall show, Nin explores the ways in which women act as 'mirrors' for each other: mirrors which reflect back aspects of the self that cannot be acknowledged or cannot be lived out, fantasies that can be lived through the other but remain problematic for the self. I shall argue that Nin's focus on *faces* and on *costumes*

[1] Brenda Silver, *Virginia Woolf Icon*, 252 (partly quoting from Mario Praz). Reading Silver's fascinating book after researching this chapter I was struck by the similarities between some of the 'versions' of Woolf and Nin, particularly the associations of monstrosity and double-sidedness explored in Silver's chapter 'The Monstrous Union of Virginia Woolf and Marilyn Monroe' (236–72). The obvious difference between Woolf and Nin is the association of Woolf with intellect: she is the archetypal intellectual woman, most often represented, as Silver notes, as a disembodied head (see e.g. p. 238). Nin, like Monroe, is more usually associated with body and sexuality. Her status as a writer, however (unlike Monroe's status as pure visual icon), pulls her back towards Woolf. The dominant 'version' of Nin that I have encountered in general conversation is that of 'writer of erotica', which obviously combines sexuality and textuality.

as signifiers of identity and identification raises questions of surface and depth which can be analysed in terms of what Talia Schaffer, following on from Judith Butler, calls 'masquerade logic'.[2]

Schaffer uses concepts of costuming and masquerade in her study of the photographs that accompany the text of Virginia Woolf's *Orlando*, drawing out the ways in which Woolf plays text and photographs against each other and in support of each other around the issues—central to the novel—of costume and identity, fiction and biography. Interestingly, Nin attempted to use photography in a similar way when, writing *This Hunger* in 1945, she posed as all the book's female characters and 'as the author', using the photographs in 1946 as publicity material for *Ladders to Fire*. I shall analyse the ways in which this use of photographs, like Woolf's, brings to the fore questions of costuming and identity; and, in staging an interplay between Nin and her characters, highlights the complex interactions of fiction and (auto)biography, setting up what Schaffer calls 'successive layers of masquerade'.[3]

Finally, I shall look at some of the very different responses Nin has provoked, and continues to provoke, from women—the 'versioning' of Nin. In particular, I shall consider feminist responses to Nin in the 1970s, the fanzine-style tributes to Nin found on the several websites currently devoted to her, and the images of Nin produced by critics reviewing the two major biographies of Nin by Fitch and Bair. These responses to Nin are frequently characterized by their extremeness, whether in a positive or negative direction. As a means of accounting for this phenomenon, I shall argue that, just as Nin in her texts depicts one woman as playing out another's fantasies of femininity, so Nin herself comes to function in this way for other women, becoming a kind of symbolic place-holder for a variety of fantasies and images—both strongly positive and strongly negative—of femininity. We can thus see, enacted on another level, the issues of mirroring and of different 'faces' of femininity that are so central to Nin's fictional explorations of womanhood.[4]

[2] Talia Schaffer, 'Posing *Orlando*', in Ann Kibbey, Kayann Short, and Abouali Farmanfarmaian (eds.), *Sexual Artifice: Persons, Images, Politics* (*Genders*, 19; New York: New York Univ. Press, 1994), 31.

[3] Ibid.

[4] This image of 'mirroring' is also the governing metaphor for Paul Herron's *Anaïs Nin: A Book of Mirrors* (Huntingdon Woods, Mich.: Sky Blue Press, 1996), an anthology of writings about Nin—including essays, poems, interviews, and personal recollections—in which the contributors describe the various ways in which they see themselves 'reflected' in Nin and her work.

'YOU ARE THE WOMAN I WANT TO BE'

In Chapter 3, I discussed the way in which Nin's attraction to June Mansfield was grounded in her (not unproblematic) identification with June—June's ability to represent for Nin a particularly seductive fantasy of femininity, the myth-making *femme fatale*. Nin sees in June an aspect of herself taken to the extreme; she apostrophizes June: 'Deep down, I am not different from you. I dreamed you, I wished for your existence. You are the woman I want to be. I see in you that part of me which is you' (*Journals*, I, 28). Knowing that she could never, in reality, live June's life, Nin nevertheless lives out vicariously through June, or her construction of June, her own fantasy of a particular kind of femininity—amoral, unfettered, dramatically mysterious. She also sees June as attracted to her in the same way, each standing as a fantasy self for the other. Depicting this relationship in the prose poem *House of Incest*, Nin shows Sabina and the narrator drawn together as the two faces, the two halves, of each other. They each see in the other the 'lost' half of themselves, the submerged or shadow self: 'I become you. And you become me. Silence the sensational course of your body and you will see in me, intact, your own fears, your own pities. You will see love which was excluded from the passions given you, and I will see the passions excluded from love' (185).

Nin would later restage, with other women, the relationship she experienced with June. The same dynamics of identification and projection can be seen, for instance, in her diary portrayals of her relationships with Thurema Sokol in 1936 and with Luise Rainer in 1941. In both cases, Nin depicts a passionate friendship based on a mutual fantasy of identification (she tells Luise, ' "We are like sisters. We need each other" ' [*Journals*, III, 143]; Luise, after reading parts of Nin's diary, writes to her, ' "I am like you. How alike we are! Why, you are writing *me*" ' [160]), followed by inevitable disillusionment and withdrawal.

Beginning with the figure of June Mansfield, Nin transposed these relationships into her fictional explorations of the complex issues of identity, fantasy, and projection at work in relationships between women; almost all of her fiction is to some extent (auto)biographical, her characters 'composites' (*Novel*, 123) or distillations both of people that she knew and of aspects of herself.[5] In particular, the *roman fleuve* form,

[5] I would, however, reject as too one-directional the model proposed by Suzanne Nalbantian in *Aesthetic Autobiography*. Nalbantian analyses Nin's work in terms of a 'process of transformation from the real to the artistic' (173), arguing that we can trace 'four

with its structure of loosely interwoven narrative threads, focused on a small group of characters, allowed Nin to return again and again to the issues of self and other, identity and identification, that preoccupied her.

Thus, in *Ladders to Fire*, the powerful attraction between Lillian and Djuna is based on a mutual recognition of the submerged aspect of self in the other. The controlled Djuna is drawn to Lillian, with her 'violence' and 'explosions', because she lives out her own repressed 'violence' vicariously through the other woman: 'Djuna contained within herself a Lillian too, to whom she had never given a moment's freedom, and it made her strangely free when Lillian gave vent to her anger or rebellions' (35). For Lillian, Djuna represents the 'femininity' she cannot access in herself: 'In front of Lillian walked Lillian's lost femininity' (42). So Djuna interprets Lillian's desperate courtship of her as an attempt at identification or appropriation, a way to regain her 'femininity' (and therefore her proper place and function within the heterosexual system) by literally possessing Djuna as her own: 'She wants something of me that only a man can give her. But first of all she wants to become me' (42).

Later in the book, Lillian's identification is with Sabina, the apparently unfettered, mysterious, and erotic *allumeuse*. When Sabina, uneasy with Lillian's 'directness', says to her '"You want to unmask me"', Lillian replies, '"If I were to unmask you, Sabina, I would only be revealing myself: you act as I would act if I had the courage"' (97). Again the eroticism of their encounter is ultimately a desire 'to become each other', because they see in each other the self they want to become or regain:

> They both wanted to exchange bodies, exchange faces. There was in both of them the dark strain of wanting to become the other . . . Sabina looked at the whiteness of Lillian's body as into a mirror and saw herself as a girl, standing at the beginning of her life unblurred, unmarked. She wanted to return to this early self. And Lillian wanted to enter the labyrinth of knowledge . . . (105–6)

Their attempted lovemaking fails because they desire not each other but the self in the other: 'Their bodies touched and then fell away, as if both of them had touched a mirror, their own image upon a mirror. They had felt the cold wall, they had felt the mirror that never appeared when they were taken by man. Sabina had merely touched her own youth, and Lillian her free passions' (106). Here Nin makes explicit the mirroring

different levels of expression through which Nin travelled': from 'life facts', to the original diaries, to the edited diaries 'for public consumption', and finally on to 'the permanence of her art' (196–7). As I have argued throughout this book, for Nin 'life' was always already strongly narrativized; she had an acute sense of the spiralling interactions of 'text' and 'life' and of the fictionality of selves, to which Nalbantian's model does not, I think, do justice.

effect that, I want to argue, structures all of these phantasmatic identifications. What appears in the 'mirror' may be a fantasy in the sense of an *ideal*, something which the woman consciously wants to become but cannot: thus Lillian desires Djuna's femininity, and Sabina longs for Lillian's 'innocence'. Or it may be a more problematic fantasy, desired in the other because it is repressed in the self. It is Sabina, particularly, who represents for other women a model of femininity and sexuality that they may identify with in fantasy but cannot act out in reality—or which they can identify with only unconsciously, while consciously repudiating it. Djuna voices this in *The Four-Chambered Heart*:

> Sabina is only behaving as all women do in their dreams, at night. I feel responsible for her acts, because when we walk together and I listen to her telling me about her adventures, a part of me is not listening to her telling me a story but recognizing scenes I have dreamed and which therefore I have committed. What is dreamed is committed. In my dreams I have been Sabina . . . Sabina cannot be made alone responsible for acting the dreams of many women, just because the others sit back and participate with a secret part of their selves. Through secret and small vibrations of the flesh they admit to being silent accomplices to Sabina's acts. (166–7)

FACES AND COSTUMES

In her depictions of this 'mirroring' between women, Nin often places particular emphasis on *faces* and *costumes* as signifiers of identity. In *Ladders to Fire*, Lillian and Sabina want to 'exchange faces'. In *House of Incest*, the narrator sees herself as 'the other face' of Sabina; the image is that of two faces, two 'profiles of the same soul', revolving like day and night. This image is picked up again in the second volume of the *Journals*, where Nin describes a woman called Hélène: 'She really has two faces: one at home, sewing, serious, tragic, the Catholic woman who is afraid of sinning, and the other outside, with mocking eyes, a sardonic mouth, a daring and voluptuous appearance . . . the different aspects of her personality are like women on a revolving stage' (*Journals*, II, 193). There is an ambiguity here, a problem of surface and depth, seeming and being: a face is both a mask, a surface which disguises a deeper truth, and the key site of that truth, that identity—so that if Lillian and Sabina 'exchange faces', they are exchanging selves.

Problems of surface and depth are also central to the imagery of costume which Nin deploys. On the one hand, a costume can function to disguise what is 'underneath'; so Djuna disguises a 'masculine' self with a 'costume' of femininity: 'While wearing the costume of utter femininity . . . she nevertheless disguised in herself an active lover of the world' (*Ladders*, 34). Here the costume is both literal (Djuna wears 'feminine' clothes and trappings) and metaphorical, a 'costume' in the sense of a surface self at odds with some 'deeper' or more 'real' identity. Similarly, Lillian is described as 'hidden in her coat of armour' (43), disguising vulnerability behind violent activity. The metaphor depends on an understanding of 'costume' as a surface which may be at odds with what is underneath, a level of mere 'seeming' which hides a deeper 'being'.

On the other hand, Nin also undercuts this model of surface and depth, seeming and being, by suggesting that the 'reality' of the self may in fact be *constituted* by, or through, an 'appearing'. So, while Nin describes Lillian's 'lost femininity' as 'imprisoned in the deepest wells of her being', she also suggests that Lillian will recapture this femininity 'by way of Djuna. By wearing Djuna's feminine exterior, swaying her hips, becoming Djuna' (*Ladders*, 42). Paradoxically, then, while Lillian's femininity is somewhere in the 'depths' of her being, she can, as it were, reconstitute herself as feminine by 'wearing' femininity like a dress, a costume. What seems to be a 'depth' is constituted, or reconstituted, by means of a 'surface'.

The best expression of this ambiguity comes in a passage from *Children of the Albatross*, when Lillian, feeling tied and constricted by her relationship with Jay (the male character based on Henry Miller), attempts to 'escape' by putting on her black cape, 'copied from Sabina's', and embarking on a casual sexual encounter in a hotel room. The attempt at freedom fails because Lillian realizes that she is only 'being Sabina', in a futile 'borrowing' of costume and identity:

> Escape escape escape—into what? Into borrowing the self of Sabina for an hour. She had donned the recklessness of Sabina, borrowed her cape for a shy masquerade, pretending freedom.
>
> The clothes had not fitted very well. (*Albatross*, 141)

There is already an ambiguity here: while Sabina's cape can be identified with her 'self', for Lillian it is only a cloak, a costume which fails to 'fit' the reality underneath. The passage continues:

> But after a while, would this cease to be a role and did the borrowing reveal Lillian's true desires?
>
> The possibility of being this that she borrowed.

> Blindly ashamed of what she termed unfaithfulness . . . she discarded all the elements of this charade, cape, bracelets, then bathed and dressed in her own Lillian costume and went to the café . . . (141–2)

Just as Lillian could regain femininity by 'wearing' Djuna's femininity, so here the suggestion is that she could become the free woman she wishes to be by wearing the costume of Sabina. But the crucial ambiguity lies in the final description of Lillian, discarding the masquerade, the 'charade', and dressing again 'in her own Lillian costume'. If her attempt at freedom was only a game of dressing up, a masquerade, nonetheless her 'own' identity as Lillian may also turn out to be constituted (at least partly) through a performance, a dressing-up—a further layer of masquerade.

Virginia Woolf's *Orlando* provides the exemplary textual exploration of issues of costume and identity—more particularly, in this case, of gender identity, what it means to be a man or a woman. Talia Schaffer notes that the emphasis, in critical studies of *Orlando*, on 'dress and portraits' is significant in relation to the novel's own focus, its 'sartorial economy': '[*Orlando*] is about costuming precisely because costuming is what gender is all about'.[6] Both Schaffer and Rachel Bowlby discuss Woolf's account of the relations between clothing, identity, and sexual difference. Both argue that *Orlando* ultimately sets up a model of 'a potentially endless series of layers':[7] clothes may or may not accurately reflect the biological 'reality' underneath, but this level of identity may itself conflict with a further level. Woolf writes: 'Clothes are but a symbol of something hid deep beneath. It was a change in Orlando herself that dictated her choice of a woman's dress and of a woman's sex.'[8] Here, gender identity itself functions as a costume which may 'fit' or not, matching or disguising what is thought to be 'underneath', just like (literal, material) clothing. This recalls Nin's descriptions of Djuna, in *Ladders to Fire*, as 'wearing the costume of . . . femininity': femininity for Djuna is a matter of dressing up on both a literal and a psychological level.

Schaffer uses Judith Butler's theory of performativity, and in particular the concept of masquerade, in her analysis of *Orlando*'s play with costume and identity. The crucial aspect of the concept of masquerade is the way in which it problematizes models of surface and depth: thinking

[6] Schaffer, 'Posing *Orlando*', 28, 36.

[7] Rachel Bowlby, 'Orlando's Vacillation', in *Feminist Destinations and Further Essays on Virginia Woolf* (Edinburgh: Edinburgh Univ. Press, 1997), 47.

[8] Woolf, *Orlando*, 121.

about masquerade, as Butler writes, brings up 'the mobile possibilities of the slippery distinction between "appearing" and "being"'.[9] Butler analyses the ambiguities of the idea of 'masquerade' in the context of Lacan's account of masculine and feminine positions within heterosexuality: on this account, women 'masquerade' as 'the Phallus'. She writes: 'On the one hand, masquerade may be understood as the performative production of a sexual ontology, an appearing that makes itself convincing as a "being"; on the other hand, masquerade can be read as a denial of a feminine desire that presupposes some prior ontological femininity regularly unrepresented by the phallic economy.'[10]

In other words, the concept of masquerade may imply a hidden depth, a level of 'being' behind or underneath a masking surface of 'appearing'; or it may suggest that, in fact, 'appearing' *is* 'being'. Returning to the analysis of *Orlando* and its accompanying photographs, Schaffer argues that it is 'masquerade logic' itself that produces the idea of a hidden reality, a real identity: 'The idea of a real, hidden self is a phantasm that the masquerade actually constructs, for the layers of disguise produce the desire for a "real identity" on the part of the bewildered reader'.[11]

This connects to Nin's explorations of the idea that what seems to be a 'deep-level' identity (a gender identity, in the case of the 'femininity' at stake between Lillian and Djuna, or a personal identity, in the case of Lillian's sense of herself 'as Lillian' rather than 'as Sabina') may actually be constituted through a 'surface' enactment or stylization, analogous to the wearing of a costume. It is, in Butler's terms, *performative.* Gender identity, Butler writes, must be understood as 'the repeated stylization of the body, a set of repeated acts within a highly rigid regulatory frame that congeal over time to produce the appearance of substance, of a natural sort of being'.[12] This stylization, rather than *expressing* an 'abiding gendered self', a 'substantial ground of identity',[13] in fact *constitutes* gender or personal identity: 'the *appearance of substance* is precisely that, a constructed identity, a performative accomplishment which the mundane social audience, including the actors themselves, come to believe in and to perform in the mode of belief'.[14]

[9] Judith Butler, *Gender Trouble: Feminism and the Subversion of Identity* (London: Routledge, 1990), 47. The *locus classicus* for the concept of masquerade, specifically in relation to femininity, is Joan Riviere, 'Womanliness as a Masquerade' (1929), repr. in Victor Burgin, James Donald, and Cora Kaplan (eds.), *Formations of Fantasy* (London: Methuen, 1986), 35–44. See also Stephen Heath, 'Joan Riviere and the Masquerade', in Burgin, Donald, and Kaplan (eds.), *Formations of Fantasy*, 45–61.

[10] Butler, *Gender Trouble*, 47.

[11] Schaffer, 'Posing *Orlando*', 31.

[12] *Gender Trouble*, 33.

[13] Ibid. 140, 141.

[14] Ibid. 141.

Butler's emphasis on stylization (she later uses the expression '*stylized repetition of acts*'[15]) resonates well with Nin's emphasis on costuming and on the bodily performance of identity. So Lillian commands Djuna to walk in front of her ('"Walk in front of me, so I can see how you walk. You have such a sway of the hips!"' [*Ladders*, 42]), because 'in front of Lillian walked Lillian's lost femininity' (42). In her masquerade as Sabina, Lillian is aware that her 'words and gestures' are those 'prescribed by Sabina' (*Albatross*, 140); she returns home after her encounter in the hotel room 'to shed her cape and her acts' (141)—to shed the stylization which is Sabina's and not her own. Lillian feels that she has played out a 'charade' (141), merely masking her real self by acting 'in disguise' (141). But there remains 'the possibility of being this that she borrowed'—the possibility that the borrowing would, over time, 'cease to be a role'. What Nin envisages here is Butler's 'performative accomplishment', whereby it is precisely the repeated performance or enactment, over time, of 'an identity' which produces the experience of and belief in that identity as an abiding, underlying substrate, a 'real self'. This is the significance of the final image of Lillian in this passage: having taken off one costume, she must put on another, dress herself again 'in her own Lillian costume', the series of acts and styles to which she has become habituated.

This focus on costuming and masquerade, then, allows us to explore from another angle the paradoxes of identity discussed in Chapter 3 in relation to acting: in Rachel Brownstein's words, questions of 'whether and how coherent, integral identity hangs on performances and fictions'.[16] Talia Schaffer argues that this is Woolf's 'project' in *Orlando*: '*Orlando* shows that the categories by which we locate ourselves (gender, identity, history, language) are perpetual performances, proliferating self-reproductions'.[17] But her main interest is in Woolf's use of 'masquerading' photographs alongside the text; and I now want to look more specifically at this in relation to Nin's own intriguing use of photographs of herself posing as her fictional characters.

15 Ibid. 140. 16 Brownstein, *Tragic Muse*, p. x.
17 Schaffer, 'Posing *Orlando*', 26.

MASQUERADING PHOTOGRAPHS

In a passage from the fourth volume of the *Journals*, Nin describes the origin of these photographs (see Fig. 1) as follows:

Town and Country magazine had published a photograph of me dressed fashionably by Henry La Pensée. The photographer heard me describe the four women

FIGURE 1. *'The roles women play': the collage for* This Hunger *in which Nin posed as her characters and as 'the novelist'*

of my next book[18] and wanted to experiment with a photograph in which I would dress differently for each character, and then as myself, Anaïs, the novelist, in the center. I assembled the clothes which seemed to fit Lillian, Djuna, Stella, Hejda. For Lillian I chose the evening suit altered to fit me . . . with a more severe shirtwaist. I dressed my hair severely, and what did I see in the mirror? A resemblance to my father, who wore his hair long in the back, as artists of his time did. This amused me, and appealed to my love of disguises. Then I dressed as Hejda, oriental, with a veil across the face. Stella, of course, was soft and feminine, pliant; and the novelist in the center was dressed simply, and looked up naturally between her 'characters'. All this was done in a playful, surrealist mood. The photographer made a collage. But *Town and Country* was not amused. Nothing came of it. The photographer gave me the photograph. (*Journals*, IV, 47 [January 1945])

Nin returned to the photographs the next year, when E. P. Dutton were publishing *Ladders to Fire*:

When *Ladders to Fire* came out, and I could not afford new photographs, I thought of the surrealists' playfulness and gave Dutton the photographs taken by the *Town and Country* photographer . . . I explained to the publicity department that I wanted them titled by the names of the characters, and only the center one identified as myself. The photos went out, and either through carelessness or malice they all appeared as photos of me . . . The reaction was totally negative. Not one smile, not one recognition of the roles women play, of disguise and play. The picture in which I posed as the author was not used. The one of me acting out Lillian was misunderstood, and gave rise to the legend that I was a Lesbian. (*Journals*, IV, 196–7 [December 1946])

The most obvious difference between Nin's use of photography here and Woolf's in *Orlando* is that, whereas Nin poses for the pictures herself, Woolf orchestrates the posing of close friends and relations—Angelica Bell as 'the Russian princess', Vita Sackville-West herself as Orlando (in both male and female guises). The points of similarity are the ways in which both Woolf and Nin use photographs to set up what Schaffer calls 'successive layers of masquerade',[19] to suggest the fundamental imbrication of 'fiction' and 'biography', and to play with conventions of photography itself, unsettling expectations about how photographs depict their subjects.

[18] The book was *This Hunger*, privately published by Nin's own Gemor Press in 1945. Philip K. Jason (*Anaïs Nin*, 55–6) summarizes the complicated subsequent history of the three sections of this novel ('Hejda', 'Stella', and 'Lillian and Djuna'): 'Hejda' ended up in *Under a Glass Bell*, 'Stella' in *Winter of Artifice*, and 'Lillian and Djuna', retitled 'This Hunger', as the first part of *Ladders to Fire*.

[19] 'Posing *Orlando*', 31.

Schaffer uses the example of the photograph of Angelica, captioned 'The Russian Princess as a Child', to illustrate her argument as to the complex layers of the masquerade going on here. Citing Woolf's letters to Sackville-West, she describes how Woolf originally wanted to use Sackville-West's current lover Valerie Taylor to pose as the character—Sasha—who is a fictional 'portrait' of Sackville-West's *former* lover, Violet Trefusis. But she finally decided to ask her sister Vanessa to photograph Angelica, who was, Schaffer reports, 'devot[ed] to the masquerade' and frequently photographed in 'elaborate disguises' by her mother.[20] Angelica plays the part to the hilt: her pose, Schaffer writes, 'parodies the sultry glare of the practiced siren'.[21] The final image, then, is 'remarkably complex: a "disguised" Valerie Taylor is replaced by Angelica Bell [herself a devoted 'masquerader' in 'real life'], who masquerades as Sasha, who is really a disguise for Violet Trefusis'.[22]

As well as multiple layers of masquerade, we can see here the complicated interactions between the fictional and the biographical that Schaffer discusses. She elaborates elsewhere in the article on the impossibility of separating the two, establishing a one-way relation of cause and effect:

> History and fiction (re)produce each other; the real history of Sackville-West's lifestyle may have generated the fictional history of Orlando's, but Orlando's fiction may have made Sackville-West reinvent herself. Did Woolf invent Orlando's emerald ring because it figures in the photograph Sackville-West sent her? Or did she deliberately dress Sackville-West in Orlando's costume for her photograph?[23]

This 'conflat[ion of] the fictional with the biographical' is 'uncomfortable' not only because we want to be able to separate those two domains, but also because it operates through photography, the very medium from which we expect 'truth', an accurate depiction of reality. *Orlando*'s photographs, Schaffer argues, destabilize such expectations, 'question[ing] the opposition between truth and fantasy . . . They actually indulge in artifice, satire, masquerade, and self-contradiction. We expect this sort of behavior from textuality, not photography.'[24]

Nin's account of the negative reception her 'playful' photographs received clearly suggests precisely this response: the journalists, she claims, rejected the experiment as a 'sensationalist prank', part of the 'decadent surrealism they hated' (*Journals*, IV, 197). Photographs should not 'indulge' in 'this sort of behaviour'. Indeed, Nin's account suggests

[20] 'Posing *Orlando*', 31. [21] Ibid. 35. [22] Ibid. 32–3. [23] Ibid. 57.
[24] Ibid. 31.

that she was annoyed because the pictures were understood (and perhaps partly presented) too literally, simply as pictures of Nin (hence giving rise to the belief that she was a lesbian). If these hostile critics related the pictures to the text at all, perhaps we could say that they used them to collapse the fictional into the biographical: all the pictures are pictures of Nin, and all the characters in the text simply 'are' Nin too.

I would argue that Nin intended these pictures to suggest the conflation of the fictional and the biographical in more interesting and more complex ways. The photographs could be, in Laura Marcus's words, 'a way of suggesting how much fiction is involved in all self-representations';[25] returning to the focus on costuming, they could be used to suggest the ways in which an identity is enacted through stylization, constituted in performance. So, while Nin describes assembling the costumes which seemed to 'fit' the various characters, we have already seen the ways in which she examines the possibility that this relation may be, in Butler's terms, performative rather than expressive: 'being' Lillian is always (at least partly) a matter of acting as Lillian, dressing as Lillian; 'being feminine' may be achieved through '*wearing* femininity'. Even being the author rather than a fictional character requires a pose, a particular stylization: 'the novelist . . . was dressed simply, and looked up naturally' (*Journals*, IV, 47).

Nin's photographs, like Woolf's, record multiple layers of masquerade. Like *Orlando*, Nin's novels can clearly be seen as quasi-(auto) biographical fiction. This immediately complicates the images in the photographs, producing the layering effect Schaffer describes: they are pictures of Nin, posing as various characters, who are themselves fictional 'portraits', partly of Nin, partly of other women of her acquaintance (such as June Mansfield); or, in the case of the pose as the author, a picture of Nin—who really is the author—styling herself as 'Anaïs, the novelist' (47). The pictures stage the interplay of costume and identity, an interplay which is both central to Nin's own self-constructions and explored in her fiction. They depict the 'series of performances' that Schaffer associates with masquerade. Noting Woolf's deliberate imitation of earlier styles of portrait photography (including that of her great-aunt, Julia Margaret Cameron), Schaffer writes: 'The present . . . reiterates a past that is nothing more than a collection of stylistic quirks, and that past in turn reveals

[25] Marcus, *Auto/biographical Discourses*, 280. I cite this passage more fully in Chapter 1; Marcus is discussing women writers' blurring of the fictional and the autobiographical, and the use of 'the fictional' as a space for exploring identity and identifications. I am arguing that Nin here uses photography in a similar way.

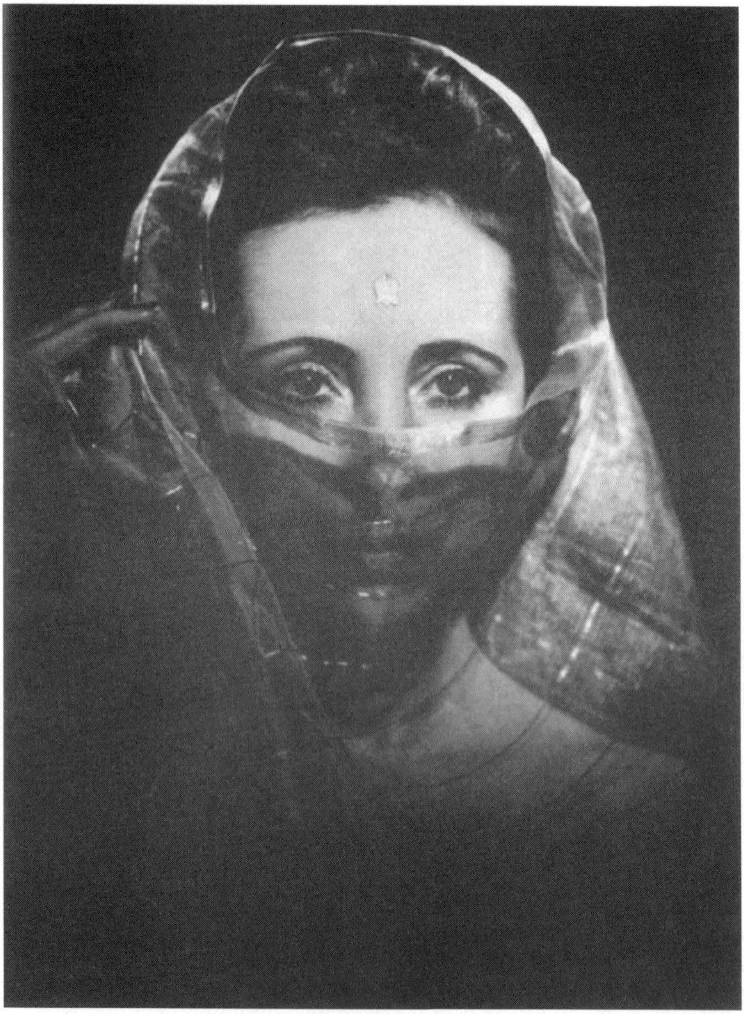

FIGURE 2. *'Rank wants me as "the dancer"': Nin posing as the Oriental* femme fatale *in 1934* (photograph by Brassaï)

itself to be a performance of some previous style no more solid than itself'.[26] This idea is interestingly echoed in Nin's amused recognition of her resemblance, in her 'severe' guise as Lillian, to her father. Here, a collection of 'stylistic quirks' produces cross-generational, cross-gender

[26] Schaffer, 'Posing *Orlando*', 27.

echoes—a resemblance between a (characteristically 'feminine') woman dressed up as a fictional 'masculine' female character, and a man with the 'feminine' image of a previous generation's dandies.

Another of the images in the collage, that of the veiled woman, demonstrates particularly well both this complex layering of images and styles and the interplay of the fictional and the biographical. Nin describes herself posing as Hejda, 'oriental, with a veil across the face' (47). The photograph that appears in the collage, however, is one that Nin had taken and sent to her then lover, Otto Rank, in 1934.[27] The image is a striking one, showing Nin veiling the lower part of her face with what she describes in the diary as an 'Indian shawl' (*Incest*, 394) and wearing a *bindi* on her forehead (see Fig. 2). Just visible at the edge of the photograph is her gloved hand, holding up the veil—or about to remove it. In its ambiguity, the gesture highlights perfectly (and presumably deliberately) the dialectic of revealing and concealing that, as we saw in Chapter 2, structures the veil, the striptease, and the image of the *femme fatale*. Nin thus presents herself, in this photograph, playing the *femme fatale* for her lover, Rank. She also clearly enacts the Orientalism inherent in this figure of exotic, mysterious femininity. In the diary, she describes the way this particular image comes into being as a result of Rank's fantasy of her, combined with her own fantasies: 'Rank wants me as "the dancer". He wants the color, the odor, the illusion, and the gaudiness . . . Thus a new image and a new me are formed by his desire, out of elements lying dormant in me for several years . . . I sit at the table with the Indian shawl over my head, eating figs and dates' (21 October 1934 [*Incest*, 395]).

It seems impossible to determine exactly how this earlier photograph came to feature in the later collage (did Nin, for instance, pose in 1945 as Hejda and then remember the earlier, perhaps better pose?).[28] But it does set up an intriguing series of performances: an image of Nin supposedly posing as her fictional character Hejda turns into an earlier image of Nin

[27] The caption to this picture in the Peter Owen edition of *Incest* states that Nin 'presumably sent this 1934 photo to Dr Rank while he was in New York'. On Oct. 24 1934, Nin writes, 'I mail [Rank] a photograph of myself, in the Hindu shawl, the only successful one taken by Brassaï' (*Incest*, 397).

[28] Gunther Stuhlmann, Nin's agent and representative, could not shed any light on my question as to whether there was a separate 'Hejda' photograph, but confirmed the symbolic connection between the earlier photograph and the later context: 'The symbolic effort here [in the 1934 picture] seems to have been what years later she called in the "Hejda" story the subject of "veils and labyrinthian evasions". She obviously was always concerned with her evasions and this was true with Rank and the various characters she assembled in her writing. The oriental veiled head with the jewel hovered over the three different women she portrayed' (personal communication from Gunther Stuhlmann, 12 June 2001).

enacting for her lover a particular fantasy of self which is (as the quotation marks around 'the dancer' show) recognizably put together from previously existing typologies and stylistic clichés. Nin describes, in the passage from *Incest*, the formation of 'a new image and a new me'. The photographs, like *Orlando*'s photographs, stage the interrelations of identity and image, fiction and 'reality', 'truth and fantasy'.[29] They provide another arena for the exploration of 'masquerade logic'—the questions of surface and depth, seeming and being, which come up again and again in Nin's writing and were so central to her own self-constructions.

FACES OF FEMININITY: NIN AS SYMBOL

In her fiction, then, Nin explores the ways in which women act as mirrors for each other, standing as each other's fantasies, enacting each other's dreams. In a 'portrait' published in *Mademoiselle* magazine in 1970, Susan Edmiston wrote in strikingly similar terms of Nin herself: 'Much of her appeal must come . . . from the fact that she has lived out many almost universal dreams: she is the complete woman'.[30] Just as Nin portrays Sabina as the embodiment of other women's (conscious or unconscious) fantasies of womanhood, so here Nin is portrayed in a similar way; and this symbolic role is central to understanding women's responses—both positive and negative—to Nin.

In the introduction to her biography, Deirdre Bair explains that one of the starting-points for her work was the attempt to understand the 'vehemence' of responses to Nin among people who knew her:

> I tried to talk to the many persons who figured throughout [Nin's] life, and I was astonished at the range of their responses, especially how, in many cases, the mere mention of her name provoked vehemence and outrage. I was puzzled, because the emotional expression seemed far greater than I thought appropriate. So a crucial issue became my trying to understand what there was about Anaïs Nin that made people react so strongly even though she had died more than a decade earlier.[31]

Later in the book, Bair records that 'people either loved or hated Anaïs Nin when they met her. No one was able to respond to her with any degree

[29] Schaffer, 'Posing *Orlando*', 31.

[30] Susan Edmiston, 'Portrait of Anaïs Nin' (1970), reprinted in DuBow (ed.), *Conversations*, 45.

[31] Bair, *Anaïs Nin*, p. xv.

of neutrality.'[32] Similarly, Fitch notes in the introduction to her biography that 'much like her first liberator, D. H. Lawrence, [Nin] inspires extremes of attack and adoration'.[33] If we widen the context to include contemporary responses to Nin from critics and fans who are, in the main, too young ever to have encountered Nin in person, we find the same extremes of adulation and hostility. I shall argue that the way to understand this exaggerated response is in terms of Nin's function as a mobilizer of fantasies, a kind of symbolic place-holder.[34] Just as Nin created for herself an identity (or non-identity) in the realm of legend and fantasy, so too, I suggest, many women respond to her in the same register: Nin becomes a mirror reflecting various faces of femininity and feminine sexuality, including 'liberated' woman, enigmatic *femme fatale*, garish old hag, and predatory monster.

With the publication of her edited diaries in the late 1960s and the 1970s, Nin achieved not only fame, but a certain symbolic status. In a radio discussion with Nin in 1971, the interviewer Milton Hoffman introduced her as 'one of the extraordinary women of our time', and picked up on this symbolic role, saying, 'You've somehow embodied the notion of personal freedom'.[35] Nin concurred: 'I realize that I've been made a symbol of a woman who struggled individually for her emancipation and was very independent and was a rebel'.[36] In Diane Richard-Allerdyce's words, Nin was transformed from 'a little-known coterie writer of abstract fiction' to 'a cultural heroine', surrounded by 'a devoted circle of readers'.[37] She had struggled throughout the 1940s and 1950s for literary success, which had eluded her; she had difficulty finding publishers for her novels, which received bad reviews and sold poorly, and she frequently had to resort to self-publishing.[38] With the dramatic social and

[32] Ibid. 484. [33] Fitch, *Anaïs*, 5.

[34] In the first chapter of her *Feminist Destinations* Rachel Bowlby argues that the same extremes are found in responses to Virginia Woolf: deployed by critics 'of all casts' as the 'exemplary woman writer', Woolf is 'vehemently celebrated or denounced from all sides' (*Feminist Destinations*, 12). Brenda Silver acknowledges Bowlby's postmodern readings of Woolf in the Introduction to *Virginia Woolf Icon* (26).

[35] Hoffman, 'An Interview with Anaïs Nin', 149. [36] Ibid. 144.

[37] Richard-Allerdyce, *Remaking of Self*, 146.

[38] Nin's first works of fiction, *House of Incest* and *Winter of Artifice*, were self-published; New York company Dutton published *This Hunger* (1945), *Ladders to Fire* (1946), and *Under a Glass Bell* (1948), but then dropped her because of poor sales and hostile reviews. *The Four-Chambered Heart* was published by Duell, Sloan and Pierce in 1950, but again received poor reviews, and Nin was forced to self-publish *A Spy in the House of Love* (1954) and *Solar Barque* (1958, the first part of what was later titled *Seduction of the Minotaur*). Nin managed to secure a distribution deal with the British Book Centre for *Spy*, but the book was dropped by them after selling a mere 1,500 copies (Bair, *Anaïs Nin*, 378). Philip K. Jason's *Anaïs Nin and her Critics* is a useful source for the complex publishing history of Nin's work.

cultural changes of the 1960s, however, and particularly with the rise of the women's liberation movement in the US, Nin found a vastly more receptive climate, not primarily for her novels, but for her diaries—carefully edited, and promoted, to tell precisely the story of the independent woman artist's struggle for emancipation and recognition that Milton Hoffman picks up on. The success of this strategy—the *power*, at that cultural moment, of this story—can be seen in Kate Millett's response to Nin's *Diary* (a response explicitly framed on behalf of an 'us', a collective female audience):

> the sight of a woman so alive, so immersed in life and art, and working so damn hard too, striving for the terms of her art: rewriting, being rejected and going at it again, fighting obscurity, publishers' brush-offs, the ten year hell of being entirely out of print, the delicate crumbs of a chance compliment, the support of comrades without which one can scarcely live. She gives us the first real portrait of the artist [as] a woman that we have ever had.[39]

In speaking to Milton Hoffman, Nin—unsurprisingly—plays down her own role in this process of symbolization, the way in which her published diaries were constructed to tell this story of heroic liberation.[40] But she is certainly correct to make the point that the diaries 'came out at the right time to match the consciousness of the new generation . . . *this time* the time was right'.[41] We can say that Nin, correctly perceiving this match, did her best to enable, or maximize, her symbolic standing as the ultimate liberated woman. For the first time in her life, she became a bestseller.[42] More than that, she became a high-profile figure, a representative of the women's movement, fêted, interviewed in magazines (especially feminist and women's arts magazines), on radio and TV, and in demand on the lecturing circuit.[43] As I showed in Chapter 1, the felt need within the women's movement for textual voices with which to identify, accounts of other women's experience in which to read and make sense of one's own, helped to construct Nin as, in Kate Millett's

[39] Millett, 'Anaïs', 7.

[40] Cf. my discussion in Chapter 1 of Nin's emphasis, in the 1970s feminist context, on the 'spontaneous' and 'authentic'.

[41] Nin, in Hoffman, 'An Interview with Anaïs Nin', 149.

[42] When the first volume of the *Diary* appeared in 1966, the first (hardback) printing of 3,000 sold out within weeks (Bair, *Anaïs Nin*, 495). According to figures cited by Bair (495), paperback sales in the US of the first four volumes of the *Diary* had reached almost 125,000 by the end of 1973.

[43] Wendy DuBow's *Conversations with Anaïs Nin* reprints a selection of these interviews from the early 1970s, including pieces from *US Vogue*, *New Woman*, *Everywoman*, *The Second Wave: A Magazine of the New Feminism*, *Mademoiselle*, and the *Chicago Review*.

terms, 'mother', 'elder sister' and (rather astonishingly) 'goddess': the one who 'tells it like it is', 'lays out her life' as inspiration for the new generation of women.[44]

Above all, Nin was seen as representative not just of the women's movement but, particularly, of 'femininity'; as, in the words of one 1971 interviewer, 'the very essence of femininity'.[45] It was precisely this association of Nin with 'femininity' which rendered her, while a heroine for many women, simultaneously a highly controversial figure in relation to feminism; and which continues to inform both positive and negative responses to her.

Questions of femininity—what it is, what it ought and ought not to be, and how women are to relate to it, what they are to 'do' with it—represent an important, if tangled, thread running through the very different responses to Nin. Claire Messud, in a 1995 review of Deirdre Bair's biography, writes that Nin 'was, above all, preoccupied with creating an ideal feminine self, an embodiment of femininity as masquerade'[46]—a suggestive comment which already seems to raise the possibility of different, perhaps conflicting, understandings of femininity. Feminist critic Julia Casterton, writing in 1982, focused on the 'uneasiness' of Nin's place in the history of women's writing and feminist thinking, particularly in relation to Nin's own self-representations as a woman. She sees Nin as a 'dissonant element', a 'clanging cymbal' (or symbol), standing as an awkward reminder that feminist 'harmony' may conceal tensions and discords. She is, Casterton writes, a voice 'making different meanings and

[44] Millett, 'Anaïs', 4, 7, 8. Millett's 'goddess' rhetoric here is all the more striking given her witty and scathing critique of the 'goddess'/'whore' dichotomy in *Sexual Politics* (London: Abacus, 1972 [1969]; see e.g. p. 250 for her sardonic account of the poetic strategies of Tennyson, D. G. Rossetti, and Swinburne in relation to wanton Roses and decorous, virginal Lilies). One of Millett's prime targets in *Sexual Politics* was of course D. H. Lawrence, whose cosmic mythification of sexuality is described as 'sexual politics in its most overpowering form' (238): in the classic structure of reversal, the 'veritable hymn to the feminine mystique' in *The Rainbow* performs a volte-face to produce the phallic 'cult' of Lawrence's later writings (258). Nin, in the 1970s, frequently found herself parrying questions about her high regard for Lawrence (and for Henry Miller, another of Millett's key targets: Lawrence, Miller, and Norman Mailer are named by Millett as 'the counter-revolutionary sexual politicians' [233]). She usually conceded Millett's point that Lawrence's sexual politics were, from a feminist perspective, problematic, while insisting on the value of his art (see, e.g., *A Woman Speaks*, 94–5). It seems highly ironic, then, that we find Kate Millett, iconic figure of 1970s feminism, praising Nin's art while others (such as Estelle Jelinek) attack Nin's sexual politics in the name of feminism.

[45] Susan Stocking, 'Personas Unmasked in Visit with Anaïs Nin' (1971), in DuBow (ed.), *Conversations*, 98–103.

[46] Claire Messud, 'Dear Oh Dear Diary', *Guardian*, 20 April 1995, G2, 6.

representations of women . . . She seems to be one of those stereotypes (mother/witch/child/whore) we thought we had cast off.'[47] Indeed, Casterton goes on to suggest, Nin seems to be—and to deliberately construct herself as—*all* these stereotypes:

> Anaïs Nin seems to define herself as [Julia] Kristeva [in *About Chinese Women*] claims femininity is defined under patriarchy: witch-enchantress, perfumed, with kohl on her eyes; tiny, bird-like woman, too small to bear children; all-giving mother who buys spectacles for Henry Miller and so cannot afford stockings for herself; martyr, writing erotica against her will, for money, to keep her 'children'. She presents herself as a problem because she *uses* these labels, rather than refuses them . . . In the Journals these definitions of femininity, which we now reject as constricting, are the means by which she writes about herself, the means by which she effaces herself. It is as though she were posing before them, playing with them, seeing if they fit.[48]

Casterton here imagines Nin playing with the various 'costumes' of femininity, or representations of womanhood; trying them on, 'seeing if they fit'—or, perhaps, demonstrating that they can never quite 'fit'. The passage also highlights the difficulty of pinning down 'femininity', its contradictory and protean nature: the 'definitions of femininity' that Casterton sees Nin employing veer from enchantress to martyr, power to fragility, seductiveness to maternal selflessness. It seems that Nin is defined by—and defines herself by—'femininity', but that 'femininity' is impossible to define.

This paradoxical situation is evident in earlier feminist attempts to get to grips with Nin and what she represents. Estelle Jelinek, writing in 1974 from a radical feminist point of view, was highly critical of Nin on many counts, accusing her of being snobbish, elitist, opportunistic, apolitical, and even 'sexist'. This latter accusation is bound up with the charge of an 'essentialist' view of sexual difference, and with Nin's 'emphasis on, and embodiment of, conventional femininity'.[49] But what *is* this 'conventional femininity'? In terms of Nin's 'embodiment' of femininity, her self-representation, Jelinek focuses on *seductiveness* as the key characteristic. In Robert Snyder's film *Anaïs Observed*, she notes, we see Nin 'posing seductively in a field'; more generally, Jelinek claims, Nin 'needs to present herself as almost professionally seductive'.[50]

In relation to Nin's 'emphasis' on femininity, however, Jelinek attacks her espousal of the idea that 'women have a special and unique nature,

[47] Molyneux and Casterton, 'Looking Again', 86.
[48] Ibid. 95.
[49] Jelinek, 'Anaïs Nin', 318.
[50] Ibid. 313, 319.

one that will transform the world':[51] the notion of femininity as intuitive, relational, compassionate, and therefore redemptive. This model of gender difference, Jelinek argues, is 'really an alternate form of sexism', simply transvaluing characteristics which have always been imposed on women as 'feminine': 'Where usually men have used the traits she celebrates against women, Nin puts women on a pedestal because they (seemingly) possess these traits, as though they were innate in women and absent in men'.[52]

For radical feminist critics such as Jelinek, women's enthusiasm for Nin appeared to be a kind of false consciousness, the women themselves duped and misguided. Jelinek calls Nin's fans 'blind', 'hoodwinked', 'in a daze'; they 'swoon at her words and applaud her "feminine" virtues'.[53] What is needed, Jelinek argues sternly, is less swooning and more rationality, more political consistency: 'These women seem incapable of discerning the inherent contradictions between their sexual and/or radical politics and her views . . . I think it is time women began to look at Anaïs Nin with some objectivity.'[54]

Although Jelinek attributes these objectionable 'views' simply to Nin as an individual, we can clearly see here the outlines of the clash between 'radical feminist' and 'cultural feminist' positions—a major schism within American feminism through the 1970s and into the 1980s. Whereas radical feminism sought to de-emphasize gender difference, understanding 'femininity' as a set of conventions imposed upon women by men and subsequently internalized, cultural feminists promoted, in Mari Jo Buhle's words, 'a renewed vision of femininity as an essential quality and relatedness as its essence'.[55] Cultural feminism was above all an affirmation of women's *difference* from men and a celebration of a sublime femininity, understood to signify women's 'artistic, intuitive, integrative, subjective, playful, and above all relational . . . conceptual modes'.[56]

We can see these tensions at work in Jelinek's interesting claim that Nin somehow comes to represent, for other women, their own femininity. She writes: 'Some women's reactions to my ideas on Nin's sexism are quite dramatic, as though I were, by attacking Nin, attacking their own femininity. This must be, at least partially, at the root of the adoration for Nin: the burden women still feel to prove their "femininity" in spite of their individuality.'[57] Here Jelinek, almost despite herself, acknowledges

[51] Ibid. 314. [52] Ibid. 315. [53] Ibid. 319, 320. [54] Ibid. 318, 323.
[55] Buhle, *Feminism and its Discontents*, 265. [56] Ibid. 261–2.
[57] Jelinek, 'Anaïs Nin', 318.

many women's *investment* in femininity, while simultaneously demonstrating the radical feminist investment in getting rid of femininity, ridding women of their misplaced identification with it (though the *content* of this femininity remains slippery and ambiguous). She also acknowledges Nin's status as an icon of femininity, a figure onto whom other women project 'their own femininity'—or, perhaps, from whom they derive an image of that femininity. In other words, Jelinek's text here suggests the mirroring relation I have been examining in this chapter: Nin functions as a mirror for other women, reflecting 'femininity' back at them, often in magnified and distorted forms. Yet what is most interesting about Jelinek's account is what it seems to suggest in spite of itself: both that the concept of femininity is more slippery than we would like, and—perhaps more significantly—that women's attitudes towards femininity might be more complex than a 'rational' feminist position would allow. After all, no less a figure than Kate Millett—author of surely the most thoroughgoing and influential critique of patriarchal politics and ideology to emerge from the second-wave feminist movement—could find in Nin's *Diary* not only intellectual excitement but erotic, sensuous pleasure:

> [She] brings us to an exotic world we never knew: geniuses knocking around in streets and restaurants that are fabled names to us, the excitement of young artists and writers crowing over their productions, the adventure of life on a houseboat on the Seine, long debates on the meaning of Surrealism, the great days before the War—she gives us romance. But also all that is refined and subtle and goes with it: the shade of a dress, the texture of the voile scarf, the steps in a seduction, the postures in a quarrel.[58]

'DEAR ANAÏS': FANS AND FANTASIES

If feminist critics such as Jelinek saw Nin's reception in the 1960s and 1970s as swooningly uncritical, a harsher spotlight began to fall on Nin, posthumously, in the 1980s and 1990s. With the gradual publication of her 'unexpurgated' diaries (beginning in 1986 with *Henry and June*), and the publication of two major biographies (Fitch's in 1993 and Bair's in 1995), the 'facts' of Nin's life—including her husband's financial support (not only of her but frequently of her lovers), her many affairs, her

[58] Millett, 'Anaïs', 7. The 'voile scarf' (symbolically, the veil) appears again in Nancy Scholar's picture of Nin, in her diary, 'leading us on with a seductive wave of her scarf' (*Anaïs Nin*, 40); Scholar, however, is irritated rather than seduced.

abortions, her apparent incest with her father, and her bigamous marriage in 1955 to her long-time lover Rupert Pole—began to come out.[59]

If we look at the reviews of Bair's and Fitch's biographies, then, we find that one of the central preoccupations of the critics is the disjunction between the story of independence and freedom told in Nin's published diaries and the truth as it is now revealed. The 'free spirit of the diaries', writes one reviewer, was far from free: 'The suave, enigmatic love-goddess was really a character in a farce'.[60] Another reviewer notes that Nin erased from her 'diary of liberation and solitary adventure' not only her husband's support but also her own 'desperate craving for male love and approval, her polishing of two men's shoes for nearly 30 years'.[61] The point being made here is not simply that Nin was materially, financially, and emotionally sustained by men, and that women's idealization of her as a liberated, independent woman has therefore been based on a lie; even more significantly, these critics contend, her supposedly liberated life was in fact a life of desperate promiscuity and pathological need for love and admiration. She was 'free' neither of the patriarchal structures of marriage and family, nor of her own pathology (often ascribed to the sexual and/or psychological abuse Nin may have suffered, as a child, from her father). Conceding her appeal to women in the 1970s, Nicci Gerrard writes: 'Today we cannot be so innocent about Anaïs Nin'. The life Bair has uncovered, she goes on, is 'monstrous, sad, and ridiculous'.[62]

According to these reviewers, then, we can see Nin today as a monster,[63] or a victim, or both; but certainly not as a heroine or an inspiration for women. And yet, if we turn to look at the several websites devoted to Nin,[64] we find women expressing their feelings about Nin and her work in precisely these terms, using a tone and vocabulary which are best described as adulatory—or even, as Estelle Jelinek might put it, 'swooning':

[59] Some of the lacunae in Nin's *Diary* were, however, picked up on at the time of publication. Millett, for instance, notes that 'the diarist has a husband and excises him utterly, lovers are still more conspicuous by their absence'; acknowledging that Nin has been criticized for this by her 'young readers', Millett nonetheless manages to turn Nin's omissions around into an instance of 'the very repression we were born to and resent' ('Anaïs', 7). Nin thus appears here more as a victim of her own pre-feminist consciousness and of the cultural silencing of women than (as for later critics) as a liar and hypocrite.

[60] Lucy Hughes-Hallett, 'The Story of A' (review of Fitch), *Sunday Times*, 3 April 1994, 6.

[61] Nicci Gerrard, 'A Talent to Delude' (review of Bair), *Observer*, 5 March 1995, review section, 2.

[62] Ibid.

[63] I shall return later in the chapter to this image of Nin as monster.

[64] My sources here include the 'Guestbook' feature in the 'Thinking of Anaïs Nin' site at www.anaisnin.com, and the 'letters' to Nin formerly at www.adeleart.com/AnaisLetters/DearAnaisNin.html (this page has subsequently been taken down by the website creator).

Anaïs Nin has forever changed my life . . . blessed be to Anaïs Nin! (Annastacia Arthy, 9 June 1999)

Her life was a sparkling, rare jewel that has forever altered the course of my own life. (Marion Lawless, 25 May 1999)

Discovering Anaïs has been an inspiration to me. (Butterfly Witch, 8 May 1999)

There aren't enough pages in the world to describe the beauty and life that was Anaïs. (Melissa Barjam, 4 April 1999)

Thank you Anaïs for reaching out to my soul. (Denise Heid, 25 January 1999)

Anaïs is my air. She takes my breath and breathes it in. (Amy, 16 January 1999)

Words do not begin to encompass what her work truly means to me. (Marie, 13 January 1999)

I absolutely adore Anaïs Nin . . . (Daria Dawson, 29 December 1998)

You [Nin] are the true beauty of woman . . . You are an inspiration to me . . . Querida I love you. (Yolanda De Leo'n, 4 December 1997)

More than twenty years after her death, Nin clearly remains a powerful and inspirational figure for these women. Further, the contributors to these sites are not unaware of the controversial revelations about Nin's life. One woman explains her feelings about Nin as follows: 'I am grateful to all the influences in my life that have supported my uniqueness and those that love me in spite of it or because of it but to Anaïs especially because she knew that what she lived was her truth. She has taught me to know my own truth and to take possession of it' (Laura Phillips, 15 November 1998). In a second posting on the same day, she goes on: 'PS on her critics and her lies . . . her gift to those who loved her was her unconditional truth of passion . . . if you must lie to be passionate then by all means lie for that is a gift, for passion is truth and certainly the greatest gift in relationship.'

For this writer, Nin's life of 'passion' represents a kind of personal truth that is more important than ordinary considerations of truth and lies; she serves as a role-model in terms of self-possession ('she has taught me to know my own truth and to take possession of it'). Another woman (old enough to have met Nin in the mid-1970s) writes: 'I read the recently published bio of her . . . I don't care what she did and censored/edited what she published. She managed to live a life few of us dream about. A remarkable woman who influenced me as a young woman artist. Should be mandatory reading for all women, especially creative ones' (Jenny Lens, 15 August 1998). In this somewhat contradictory statement, the writer both appeals to Nin's life as the ground for her status as a role-model, a 'remarkable woman', and discounts the (unpleasant or morally reprehensible) realities of that life as irrelevant ('I don't care what she did'). Significantly, she also discounts as irrelevant the fact that Nin's diary was 'censored' for publication, and goes so far as to recommend it (or Nin's writing as a whole) as 'mandatory reading' for women.

Another woman makes more of an attempt to acknowledge the problem, while simultaneously arguing that Nin must be forgiven because of her 'inestimable gift to humanity'. In terms of her own feelings about Nin, she resorts to a somewhat tendentious distinction: 'With all the . . . revelations about your life, my admiration for you is tempered, but undiminished'. She goes on: 'In your time, you explored some of the furthest reaches of the human spirit, at great cost to yourself and doubtless to others. Like Ariadne's thread, your writing is a tendril to be grasped by those who would share at least part of your journey in times to come. For such an inestimable gift to humanity, you have a right to be forgiven and exonerated' (Jan Sinstadt, 23 June 1999).

There seems to be a kind of doublethink involved here: a recognition of a highly problematic dimension to Nin's life, and at the same time a determined minimizing of this aspect. What happens, then, to Nicci Gerrard's claim that, today, 'we cannot be so innocent about Anaïs Nin'? These women cannot be said to be 'innocent' of the problems raised by Nin's life. What their accounts suggest, I believe, is that Nin's importance to them lies in her iconic status as a figure of female creativity, freedom, and passionate adventure: and that the *cost*, in reality, of the pursuit of these goals (the cost, that is, both to Nin herself and to those around her) is minimized or disregarded. Nin is important to these women, I would argue, to the extent that she mobilizes a particular fantasy (which may be only partially realizable, if at all) of a passionate, creative, unfettered life; just as June Mansfield represented, for Nin, her own fantasy of woman, and just as Sabina, in *The Four-Chambered Heart*, is said to play this role for other women. This investment in Nin cannot be undermined to any great extent by revelations about sordid aspects of her 'real life' because its motivating and sustaining power does not come from that sphere.[65]

[65] In a fascinating article about his experiences of discussion groups devoted (in more than one sense) to Nin on the internet, Paul Herron describes the extreme defensiveness and proprietorial attitude that he encountered when he mentioned some of Deirdre Bair's criticisms of Nin: '"Who gives a flying fuck what Deirdre Bair thinks about our Anaïs?" [one woman responded]. Whoa, I thought. What have I gotten myself into?' (Paul Herron, 'The Café in Space: Anaïs Nin on the Internet', *Anaïs: An International Journal*, 19 [2001], 55). Herron discusses many of the issues that I consider here around women's identification with Nin.

There is a strong sense of identification apparent in many of these tributes to Nin; in particular, an identification in terms of womanhood, the sense of oneself 'as a woman':

Reading her books made me feel utterly more woman than ever. Spending time uncovering more about this amazing woman is time spent uncovering the amazing woman in me. (Alysia Smith, 24 September 1999)

Her words trace new and brave paths to womanhood, sexuality and self-discovery. (Nancy Lutz, 29 September 1999)

I swear that Anaïs wrote a prophecy of my life. It is not only my prophecy, but every woman's prophecy. (Geneva, 26 May 1999)

Passion and sexuality are particularly important to Nin's 'inspirational' status (and, as we shall see, sexuality is equally crucial in the most strongly *negative* constructions of Nin). Many of the tributes to Nin on the websites convey the importance of body and sexuality in her work and in the readers' response to it:

Anaïs's words allowed me to reach inside the depths of my soul and bring forth a woman, a sexual being . . . (Jennifer Andrews, 14 January 1999)

I absolutely adore Anaïs Nin . . . when I am reading her work I feel as though everything that dwells deep inside [the] core of my cells and membranes is being exposed . . . it is an explosive feeling to experience such unencumbered beauty through someone else's eyes, tongue, heart and soul . . . (Daria Dawson, 29 December 1998)

Delta of Venus changed the way I thought about my body, my writing . . . (Kristi Sprinkle, 28 December 1998)

Clearly, Nin's erotica are particularly important here: these statements pay tribute to the ability of Nin's writing to evoke a powerful sense of female sexuality and sensuality, actually to inspire a sense of a sexual self—'a woman, a sexual being'. However, we can also see in many of these accounts a perceived continuum between 'Nin', her life, and her writing.[66] In some cases this is made explicit: 'I have a love affair with her books that extends beyond the printed page to her very spirit' (Kimmy Beach, 28 December 1998). In other cases the continuum is implicit, the writers responding to an 'Anaïs Nin' (or, frequently, just 'Anaïs') who encompasses both the textual and the personal.

[66] Again, Bowlby finds the same continuum in responses—both positive and negative—to Woolf: 'criticism frequently takes the form of violent attack or defence—of Virginia Woolf herself, of what she wrote, or (most often) of some nebulous fusion of the two' (*Feminist Destinations*, 13).

This was brought out particularly well by one website set up in the form of letters to Nin, under the title 'Dear Anaïs'.[67] The organizer of the site, Adele Aldridge, addresses Nin as follows: 'I would like to thank you again for creating and leaving us your *Diaries* . . . It is because of your magic that I am now inviting all readers of your work who would like to write a letter to you to do so here' (12 September 1997). This format thus allows fans the fantasy of addressing Nin directly: Nin becomes 'you', and this 'you' is both *a person*, someone to be addressed in an intimate way ('Querida I love you'), and at the same time mediated through texts: 'I found you in 1974. Someone handed me your book, *[The] Four-Chambered Heart*' (Canary Burton, 9 October 1997).

The all-inclusiveness of this response is well conveyed in a 'letter' from Rebecca-Starr Price: 'From all your journals, edited and not, letters, essays, biographies and novellas, I have ravenously sought out your work, finding a kindred spirit from over 80 years ago! It is so wonderful to be able to see your life from beginning to end, laid out before us in your own words as well as in other writers and friends' (14 April 1998). In a PS, she writes: 'I would love anyone to email who adores Anaïs, her work, life, etc.'. Clearly, she is not interested in making distinctions between Nin's 'work' and her 'life' (or, indeed, anything else that could conceivably relate to her, enthusiastically covered by the 'etc.'). She seems undisturbed by discrepancies between the various accounts of Nin's life found in the originally published diaries, the more recent 'unexpurgated' volumes, and even the biographies (the inclusion of the latter suggesting once again that any negative aspects of the story are simply discounted or ignored). Importantly, Nin's fiction is also part of this list: like Canary Burton, who 'found' Nin (or, as she calls her, 'Anaïs') initially through one of her novels, Rebecca-Starr Price locates her 'kindred spirit' in diary and fiction alike.

Claire Messud calls Nin 'her own finest character', and this suggests, I would argue, the best way to understand Nin's iconic status for these women. Certainly, for Nin's fans there is a continuum linking Nin and her writing (both fiction and diary), her 'life', and her 'work': they feel that they 'know' her through her texts. But rather than a desire to access the 'real' woman (with all the inevitable disappointments and disillusionments that that would entail), I think we can see here a response to an 'Anaïs Nin' understood primarily as an extension, or (to employ Nin's

[67] Although this page has been taken down, the site still features personal reminiscences of and views on Anaïs Nin by the site coordinator, Adele Aldridge (www.adeleart.com/NinPage/RememberAnais/html).

own alchemical imagery) a distillation, of her writing. Lucy Hughes-Hallett, while acknowledging the problem of 'misrepresentation' in Nin's published diaries, concedes that Nin did have 'remarkable talents', among them the ability to inspire other women through her own self-constructions. She portrays Nin's diary as a kind of soft-porn fantasy text, with Nin as its protagonist: 'It shows a woman, talented, independent, infinitely desirable, moving in her capes and velvet dresses through voluptuous settings . . . and enjoying a multiplicity of passionate but exquisitely refined relationships with illustrious men'.[68] She goes on to state that the image Nin created, 'of a dignified and adventurous, sensually and intellectually stimulating life, proved inspirational to many women'.

Nin was, in fact, a consummate performer. Writing in the *Guardian*, Maureen Freely lists Nin along with Sarah Bernhardt, Isadora Duncan, and Zelda Fitzgerald as the women who, she says, 'reinvented the modern erotic female', and did so through *performance*: 'They worked very hard to look and live up to the part, and it is, in the end, their performances we remember them for'.[69] It seems to me that it is precisely Nin's 'performance'—both textually and extratextually—of the role of the erotic, rebellious, unfettered woman that so many women have responded to—and, as the websites show, continue to respond to. I would also argue that the fans for whom 'Anaïs Nin' remains a powerful representation of erotic femininity are responding to her performances *as* performances, rather than being duped *by* them: rather than being unaware of the 'sordid' facts about her life, they are simply not concerned with this level of reality. This suggests a reading strategy on the part of Nin's admirers such that, rather than searching for the 'real woman' behind the iconic figure, the protagonist of the diaries or even the women of the fiction, they read 'Anaïs' back into those representations. Rather than simply being duped by Nin, they collude with her in producing and playing with particular fantasies of the feminine.

[68] Hence the title of her review, 'The Story of A', alluding to the pornographic *Story of O*.

[69] Maureen Freely, 'Pleasure of the Flesh' (article about Alina Reyes), *Guardian*, 13 June 1995, G2, 4. Similarly, I would argue that the idea of performance underlies the connection made by one contributor to the 'Dear Anaïs' website between Nin and Mick Jagger (Henk Huisman, 11 July 1998). Particularly relevant here is Jagger's self-parodying portrayal of the decadent former rock star Turner in Nic Roeg's 1970 film *Performance*.

'ESSENCE' AND 'EXCESS'

Another account of Nin from the early 1970s paints an intriguing picture of the definitional and ontological difficulties surrounding 'femininity'. Susan Stocking, interviewing Nin for the *Los Angeles Times* in 1971, wrote that '[in] person, Nin is the very essence of femininity'.[70] The statement is suggestive both in its claim that Nin embodies femininity, and in the promise it holds out—that femininity *has* an 'essence', and that we can know what it is. Stocking's descriptions of Nin, however, imply that this 'essence' is a strange one, involving self-contradiction and masquerade. She begins by noting that Nin 'speaks in a small tremulous voice, like an adolescent girl who is embarrassed to draw attention to herself'; her voice retains 'the trace of a French accent'.[71] She goes on to describe Nin's hair, 'sweeping in gentle half-moons from the center of her wide forehead, back over her ears and up into a modest roll atop her head'; her skin, which 'though wrinkled and masked by makeup, seems ageless and opalescent'; and her eyes, 'edged in heavy black mascara under Jean Harlow eyebrows'.[72] We can see a tension at work in these descriptions: Nin's 'femininity' seems to be constituted on the one hand by 'gentleness' and 'modesty', a kind of self-effacing meekness and lack of assertion more befitting an adolescent than a grown woman; and on the other hand by glamour and artifice, the seductiveness of a film star (with an exotic hint of Frenchness to boot).

We can also see the ways in which Stocking's account of 'the essence of femininity' so frequently invokes both artifice and dissimulation. Nin's skin is 'masked' by make-up; her eyes are emphasized with 'heavy' mascara; her eyebrows have been plucked and reshaped. Even her voice dissembles: she speaks like an adolescent girl who is 'embarrassed to draw attention to herself', though she is in fact a 68-year-old woman giving a publicity interview to promote her published diaries. This clearly recalls

[70] Stocking, 'Personas Unmasked', 99.

[71] It seems likely that Nin—who had, in 1971, been living in the US for over 30 years—deliberately clung to this linguistic trace of her European (rather than American) identity, embracing the 'exoticism' it conferred on her even as she complained about America's insularity and anti-Europeanness (see e.g. *Novel*, 1). Fitch notes that, on arriving in America as a child, fervently patriotic towards France, Nin '[clung] to her accent, while her brothers [lost] theirs', refusing to assimilate and adopting an affectedly 'French' image (*Anaïs*, 13). Fitch also quotes Wallace Fowlie as recalling that when he met Nin in 1945 he was 'struck by her youthful beauty, skillful makeup, and unique accent' (267).

[72] Stocking, 'Personas Unmasked', 98, 99.

the 'subterfuge' of one of the subjects in Joan Riviere's original discussion of masquerade, a capable 50-year-old woman who deals with tradesmen by affecting an 'innocent and artless manner': 'even with the butcher and baker, whom she rules in reality with a rod of iron, she cannot take up a firm straightforward stand; she feels herself as it were "acting a part", she puts on the semblance of a rather uneducated, foolish and bewildered woman, yet in the end always ends up making her point.'[73]

In Stocking's account, Nin embodies the paradoxes of masquerade: she speaks like a shy girl, while plainly being an adult woman in the public arena; she wears make-up which 'masks' her ageing face and simultaneously draws attention to itself as make-up. This lends a suggestive irony to Stocking's description of Nin as 'the very essence of femininity': is it, in fact, the 'essence' of femininity to wear a mask—and furthermore, a mask which clearly shows itself to *be* a mask?

In Riviere's essay, the 'masquerade' involves the *inappropriate* and *excessive*, or *exaggerated*, display of 'femininity' (the first woman she discusses 'ogles', flirts, and 'coquettes' with her male professional colleagues; another woman, a university lecturer, 'chooses particularly feminine clothes' and behaves in an inappropriately flippant manner[74]). Mary Ann Doane develops the theme of exaggeration, describing a 'masquerading' woman as one who 'produce[s] herself as an excess of femininity'; the masquerade is 'constituted by a hyperbolization of the accoutrements of femininity'.[75] Doane argues that masquerade thus has a certain radical potential insofar as it 'effects a defamiliarization of female iconography', caricaturing the image of femininity and thereby showing it up *as* an image, a structure of representation rather than a natural essence.[76]

This understanding of masquerade as 'excessive' femininity provides a suggestive way of reading both Nin 'herself' and some of the highly charged responses to her from various points on the feminist spectrum. If, as Estelle Jelinek perceptively noted, Nin functions as a 'mirror' for other women, reflecting 'femininity' back to them, this frequently appears as a *hyperbolic* femininity, which draws attention to itself as such.

[73] Riviere, 'Womanliness as a Masquerade', 39.

[74] Ibid. 36, 37, 39.

[75] Mary Ann Doane, 'Film and the Masquerade: Theorizing the Female Spectator' (1982), in *Femmes Fatales*, 25, 26.

[76] In a later article, however, Doane is more hesitant on this point. In particular, she discusses the possible psychic *difficulty*, for the woman, of masquerade, noting that 'masquerade is not theorized by Riviere as a joyful or affirmative play but as an anxiety-ridden compensatory gesture, as a position which is potentially disturbing, uncomfortable, and inconsistent, as well as psychically painful' ('Masquerade Reconsidered: Further Thoughts on the Female Spectator' [1988–9], in *Femmes Fatales*, 38).

It thereby foregrounds the tensions and difficulties involved, as Doane says, 'in *any* concept of femininity'[77]—and especially in women's relations to it.

We can see the ways in which Susan Stocking's depiction of Nin hints at this exaggerated femininity. More recent—and more hostile—critics have focused precisely on the excessive and/or inappropriate characteristics of Nin's femininity. Claire Messud gives a sardonic account of her (male) university professor swooning over Nin in the 1970s: 'What had so utterly charmed him was the woman herself, bejewelled and perfectly made up, her slim figure swathed in an elegant cape. She was, at the time, over 70 years old—though he insisted that she didn't look a day over 50. And she was sexy.'[78] Messud's repeated use of 'perfectly'—Nin is also described as 'perfectly turned out', with 'perfectly manicured hands'—ironically suggests the exaggerated nature of her feminine appearance. This femininity is also inappropriate because of Nin's age at the time, which Messud mentions three times in her review. A description by Deirdre Bair of Nin in the 1960s brings this out even more clearly:

> there were not many sixty-three-year-old women who walked those streets [of Greenwich Village] in broad daylight with hair entwined with ribbons and flowers and piled high on their heads, who wore long flowing gowns of white cashmere or silver lamé covered with dramatic capes that once belonged to parish priests or French policemen, and who painted their faces and lips dead white in the fashion of the day and darkened their eyes so heavily they were startling when glimpsed unexpectedly on a sunny afternoon.[79]

Here Nin appears as a grotesque caricature of a glamorous and sexy young woman, a freakishly exaggerated vision of femininity that should not be walking the streets in 'broad daylight'. For both Bair and Messud it is Nin's age that renders her use of the trappings of femininity particularly inappropriate: she is that grotesque figure, an old woman masquerading as a younger woman.[80] This adds yet another level to the problem of seeming and being: Nin here is an old woman, 'producing herself' as a young, glamorous woman—a masquerade of a masquerade. It seems clear that the unease produced by Nin's 'flaunting' of femininity

[77] Ibid. 33. [78] Messud, 'Dear Oh Dear Diary', 6. [79] Bair, *Anaïs Nin*, 481.

[80] Cf. the description, in *1984*, of Winston Smith's encounter with a heavily made-up prostitute whom, in the dim light, he takes to be a young woman: 'What he had suddenly seen in the lamplight was that the woman was *old*. The paint was plastered so thick on her face that it looked as though it might crack like a cardboard mask. There were streaks of white in her hair; but the truly dreadful detail was that her mouth had fallen a little open, revealing nothing except a cavernous blackness. She had no teeth at all' (George Orwell, *1984* [London: Penguin, 1983 (1949)], 63).

(to use Doane's description of the masquerading woman) is exacerbated by the fact that she continued to present herself in this way—indeed, became for the first time a highly public figure of femininity—when she was in her sixties and seventies. We might read the staginess and excess of the elderly Nin's appearance as subversive in the way that Doane suggests, effecting the 'defamiliarization' of femininity through performance to excess, a kind of caricature. On the other hand, accounts such as Messud's and Bair's might suggest rather the desire to reinscribe femininity as 'natural'—to *young* women but not to old women; a masquerade perhaps, but one which can be seen as appropriate within its proper sphere.

THE MONSTER IN THE MIRROR

Bair's description of Nin stalking the streets of Greenwich Village in her cape and pancake make-up is redolent of Hammer horror, an image of something vampiric which ought not to appear in daylight hours. I now want to look in more detail at the way in which Nin is explicitly portrayed, by several female critics, as a monster—as, to use Barbara Creed's terminology, an incarnation of the sexually predatory 'monstrous-feminine'.[81]

In reviews of Bair's and Fitch's biographies of Nin, the recurrence of the terms 'monster' and 'monstrous' (the reversal of Millett's term 'goddess') is striking. Nin is described as a 'female monster', a 'monster of self-centredness', a 'monster of narcissism, deceit and vanity'; her behaviour and her life are 'monstrous'.[82] While it is not surprising that negative characteristics such as selfishness, narcissism, and deceitfulness are ascribed to Nin (indeed, it would be surprising if they were not), the repeated and explicit use of the term 'monster' suggests an affective response going beyond mere condemnation of dubious or immoral behaviour. Whether the writers are conscious of it or not, by describing Nin as a monster they are invoking a powerful image with a very long cross-cultural history. Creed writes: 'All human societies have a concep-

[81] Barbara Creed, *The Monstrous-Feminine: Film, Feminism, Psychoanalysis* (London: Routledge, 1993).

[82] Gerrard, 'A Talent to Delude'; Nigella Lawson, 'Adventures of a Superfluous Woman' (review of Bair), *The Times*, 11 May 1995, 35; Michèle Roberts, 'Naughty but Anaïs' (review of Bair), *The Sunday Times*, 30 April 1995 (in her use of the term 'monster' Roberts is summing up common views of Nin rather than giving her own); Hughes-Hallett, 'Story of A'.

tion of the monstrous-feminine, of what it is about woman that is shocking, terrifying, horrific, abject'.[83] The monstrous-feminine may appear in many different forms: 'archaic mother, monstrous womb, vampire, possessed monster, femme castratrice, witch, castrating mother'.[84] All, crucially, are defined in terms of sexual difference and sexuality. But, Creed suggests, representations of the monstrous-feminine generally fall into two groups: those in which the woman's monstrousness is related to mothering and reproduction, and those, centred around the image of woman as castrator, in which monstrousness is directly linked to sexual desire. The most common images of the monstrously desiring woman, Creed suggests, are 'the deadly femme castratrice, the castrating mother and the *vagina dentata*'.[85]

In none of the reviews I am considering is Nin's 'monstrousness' overtly linked to her sexuality (though the deceit, vanity, and narcissism ascribed to her are certainly connected, by the writers, to her sexual relationships). However, I would argue that Nin is implicitly presented, by these reviewers, in the terms of Creed's second type of monstrous-feminine: she is the sexually predatory woman defined in terms of her devouring (if not actually toothed) vagina. Almost all the reviews (again, not surprisingly) emphasize Nin's promiscuity. Messud writes that 'in her thirties, [Nin] juggled half a dozen lovers at one time'; Gerrard refers to her 'orgiastic affair' with her father and her seductions of 'five or six men in a single week'. Nigella Lawson writes that 'Nin's promiscuity required dedication and skill: she would flit from hotel to hotel, from house to house, keeping as many as four lovers (and her husband) happy in one day'. Hughes-Hallet writes that Nin was, at one point, 'regularly bedding three men a day', and was 'for 25 years an undiscovered bigamist'.

Further, Nin's promiscuous sexuality is the non-reproductive sexuality of the *femme fatale*, who is frequently represented as, in Mary Ann Doane's phrase, 'the antithesis of the maternal'.[86] Lawson describes the 'petulant brutality' of Nin's abortions, 'the first one when she was six months pregnant and had to try repeatedly to kill a foetus which seemed to go on living

[83] Creed, *The Monstrous-Feminine*, 1. Creed explains that she uses the term 'monstrous-feminine' to convey the important point that she is not talking about monsters who just happen to be female: sexual difference, the femaleness of the monstrous-feminine, is essential to its 'monstrosity' (3).

[84] Creed, *The Monstrous-Feminine*, 151.

[85] Ibid. 7.

[86] Doane, *Femmes Fatales*, 2. Here again Nin shares an important characteristic with Brenda Silver's female monsters, Woolf and Monroe: childlessness (see *Virginia Woolf Icon*, 260).

despite her best efforts'. Bair herself writes that, 'The account of the birth in the diary almost defies interpretation. It is a portrait of *monstrous* egotism and selfishness, horrifying in its callous indifference' (though she goes on to acknowledge that 'the birth episode is probably [Nin's] finest writing').[87] Nin here becomes simultaneously the 'antithesis of the maternal', in that she kills her child, and the 'terrible mother' of mythology, the child-murdering witch. (It also seems significant that Bair's account has Nin, in killing her child, producing 'probably her finest writing'—Bair's over-determined comment conjures with all the oppositions and parallels between motherhood and writing, babies and books.)

Finally, and most strikingly of all, Nin is represented as the ultimate victim of her own devouring sexuality. She died, in 1977, from cancer which began in the cervix and spread through her body. Both Nigella Lawson and Nicci Gerrard—among the reviewers most hostile to Nin—explicitly describe her death from 'cancer of the vagina'. Nin died, Gerrard writes, 'of a cancer that ate into her vagina and wiped out her carefully-preserved, strangely youthful beauty'. This description, I would argue, takes a certain sadistic pleasure in suggesting a brutal kind of justice: Nin, Gerrard implies, lived by the cunt and died by the cunt. Just as she used her sexuality to 'devour' those around her, so in the end that sexuality turns in on itself, becoming the cancer that devours ('eats into') her, destroying in the process her 'strangely youthful' beauty—a beauty which, like that of Dorian Gray, belies the corruption beneath.

In her own writing, Nin uses the image of the monster to represent one's own unconscious 'demons', which must be acknowledged and grappled with: 'the modern hero is one who would master his own neurosis . . . who would enter the labyrinth and fight the monster' (*Journals*, II, 347). This theme is central to the last novel of Nin's *roman fleuve*, *Seduction of the Minotaur* (1961), in which Lillian travels to Mexico in an attempt to escape the difficulties of her life, but finds herself compelled to embark on a psychic journey of exploration, confronting her 'monsters' rather than simply repeating the same patterns. Towards the end of the novel, as Lillian is returning home on an aeroplane, she has a vision of the 'Minotaur' whom she had feared to confront:

[87] Bair, *Anaïs Nin*, 200, 202, my emphasis. It is noteworthy that—despite their general view of Nin as a highly unreliable narrator of her own life—all of these critics take at face value Nin's declared lack of interest in the stillbirth/abortion. In contrast, Diane Richard-Allerdyce argues, far more convincingly in my opinion, that 'the frequent reference to themes of stillbirth, birth, and mothering in Nin's writing . . . indicate[s] the degree to which she was traumatized by her abortion experience' (*Remaking of Self*, 183 n. 41).

Lillian had felt the existence of the labyrinth beneath her feet like the excavated passageways under Mexico City, but she had feared entering it and meeting the Minotaur who would devour her.

Yet now that she had come face to face with it, the Minotaur resembled someone she knew. It was not a monster. It was a reflection upon a mirror, a masked woman, Lillian herself, the hidden masked part of herself unknown to her, who had ruled her acts. She extended her hand toward this tyrant who could no longer harm her. It lay upon the mirror of the plane's round portholes, travelling through the clouds, a fleeting face, her own, clear and definable only when darkness came. (*Seduction*, 129)

The 'monster' reflected in the mirror (the dark window) is of course Lillian's own unconscious, or (in more Jungian terms) her shadow self, repository of all that she could not acknowledge as part of herself, and therefore projected outwards onto the 'Minotaur'. Nin herself, I suggest, plays this role for other women, appearing in the mirror as the sexually devouring monstrous-feminine, a distorted fantasy of femininity which is projected outwards, ascribed to the Other. This monstrous-feminine is, I would argue, the 'other face' of the idealizing fantasies of femininity ('mother, elder sister, goddess') which Nin *also* serves to represent—equally distorted, exaggerated images.

This is particularly interesting given that critics' hostility to Nin often appears to be an attempt to reintroduce 'reality', separating it from the 'fantasy' that they see woven around Nin. The emphasis on the 'sordid' or farcical elements of Nin's life, the desperate or compulsive aspects of her sexuality and promiscuity, is intended to suggest a *pathology* underlying the fantasy-figure of the liberated, unfettered *femme fatale* (and there is a connection here with Doane's worry about the psychical difficulties of the masquerading woman). The 'real woman' and the 'real life', Nin's critics want to emphasize, were tragic, appalling or simply ridiculous: 'The suave, enigmatic love-goddess was really a character in a farce'. But what is interesting about these critical accounts is the way in which the 'suave, enigmatic love-goddess' disappears and is replaced, not by a 'real woman', but by another, equally extreme, set of images—a child-killing, man-devouring monster, a female Dorian Gray being eaten away by her own corruption. Nin, it seems, will not stay put as a 'real woman', but maintains a posthumous existence as a representation bearing a striking resemblance to her own fictional creation, the double-faced woman of *House of Incest*, revolving like a planet or like a stage, alternately showing a day-face and a night-face.

CONCLUSION

This afterlife seems apt enough, given Nin's own lifelong interest in the fictionality and multiplicity of any 'self' and any life. I hope that this book has demonstrated the different ways in which Nin approached this issue and the different arenas—textual narratives, psychoanalysis, the actress's roles, even photographs—in which she saw these questions of identity played out. I hope also to have shown the *tension* running through Nin's explorations of subjectivity and identity: the pull, on the one hand, towards what I have called an erotics of multiplicity, a delight in 'playing a thousand roles'; and on the other hand the sometimes desperate drive for a 'whole' and 'true' self, the fear of 'dislocation' and loss of control. Nin herself summed up perfectly this fundamental conflict: 'I have always been tormented by the image of the multiplicity of selves. Some days I call it richness, and other days I see it as a disease' (*Journals*, I, 54).

This problem, in varying forms, has played a central role within feminist thought over the past three decades. Questions of identity and its assertion or subversion, coupled with seemingly intractable problems around the notion of 'femininity', have been at the forefront of feminist debate since the 1970s. There is, then, a significant parallel between these feminist questions and the central questions raised by Nin's work and by Nin herself as an iconic figure.

This parallel also highlights the historical and contextual aspects to the 'thousand roles' an individual might play. The interest of Nin as object of study lies to a considerable extent in her historical longevity and mobility, the many different contexts through which she and her work have moved. As I have shown, these different contextual 'conversations' (to return to Lisa Rado's term) produce different, often conflicting, versions of Nin and her work, as different questions produce different answers, and new framings and interpretations become possible. I think we can see, then, another parallelism, as Nin's fascination with the changing 'faces' of a self, an identity, is also staged on the broader level of historical context and critical reception.

I also hope that my final chapter has provided, if not an answer, at least some suggestions for thinking about the difficulties of Nin as an iconic feminine figure and women's highly charged responses to her. I argued that Nin sees identity as, in Judith Butler's terms, a 'performative accomplishment', a series of enactments and stylizations. In her textual explorations of identity and femininity, and in her stagings of these issues through photographs, Nin insists that there is always an element of masquerade, of performance, in any 'identity'. This is, I think, what Julia Casterton is suggesting when she describes Nin 'trying on' the various costumes of femininity: perhaps such 'play' with these identities may be an alternative both to the attempt to dispense with femininity, rid women of it once and for all, and to the (equally problematic) attempt to locate or establish an 'authentic' femininity behind or underneath the masquerade. The photograph of Nin posing in her 'veil' for Rank is so striking precisely because it combines a teasing acknowledgement of the masquerade ('Rank wants me as "the dancer"') with a genuinely compelling performance—the performance, as Maureen Freely puts it, of 'the modern erotic female'. It is, perhaps, just this combination that explains Nin's continuing power (whether this is felt as positive or negative) in the realm of representation. As she wrote in March 1932, on the brink of the most intense and tangled involvement of her life, with Henry Miller and June Mansfield: 'I affect their imaginations. It is the strongest power' (*Henry and June*, 54).

Bibliography

WORKS BY ANAÏS NIN

D. H. Lawrence: An Unprofessional Study (London: Neville Spearman, 1961 [Paris: Edward Titus, 1932]).

Winter of Artifice & House of Incest (London: Peter Owen, 1974 [*The House of Incest*, Paris: Siana Editions, 1936; *The Winter of Artifice* (different version), Paris: Obelisk Press, 1939; (this version) Denver: Swallow Press, 1961]).

Under a Glass Bell (London: Penguin, 1978 [New York: Gemor Press, 1944]).

Ladders to Fire (London: Peter Owen, 1991 [New York: E. P. Dutton, 1946]).

Children of the Albatross (London: Penguin, 1993 [New York: E. P. Dutton, 1947]).

The Four-Chambered Heart (London: Virago, 1992 [New York: Duell, Sloan & Pierce, 1950]).

A Spy in the House of Love (London: Penguin, 1973 [New York: British Book Centre, 1954]).

Seduction of the Minotaur (London: Penguin, 1993 [Denver: Alan Swallow, 1961]).

'Sabina', *Chicago Review* 15/3 (1962), 45–60.

Collages (London: Virago, 1993 [Denver: Alan Swallow, 1964]).

The Journals of Anaïs Nin (7 vols.; ed. Gunther Stuhlmann)

I. 1931–34 (London: Quartet, 1973 [New York: Swallow Press/Harcourt, Brace & World, 1966]).

II. 1934–39 (London: Quartet, 1974 [New York: Harcourt, Brace & World, 1967]).

III. 1939–44 (London: Peter Owen, 1969 [New York: Harcourt, Brace & World, 1969]).

IV. 1944–47 (London: Quartet, 1976 [New York: Harcourt Brace Jovanovich, 1971]).

V. 1947–55 (London: Quartet, 1976 [New York: Harcourt Brace Jovanovich, 1974]).

VI. 1955–66 (London: Peter Owen, 1976 [New York: Harcourt Brace Jovanovich, 1976]).

VII. 1966–74 (London: Quartet, 1983 [New York: Harcourt Brace Jovanovich, 1980]).

The Novel of the Future (New York: Macmillan, 1968).

A Woman Speaks (ed. Evelyn J. Hinz; London: Penguin, 1992 [Chicago: Swallow Press, 1975]).

In Favour of the Sensitive Man (London: Penguin, 1992 [New York: Harcourt Brace Jovanovich, 1976]).

Delta of Venus (London: Penguin, 1990 [New York: Harcourt Brace Jovanovich, 1977]).

Linotte: The Early Diary of Anaïs Nin. I. 1914–1920 (ed. John Ferrone; New York: Harcourt Brace Jovanovich, 1978).

Little Birds (London: Book Club Associates, 1980 [New York: Harcourt Brace Jovanovich, 1979]).

The Early Diary of Anaïs Nin. II. 1920–1923 (ed. Rupert Pole; New York: Harcourt Brace Jovanovich, 1982).

Journal of a Wife: The Early Diary of Anaïs Nin. III. 1923–1927 (ed. Rupert Pole; London: Peter Owen, 1984).

The Early Diary of Anaïs Nin. IV. 1927–1931 (ed. Rupert Pole; New York: Harcourt Brace Jovanovich, 1985).

Henry and June: From the Unexpurgated Diary of Anaïs Nin (ed. Rupert Pole; London: Penguin, 1990 [San Diego: Harcourt Brace Jovanovich, 1986]).

Incest: From 'A Journal of Love': The Unexpurgated Diary of Anaïs Nin (ed. Rupert Pole; London: Peter Owen, 1993 [San Diego: Harcourt Brace Jovanovich, 1992]).

Waste of Timelessness and Other Early Stories (Athens, Oh.: Swallow Press/Ohio Univ. Press, 1993).

The Mystic of Sex: Uncollected Writings, 1931–1974 (ed. Gunther Stuhlmann; Santa Barbara: Capra Press, 1995).

Fire: From 'A Journal of Love': The Unexpurgated Diary of Anaïs Nin (ed. Rupert Pole; London: Peter Owen, 1996).

Nearer the Moon: From 'A Journal of Love': The Unexpurgated Diary of Anaïs Nin (ed. Gunther Stuhlmann, Vicki Aus; San Diego: Harcourt Brace Jovanovich, 1996).

Anaïs Nin and Henry Miller, *A Literate Passion: Letters of Anaïs Nin and Henry Miller 1932–1953* (ed. Gunther Stuhlmann; London: Allison & Busby, 1988).

SECONDARY SOURCES

Abel, Elizabeth, *Virginia Woolf and the Fictions of Psychoanalysis* (Chicago: Univ. of Chicago Press, 1989).

Andersen, Margret, 'Critical Approaches to Anaïs Nin', *Canadian Review of American Studies* 10/2 (1979), 255–65.

Appignanesi, Lisa and John Forrester, *Freud's Women* (London: Weidenfeld & Nicolson, 1992).

Bair, Deirdre, *Anaïs Nin: A Biography* (London: Bloomsbury, 1995).

Barillé, Elisabeth, *Anaïs Nin: Naked under the Mask* (London: Minerva, 1993).

Barthes, Roland, 'The Death of the Author', in *Image, Music, Text* (trans. Stephen Heath; London: Fontana, 1977).

Baudelaire, Charles, *Selected Writings on Art and Literature* (Harmondsworth: Penguin, 1992).

Benstock, Shari, *Women of the Left Bank: Paris, 1900–1940* (London: Virago, 1987).

Bowker, Gordon, *Pursued by Furies: A Life of Malcolm Lowry* (London: Flamingo, 1993).

Bowlby, Rachel, 'The Feminine Female', *Social Text* 7 (1983), 54–68.

—— *Still Crazy After All These Years: Women, Writing and Psychoanalysis* (London and New York: Routledge, 1992).

—— *Feminist Destinations and Further Essays on Virginia Woolf* (Edinburgh: Edinburgh Univ. Press, 1997).

Brennan, Karen, 'Anaïs Nin: Author(iz)ing the Erotic Body', *Genders* 14 (Autumn 1992), 66–86.

Breton, André, *Manifestoes of Surrealism* (Ann Arbor: Univ. of Michigan Press, 1969).

Brooks, Peter, *Reading for the Plot* (Oxford: Clarendon Press, 1984).

Brownstein, Rachel M., *Tragic Muse: Rachel of the Comédie-Française* (Durham, NC and London: Duke Univ. Press, 1995).

Buhle, Mari Jo, *Feminism and its Discontents: A Century of Struggle with Psychoanalysis* (Cambridge, Mass.: Harvard Univ. Press, 1998).

Butler, Judith, *Gender Trouble: Feminism and the Subversion of Identity* (London: Routledge, 1990).

Chawaf, Chantal, 'Linguistic Flesh', in Elaine Marks and Isabelle de Courtivron (eds.), *New French Feminisms: An Anthology* (Hemel Hempstead: Harvester Wheatsheaf, 1980), 177–8.

Cixous, Hélène, 'The Laugh of the Medusa', in Elaine Marks and Isabelle de Courtivron (eds.), *New French Feminisms: An Anthology* (Hemel Hempstead: Harvester Wheatsheaf, 1980), 245–64.

Cottam, Rachel, 'Secret Scratching: The Diary and its Writing' (Ph.D. dissertation, Sussex University, 1996).

Creed, Barbara, *The Monstrous-Feminine: Film, Feminism, Psychoanalysis* (London: Routledge, 1993).

Dearborn, Mary, *The Happiest Man Alive: A Biography of Henry Miller* (London: HarperCollins, 1991).

Derrida, Jacques, 'Signature Event Context' (1972), in *A Derrida Reader: Between the Blinds* (ed. Peggy Kamuf; Hemel Hempstead: Harvester Wheatsheaf, 1991).

Dijkstra, Bram, *Idols of Perversity: Fantasies of Feminine Evil in Fin-de-Siècle Culture* (New York: Oxford Univ. Press, 1986).

Doane, Mary Ann, *Femmes Fatales: Feminism, Film Theory, Psychoanalysis* (New York and London: Routledge, 1991).

DuBow, Wendy (ed.), *Conversations with Anaïs Nin* (Jackson, Miss.: Univ. Press of Mississippi, 1994).

Duras, Marguerite, interview, in Elaine Marks and Isabelle de Courtivron (eds.), *New French Feminisms: An Anthology* (Hemel Hempstead: Harvester Wheatsheaf, 1980), 174–6.

Durrell, Lawrence, Preface to *Children of the Albatross*, in Robert Zaller (ed.), *A Casebook on Anaïs Nin* (New York: Meridian, 1974), 2.

Eliot, T. S., 'Ulysses, Order and Myth', *The Dial*, 70/5 (Nov. 1923).

Evans, Oliver, *Anaïs Nin* (Crosscurrents Modern Critiques; Carbondale, Ill.: Southern Illinois Univ. Press, 1968).

Felski, Rita, *Beyond Feminist Aesthetics: Feminist Literature and Social Change* (London: Hutchinson Radius, 1989).

—— *The Gender of Modernity* (Cambridge, Mass.: Harvard Univ. Press, 1995).

Finney, Gail, *Women in Modern Drama: Freud, Feminism and European Theater at the Turn of the Century* (Ithaca, NY: Cornell Univ. Press, 1989).

Fitch, Noël Riley, *Anaïs: The Erotic Life of Anaïs Nin* (Boston: Little, Brown, 1993).

——(ed.), *In transition: A Paris Anthology: Writing and Art from* transition *Magazine 1927–30* (London: Secker & Warburg, 1990).

Forster, E. M., *A Passage to India* (Harmondsworth: Penguin, 1985 [1924]).

Freely, Maureen, 'Pleasure of the Flesh', *Guardian*, 13 June 1995.

Freud, Sigmund, *The Interpretation of Dreams* (1900) (trans. James Strachey; Penguin Freud Library, 4; Harmondsworth: Penguin, 1991).

—— *Three Essays on the Theory of Sexuality* (1905), in *On Sexuality* (trans. James Strachey; Penguin Freud Library, 7; Harmondsworth: Penguin, 1991).

——'Delusions and Dreams in Jensen's *Gradiva*' (1907), in *Art and Literature* (trans. James Strachey; Penguin Freud Library, 14; Harmondsworth: Penguin, 1990), 27–118.

——'Leonardo da Vinci and a Memory of his Childhood' (1910), in *Art and Literature* (trans. James Strachey; Penguin Freud Library, 14; Harmondsworth: Penguin, 1990), 143–232.

——'The Dynamics of Transference' (1912), in *The Standard Edition of the Complete Psychological Works of Sigmund Freud*, XII (trans. James Strachey; London: Hogarth Press, 1958), 97–108.

——'On the History of the Psychoanalytic Movement' (1914), in *Historical and Expository Works on Psychoanalysis* (trans. James Strachey; Penguin Freud Library, 15; Harmondsworth: Penguin, 1993), 63–126.

——'Observations on Transference-Love' (1915), in *The Standard Edition of the Complete Psychological Works of Sigmund Freud*, XII (trans. James Strachey; London: Hogarth Press, 1958), 157–71.

——and Josef Breuer, *Studies on Hysteria* (1895) (trans. James Strachey; *The Standard Edition of the Complete Psychological Works of Sigmund Freud*, II; London: Hogarth Press, 1955).

——and C. G. Jung, *The Freud/Jung Letters* (ed. William McGuire; Harmondsworth: Penguin, 1991 [1974]).

Friedman, Ellen G., 'Anaïs Nin', in Lea Baechler, A. Walton Litz, and Elaine Showalter (eds.), *Modern American Women Writers* (New York: Charles Scribner's Sons, 1991).

——and Miriam Fuchs (eds.), *Breaking the Sequence: Women's Experimental Fiction* (Princeton: Princeton Univ. Press, 1989).

Friedman, Susan Stanford, *Psyche Reborn: The Emergence of H.D.* (Bloomington, Ind.: Indiana Univ. Press, 1981).

——*Penelope's Web: Gender, Modernity, H.D.'s Fiction* (Cambridge: Cambridge Univ. Press, 1990).

——'Return of the Repressed in H.D.'s Madrigal Cycle', in Susan Stanford Friedman and Rachel Blau DuPlessis (eds.), *Signets: Reading H.D.* (Madison, Wis.: Univ. of Wisconsin Press, 1990), 233–52.

Gerrard, Nicci, 'A Talent to Delude' (review of Bair, *Anaïs Nin*), *Observer*, 5 March 1995.

Gourmont, Remy de, *Decadence and Other Essays on the Culture of Ideas* (trans. William Bradley; New York: Harcourt, Brace, 1921).

Grosz, Elizabeth, *Jacques Lacan: A Feminist Introduction* (London: Routledge, 1990).

H.D. (Hilda Doolittle), 'The *Borderline* Pamphlet' (1930), in Bonnie Kime Scott (ed.), *The Gender of Modernism* (Bloomington, Ind.: Indiana Univ. Press, 1990).

——*Hermetic Definition* (Oxford: Carcanet, 1972 [1958]).

——*Bid Me To Live (A Madrigal)* (London: Virago, 1984 [New York: Grove Press, 1960]).

——*Notes on Thought and Vision & The Wise Sappho* (San Francisco: City Lights, 1982).

——*Tribute to Freud* (Manchester: Carcanet, rev. edn., 1985).

——*End to Torment: A Memoir of Ezra Pound by H.D.* (ed. Norman Holmes Pearson and Michael King; Manchester: Carcanet, 1980 [1979]).

——'H.D. by Delia Alton', *Iowa Review* 16 (1986), 180–221.

Heath, Stephen, 'Joan Riviere and the Masquerade', in Victor Burgin, James Donald, and Cora Kaplan (eds.), *Formations of Fantasy* (London: Methuen, 1986), 45–61.

Herron, Paul, 'The Café in Space: Anaïs Nin on the Internet', *Anaïs: An International Journal* 19 (2001), 51–63.

——(ed.), *Anaïs Nin: A Book of Mirrors* (Huntingdon Woods, Mich.: Sky Blue Press, 1996).

Hillis Miller, J., *Ariadne's Thread: Story Lines* (New Haven: Yale Univ. Press, 1992).

Hinz, Evelyn J., *The Mirror and the Garden: Realism and Reality in the Writings of Anaïs Nin* (New York: Harcourt Brace Jovanovich, 2nd edn., 1973 [1971]).

Hogan, Rebecca, 'Engendered Autobiographies: The Diary as a Feminine Form', in Shirley Neuman (ed.), *Autobiography and Questions of Gender* (London: Cass, 1992), 95–107.

hooks, bell, *Talking Back: Thinking Feminist, Thinking Black* (London: Sheba, 1989).

Hughes-Hallett, Lucy, 'The Story of A' (review of Fitch, *Anaïs*), *Sunday Times*, 3 April 1994.

Huyssen, Andreas, *After the Great Divide: Modernism, Mass Culture, and Postmodernism* (London: Macmillan, 1988).

Irigaray, Luce, 'This Sex which is Not One' (1977), in Elaine Marks and Isabelle de Courtivron (eds.), *New French Feminisms: An Anthology* (Hemel Hempstead: Harvester Wheatsheaf, 1980), 99–106.

James, Henry, *The Tragic Muse* (London: Macmillan, 1921 [1889–90]).

Jason, Philip K., *Anaïs Nin and her Critics* (Columbia, SC: Camden House, 1993).

Jelinek, Estelle C., 'Anaïs Nin: A Critical Evaluation', in Cheryl L. Brown and Karen Olson (eds.), *Feminist Criticism* (Metuchen, NJ: Scarecrow Press, 1978), 312–23.

——(ed.), *Women's Autobiography: Essays in Criticism* (Bloomington, Ind.: Indiana Univ. Press, 1980).

Jones, Ann Rosalind, 'Writing the Body: Toward an Understanding of *l'Écriture Féminine*', in Elaine Showalter (ed.), *The New Feminist Criticism: Essays on Women, Literature and Theory* (London: Virago, 1986 [1985]), 361–77.

Joyce, James, *Portrait of the Artist as a Young Man* (1916), in *The Essential James Joyce* (London: Triad Grafton, 1977).

Jung, C. G., 'On the Relation of Analytical Psychology to Poetry', in *Collected Works of C. G. Jung*, XV (London: Routledge & Kegan Paul, 1966), 97–132.

Kamuf, Peggy, *Signature Pieces: On the Institution of Authorship* (Ithaca, NY: Cornell Univ. Press, 1988).

Kristeva, Julia, *Revolution in Poetic Language* (trans. Margaret Waller, with introduction by Leon S. Roudiez; New York: Columbia Univ. Press, 1984).

Lacan, Jacques, *The Four Fundamental Concepts of Psycho-Analysis* (ed. Jacques-Alain Miller; trans. Alan Sheridan; London: Hogarth Press and the Institute of Psycho-Analysis, 1977).

Laity, Cassandra, *H.D. and the Victorian Fin de Siècle: Gender, Modernism, Decadence* (Cambridge: Cambridge Univ. Press, 1996).

Laplanche, Jean, 'Notes on Afterwardsness', in John Fletcher and Martin Stanton (eds.), *Seduction, Translation, Drives* (London: ICA, 1992), 217–23.

——'Psychoanalysis, Time and Translation', in *Seduction, Translation, Drives*, 161–77.

——and J.-B. Pontalis, *The Language of Pyscho-Analysis* (trans. Donald Nicholson-Smith; London: Hogarth Press/Institute of Psycho-Analysis, 1973).

Lawson, Nigella, 'Adventures of a Superfluous Woman' (review of Bair, *Anaïs Nin*), *The Times*, 11 May 1995.

Lejeune, Philippe, 'The Autobiographical Pact', in *On Autobiography* (ed. Paul John Eakin; trans. Katherine Leary; Minneapolis: Univ. of Minnesota Press, 1989), 3–30.

Lieberman, E. J., *Acts of Will: The Life and Work of Otto Rank* (New York: Free Press, 1985).

Lorde, Audre, *Zami: A New Spelling of My Name* (London: Sheba, 1984 [1982]).

Marcus, Laura, *Auto/biographical Discourses: Theory, Criticism, Practice* (Manchester: Manchester Univ. Press, 1994).

Marks, Elaine, and Isabelle de Courtivron (eds.), *New French Feminisms: An Anthology* (Hemel Hempstead: Harvester Wheatsheaf, 1980).

Menaker, Esther, *Otto Rank: A Rediscovered Legacy* (New York: Columbia Univ. Press, 1982).

Messud, Claire, 'Dear Oh Dear Diary' (review of Bair, *Anaïs Nin*), *Guardian*, 20 April 1995.

Miller, Henry, 'Un Être Êtoilique' (1937), in Robert Zaller (ed.), *A Casebook on Anaïs Nin* (New York: Meridian, 1974), 5–23.

Miller, Nancy K., *Subject to Change: Reading Feminist Writing* (New York: Columbia Univ. Press, 1988).

Millett, Kate, *Sexual Politics* (London: Abacus, 1972 [1969]).

—— 'Anaïs: A Mother to Us All', *Anaïs: An International Journal* 9 (1991), 3–8.

Mitchell, Juliet, *Psychoanalysis and Feminism* (London: Allen Lane, 1974).

Moi, Toril, *Sexual/Textual Politics: Feminist Literary Theory* (London: Methuen, 1985).

Molyneux, Maxine, and Julia Casterton, 'Looking Again at Anaïs Nin', *Minnesota Review* 18 (1982), 86–101.

Morgan, Janice, and Colette T. Hall (eds.), *Redefining Autobiography in Twentieth-Century Women's Fiction: An Essay Collection* (New York: Garland, 1991).

Nalbantian, Suzanne, *Aesthetic Autobiography: From Life to Art in Marcel Proust, James Joyce, Virginia Woolf and Anaïs Nin* (London: Macmillan, 1994).

—— (ed.), *Anaïs Nin: Literary Perspectives* (London: Macmillan, 1997).

Nicholls, Peter, *Modernisms: A Literary Guide* (London: Macmillan, 1995).

Nietzsche, Friedrich, *The Gay Science* (New York: Vintage, 1974 [1882]).

Nussbaum, Felicity, 'Towards Conceptualizing Diary', in James Olney (ed.), *Studies in Autobiography* (New York: Oxford Univ. Press, 1988), 128–40.

Olney, James, *Memory and Narrative: The Weave of Life-Writing* (Chicago: Univ. of Chicago Press, 1988).

Orwell, George, 'Inside the Whale' (1940), in *Inside the Whale and Other Essays* (Harmondsworth: Penguin, 1957), 9–50.

—— *1984* (London: Penguin, 1983 [1949]).

Phillips, Adam, *On Flirtation* (London: Faber & Faber, 1994).

Pound, Ezra, 'Translator's Postscript', to Remy de Gourmont, *The Natural Philosophy of Love* (1921), repr. in Ezra Pound, *Pavannes and Divagations* (London: Peter Owen, 1960).

Rado, Lisa (ed.), *Rereading Modernism: New Directions in Feminist Criticism* (New York and London: Garland, 1994).

—— *Modernism, Gender, and Culture: A Cultural Studies Approach* (New York and London: Garland, 1997).

Ragland-Sullivan, Ellie, *Jacques Lacan and the Philosophy of Psychoanalysis* (London: Croom Helm, 1986).

Rank, Otto, *Truth and Reality* (trans. Jessie Taft; New York: Norton, 1978 [orig. German edn. 1929]).
——*Art and Artist: Creative Urge and Personality Development* (New York: Norton, 1989 [1932]).
——*Will Therapy & Truth and Reality* (New York: Knopf, 1947).
——*Beyond Psychology* (New York: Dover, 1958).
——*A Psychology of Difference: The American Lectures* (ed. Robert Kramer; Princeton: Princeton Univ. Press, 1996).
Richard-Allerdyce, Diane, *Anaïs Nin and the Remaking of Self: Gender, Modernism and Narrative Identity* (DeKalb, Ill.: Northern Illinois Univ. Press, 1998).
Richards, Thomas, *The Commodity Culture of Victorian England: Advertising and Spectacle, 1851–1914* (London: Verso, 1991).
Ricoeur, Paul, *Time and Narrative*, I (trans. Kathleen McLaughlin and David Pellauer; Chicago: Univ. of Chicago Press, 1984).
Riviere, Joan, 'Womanliness as a Masqerade' (1929), in Victor Burgin, James Donald, and Cora Kaplan (eds.), *Formations of Fantasy* (London: Methuen, 1986), 35–44.
Roberts, Michèle, 'Naughty but Anaïs' (review of Bair, *Anaïs Nin*), *Sunday Times*, 30 April 1995.
Robinson, Janice, *H.D.: The Life and Work of an American Poet* (Boston: Houghton Mifflin, 1982).
Roof, Judith, 'The Erotic Travelogue: The Scopophilic Pleasure of Race vs. Gender', *Arizona Quarterly* 47/4 (Winter 1991), 119–35.
Rose, Jacqueline, *Sexuality in the Field of Vision* (London: Verso, 1986).
Roudinesco, Elisabeth, *Jacques Lacan & Co.: A History of Psychoanalysis in France, 1925–1985* (trans. Jeffrey Mehlman; London: Free Association Books, 1990).
——*Jacques Lacan: An Outline of a Life and a History of a System of Thought* (trans. Barbara Bray; Cambridge: Polity Press, 1997).
Schaffer, Talia, 'Posing *Orlando*', in Ann Kibbey, Kayann Short, and Abouali Farmanfarmaian (eds.), *Sexual Artifice: Persons, Images, Politics* (*Genders*, 19; New York: New York Univ. Press, 1994).
Scholar, Nancy, *Anaïs Nin* (Boston: Twayne, 1984).
Scott, Bonnie Kime (ed.), *The Gender of Modernism* (Bloomington, Ind.: Indiana Univ. Press, 1990).
Segal, Lynne, *Why Feminism? Gender, Psychology, Politics* (Cambridge: Polity Press, 1999).
Seymour, Miranda, 'Sex, Lies and Narcissism' (review of Bair, *Anaïs Nin*), *The Independent*, 20 May 1995.
Showalter, Elaine (ed.), *The New Feminist Criticism: Essays on Women, Literature and Theory* (London: Virago, 1986).
Silver, Brenda R., *Virginia Woolf Icon* (Women in Culture and Society; Chicago: Univ. of Chicago Press, 1999).

Smith, Sidonie, *A Poetics of Women's Autobiography: Marginality and the Fictions of Self-Representation* (Bloomington, Ind.: Indiana Univ. Press, 1987).
Spencer, Sharon, *Collage of Dreams: The Writings of Anaïs Nin* (New York: Harcourt Brace Jovanovich, 2nd edn., 1981 [1977]).
—— 'Delivering the Woman Artist from the Silence of the Womb: Otto Rank's Influence on Anaïs Nin', *Psychoanalytic Review* 69/1 (1982), 111–29.
—— 'The Music of the Womb: Anaïs Nin's "Feminine" Writing', in Ellen G. Friedman and Miriam Fuchs (eds.), *Breaking the Sequence: Women's Experimental Fiction* (Princeton: Princeton Univ. Press, 1989), 161–73.
Spengemann, William C., *The Forms of Autobiography: Episodes in the History of a Literary Genre* (New Haven: Yale Univ. Press, 1980).
Stanton, Domna C. (ed.), *The Female Autograph: Theory and Practice of Autobiography from the Tenth to the Twentieth Century* (Chicago: Univ. of Chicago Press, 1987).
Steele, Jeffrey, 'Interpreting the Self: Emerson and the Unconscious', in Joel Porte (ed.), *Emerson: Prospect and Retrospect* (Harvard English Studies, 10; Cambridge, Mass.: Harvard Univ. Press, 1982).
Stokes, John, 'Rachel Félix', in Michael Booth, John Stokes, and Susan Bassnett, *Three Tragic Actresses: Siddons, Rachel, Ristori* (Cambridge: Cambridge Univ. Press, 1996).
Thoreau, Henry David, *The Variorum Walden* (ed. Walter Harding; New York: Twayne, 1962).
Whitford, Margaret, *Luce Irigaray: Philosophy in the Feminine* (London: Routledge, 1991).
Wilde, Oscar, *Complete Works of Oscar Wilde* (Glasgow: HarperCollins, 1994).
Williams, Raymond, *The Politics of Modernism: Against the New Conformists* (ed. Tony Pinkney; London: Verso, 1989).
Williams, Rosalind, *Dream Worlds: Mass Consumption in Late Nineteenth-Century France* (Berkeley and Los Angeles: Univ. of California Press, 1982).
Wilson, Edmund, *Axel's Castle: A Study in the Imaginative Literature of 1870–1930* (London: Fontana, 1961 [1931]).
—— review of *Under a Glass Bell*, in Robert Zaller (ed.), *A Casebook on Anaïs Nin* (New York: Meridian, 1974), 3–4.
Woolf, Virginia, review of *Rachel: Her Stage Life and her Real Life*, by Francis Gribble, in *The Essays of Virginia Woolf*, I (ed. Andrew McNeillie; London: Hogarth Press, 1986).
—— 'Modern Fiction' (1919), in *The Crowded Dance of Modern Life* (ed. Rachel Bowlby; Harmondsworth: Penguin, 1993), 5–12.
—— *Mrs Dalloway* (London: Triad Grafton, 1976 [1925]).
—— 'The Cinema' (1926), in *The Crowded Dance of Modern Life* (ed. Rachel Bowlby; Harmondsworth: Penguin, 1993), 54–8.
—— *Orlando: A Biography* (London: Virago, 1993 [1928]).
Zaller, Robert (ed.), *A Casebook on Anaïs Nin* (New York: Meridian, 1974).

Index